My Bittersweet Homecoming

My Bittersweet Homecoming

Jory Berkwits

ISBN: 0692427155
ISBN 13: 9780692427156
Library of Congress Control Number: 2015938515
Atlantic Publishing, University Park, FL

CONTENTS

FOREWORD

On June 27, 2003, I became a grandfather. Naturally I felt joyful and ecstatic, just as I had when my own children were born, but on this day, I also felt pensive, reflective, and perhaps a bit bewildered. For my whole life, I had typically found myself looking ahead to the next major event or milestone: getting a driver's license, graduating from school, getting married, obtaining a job, buying a house, or starting a family and raising my children. Now, quite unexpectedly, I began to experience a sea change in attitude and perspective, reviewing in my mind's eye all of the years that had passed before. I thought of what I had accomplished and what I had not, of achievements, and of regrets. As I held this six-pound newborn in my arms, I began to think of the pathway her life might take—and the one mine had already taken.

It is strange for this grandfather to think back and picture himself a newborn, a toddler in diapers, or a child blowing out birthday candles, but I began my life's journey just like everyone else. I often think about that childhood. I remember two loving parents, Cub Scouts, bicycles, and weekly gatherings with cousins and aunts and uncles. There were Sunday drives in the family car, with "Canadian Sunset" playing on the radio. I never knew how lucky I was.

Like most boys, I was something of a fanatic when it came to sports. Often our games were unorganized and unsupervised, and they ended only when the child who owned the game ball had to go home to eat. I was a walking encyclopedia of sports statistics. I still remember that Mickey Mantle won the Triple Crown in 1956 and what his numbers were (.353

BA, 52 HR, 130 RBI). I never did get one of his baseball cards, although I tried mightily for a number of years. Unfortunately, I ended up with a collection featuring the likes of journeymen such as Wayne Terwilliger and Milt Bolling.

I hung around with a pack of boys, all of whom I considered to be my "best friends." A few years later I attended that great transitional event, the sixth-grade dance, and shortly thereafter discovered that the planet was populated by girls as well as boys.

It has all been a blur. Today I feel a little like a ghost or a time traveler, a solitary figure with a unique connection to the past—my memory. Yet I am certain many if not all of my contemporaries can clearly identify with these feelings, no matter how personal they may be to me.

I grew up in Allentown, Pennsylvania. I joke about it today as being the center of the universe. In the 1950s, it was certainly the center of my universe, but clearly, after a long decline that has spanned most of my lifetime, it became anything but. Then, Allentown was a thriving, small city, in many ways, the quintessence of post–World War II America. It has since fallen on hard times, like many midsized industrial cities in the upper Midwest and Northeast. My first visit back in 2010—for the first time in over thirty-five years—was both eye-opening and heartbreaking. In fairness, though, during my most recent stopovers, I have witnessed a genuine turnaround taking shape, one that could well prove to be the early steps of a meaningful rebirth. If so, this turnaround will have taken at least forty years.

Many baby boomers, like me, can identify with the emotions I experienced during my homecoming. The deindustrialization of America hit many of us awfully hard, and if we were lucky enough to avoid the resulting economic hardship directly, we all know someone who wasn't. It was that pervasive; there was only one degree of separation. The pain was felt especially hard in the Midwest and in the Northeast. Detroit, Cleveland, Buffalo, Syracuse, Milwaukee, and countless other cities suffered severely as traditional manufacturing jobs dried up and many of their residents began to move south and west.

The creation of *My Bittersweet Homecoming* was the result of pure chance. My mother had saved a fourth-grade class picture taken in 1956, when I was attending the Muhlenberg Elementary School in Allentown. She probably had it in her possession for twenty-five years, perhaps more, and then gave it to me with a number of papers and pictures, the kind that parents often keep tucked away in a drawer. I had long ago forgotten that I had the picture or that it was ever passed down. Worse yet, I was in complete denial that she ever gave it to me in the first place. Yet one day, it appeared serendipitously as I was rummaging through some personal files. I stared at it a long time. I was nine when I entered fourth grade and ten by the time the school year ended. It was a long time ago, indeed.

I was emotionally moved every time I looked at it. Events I had long forgotten soon began to reappear with some clarity. I remembered the name of the teacher who welcomed us to our fourth-grade class that September in 1956. Was she still living? What had become of her? What were the chances she would even be in Pennsylvania? I vaguely remembered she had to leave midyear to join her husband, whose job had taken him out of state.

Curiosity got the better of me. I did a quick search and found out that she and her husband resided in a small suburb just outside the city. I called her on the telephone, reintroduced myself, and chatted a bit. We agreed to meet the next time I was visiting. Teresa Sinko had begun her teaching career only a year or two before I entered fourth grade. I remembered just a few things about her. First, she enunciated words perfectly, making spelling tests almost a breeze. It would take her about eight seconds to pronounce "veg-e-ta-ble." Second, she won the Mrs. Eastern Pennsylvania contest, something that brought a smile to her face when I mentioned it. It was the same winning smile I recalled after all these years.

Of course, when we met, we didn't recognize each other. When I saw her last, she was in her mid-twenties, and I was still a child. Now we were both retired seniors—in every way, total strangers. Still, when I pulled into her driveway, she came out the front door and gave me a hug. We talked for about an hour without any awkwardness or a hint of hesitation.

We chatted about many different things: childhood, raising kids, careers, and of course the changes that had taken place locally since the 1950s. This conversation was the catalyst that got this project off the ground. What had been nothing more than idle thought and empty talk became action: research, writing, and ultimately, a book.

So much time has passed since the 1950s. Many cities in the United States have changed so radically that they are now virtually unrecognizable, with high-speed beltways, enclosed shopping malls, magnificent stadiums, and dramatic skylines. As recently as 2012, Allentown looked pretty much the same as it did when I was a kid, apart from the fact that everything was fifty years older. The city did not age gracefully. One might have presumed that life there had gone on largely uninterrupted and undisturbed, but in fact on a very fundamental human level, it has experienced profound changes, very often with devastating consequences.

The Allentown I remember was a gritty, thriving blue-collar city. It was a city almost entirely dependent upon manufacturing and heavy industry. Tens of thousands of workers were employed in businesses like cement, truck manufacturing, steel fabrication, and textiles. It was a place where a high school graduate could get a union job with good benefits and job security and retire on a comfortable pension. The city I remember no longer exists.

This book is in a sense about change and how it has affected me, my classmates, and the town we called home. Sometimes, there are very large-scale global events that spur change. They can be sudden and unexpected, like the terrorist attacks of 9/11, or they can be protracted and uncertain, like climate change and global warming.

If you look at Allentown through a fifty-year prism, you can identify enormous change, but month by month and year by year, it occurred very slowly. Sometimes change that takes place like this—let's call it evolutionary—is hard to discern even while it is occurring. How did a town's personality change? Why? What was the catalyst? When those proverbial forks in the road were approached, what decisions were made that virtually assured the ultimate outcome? Was the long, sad decline experienced by Allentown at all avoidable? Is it over? Are we now at the doorstep of a genuine renaissance?

My classmates and I are now well into our sixties. We were among the first wave of baby boomers, witnesses to monumental cultural changes in the 1960s and 1970s and then to unimaginable technological innovation in the years that followed. We represent the generation that was an agent of change, and now, looking back, we have a chance to evaluate what we did and how we were affected by it.

For some reason, I remember a school assembly that occurred during the 1956–57 school year. As we took our seats, Doris Day's "Que Sera, Sera" was being played over the loudspeakers.

When I was just a little girl,
I asked my mother, what will I be?
Will I be pretty?
Will I be rich?
Here's what she said to me...
Que sera, sera
Whatever will be, will be
The future's not ours to see,
Que sera, sera
What will be, will be.

It seems strange that a ten-year-old boy would hold that memory in his mind for a lifetime, but the fact is I was always fascinated with thoughts of the future, speculating about how my life would turn out, where I would live, what profession I would choose, whom I would marry. Now that much of what was in my future is part of my past, I am no less interested in it. In many ways, reflection and reminiscing have become two of my favorite pastimes.

In this book I have tried to weave together two threads. One is the story behind the steady and relatively swift economic decline of Allentown. Going in, I had no preconceived notions. I knew that conditions there had changed for the worse, and of course, the ongoing slump in American manufacturing would have had to play a huge part in what happened, but in my mind, that alone couldn't have explained everything. Our national economy has proven to be remarkably resilient over the years and, in large part, has been able to adapt successfully to global competition. Within Pennsylvania, for example, the city of Pittsburgh was able to stage a significant turnaround in spite of a domestic steel industry that entered into a seemingly endless and practically terminal decline. Even the city of Bethlehem, situated directly adjacent to Allentown, managed to withstand the failure of its largest employer, Bethlehem Steel, somewhat successfully. That it was able to survive at all is notable. This company was once the second-largest steel producer in the country, employing over thirty thousand workers in Bethlehem alone (Bethlehem's current population is about seventy-five thousand). Clearly, something had happened in Allentown that was quite unique and, perhaps, to some degree avoidable as well.

The other story concerns my link with the past, namely my former classmates. I challenged myself to try to reach out to as many as I could, to speak when possible with each of them, and to learn about their personal journeys. How were their lives shaped by the experiences of their childhood? How did the ensuing hard times affect their families or each of them individually?

As the project became clearer in my mind, I realized that the task of successfully tracking down these folks was going to be a daunting one indeed. At first, I could only identify six faces from my class picture. The Muhlenberg Elementary School and the Allentown School Department did not maintain any records such as class rosters. Internet searches did prove to be somewhat helpful, but the dead ends soon became obvious, such as women who married and assumed their husbands' surnames. Additionally, many of the males had such common names that standard search tools became almost useless, but I persevered.

One afternoon I was watching an NFL game and heard the announcer describe a play made by New York Giants receiver Jerrel Jernigan. This made me think, "Whatever happened to Jane Ellen Ternigan?" Jane Ellen was in my fourth-grade class, and I remembered her clearly. If it is possible for a ten-year-old to have a "girlfriend," she was it. Somehow I was able to locate her. She is happily married and maintains a practice as a family therapist in a small town in the western United States. We had a nice phone conversation, and she volunteered to look at our class picture to help me identify more of the children in the photo. She came up with about a half dozen additional names. Next to one of them, she wrote "Beverly Hackett." For weeks I kept looking at the name, and for some reason, it didn't seem to fit. One night while sleeping, I sat up in bed and shouted out loud (at myself, not Jane Ellen), "It's Hacker, you idiot, not Hackett." The scene could have been taken from a Steve Martin movie. In any case, my wife thought I had lost my mind.

It took a while, but I did locate Beverly, who had married and settled in Pennsylvania about an hour from Allentown. On one of my visits to Allentown, we met to catch up on the last fifty-five years. What unexpected fun! Bev had spent her life in educational administration and explained she had just retired. She also volunteered to see if she could identify other classmates in the picture, and she too was very helpful.

That's how it went. This process of identification continued in a quite unremarkable and old-fashioned way: first by locating one person, and another, then one more, and often each new contact was able to match a different face in the original class picture with a new name. Some classmates, it turned out, had been able to stay in touch with each other to this day, and these unexpected connections proved to be invaluable. The most surprising connection of all was that two of my classmates later married each other. And they had kept this very same class picture among their treasures for all these years.

I was also able to dig up pieces of information on several other contemporaries, who may not have sat in this particular fourth-grade classroom, but they did attend the same school at the same time and shared many of the same experiences. In the end, I was able to ID most of those in the class picture, and with the assistance of several other classmates, all of the rest. I was successful in reaching almost half either by phone or in person, and over the course of time, I was able to make a number of additional contacts as well.

Not surprisingly, a few people I looked up after fifty-five years had elapsed were not entirely enthusiastic about me or my project. Many were civil, but hardly welcoming, making me feel like an unwanted telemarketing solicitor. Some in fact had vivid memories of pranks that I had pulled on them, and as I spoke to more and more classmates, it became obvious that my behavior in those days was beyond atrocious. It was fairly humiliating that after fifty-five years the mere mention of my name would elicit these memories if not outright horror. I vainly tried to look upon that as a positive in that it gave me a chance to make long-overdue amends, but truthfully, it was just plain embarrassing. In the end, the apologies I did make were able to give me some sense of relief.

My greatest challenge concerned how to link together what seemed to be two very different stories: first, the deterioration and potential rebirth of a city, and second, the growth and development of a group of aging baby boomers who happened to live there when they were very young. For those who remained in the area as adults, of course there would be a very strong connection to the community and a powerful story to tell. For the rest, the association would be less direct, and much of the local narrative would be told through the eyes of others.

As my peers entered the labor force in the 1970s, cities like Allentown were already beginning to suffer as a result of global economic changes that left them vulnerable. These changes had a corrosive effect on the community at large. Financial insecurity abounded, and with it came a general feeling of defeatism. President Jimmy Carter's much-celebrated "malaise" speech, delivered in 1979, said it all. Carter put it like this: "The erosion of our confidence in the future is threatening to destroy the social and the political fabric of America."

Life presents us all with choices and challenges. This is as true for us as individuals as it is for our society at large. In my particular case, I never really chose to stay in Allentown, or even to leave it, because in a sense that decision had already been dictated by events beyond my control. My parents moved to Philadelphia in 1962 when I was fifteen. I attended boarding school in Massachusetts, college in New York, and graduate school on the West Coast. My entire adult life has been spent in New England, mostly in the Boston area. When I made the choice to settle in Boston, I was twenty-four, and the thought of returning to Allentown, Pennsylvania, as an option never even occurred to me. Aunts, uncles, and cousins had all left. I still had some roots there, but the pull wasn't very strong, at least not then.

For many years, I had no real transmission line to my hometown. Yet, as I later learned, a number of my classmates did, either as visitors staying in touch with family or as full-time residents who were working, establishing businesses, raising families, and otherwise contributing to their community. These individuals had clearly made a different sort of commitment.

Changing economic conditions, and some questionable decisions by some, ultimately overwhelmed the good intentions of many who chose to remain. As economic decay set in, many residents came to believe that the subsequent increase in poverty and crime had become an irreversible and permanent feature of daily life.

My reading of history, however, suggests that nothing in life is static. People, cities, and even civilization itself are in a continuous state of evolution and change. Even though this work is largely a pastel of recollections and anecdotal history, the past that it examines in a sense is alive today. The events and issues of that time will continue to have a lasting influence upon my generation and those that follow in the future.

My Bittersweet Homecoming is neither a conventional memoir nor a chronological history. Think of it as a collage of facts and reminiscences that speaks to the American baby boom generation. There are millions of boomers who grew up in places just like Allentown, Pennsylvania, and all of them, I am certain, can identify with my own experience and memories.

1

WHY?

WE HAVE ALL heard the cliché that hindsight is twenty-twenty, but all the hindsight in the world can often fail to answer the question "Why?" Humorist Will Rogers was asked during the Depression in the 1930s if it were possible to make money in the stock market. At the time, this was in itself a laughable proposition, since the market was performing so badly. Rogers said it was easy: "Just buy a good stock, and when it goes up, sell it...and if it doesn't go up, don't buy it."

We all know it is impossible to predict the future. Strangely enough, it is often equally hard to understand the past. Why did the stock market go up or down? How could the American Civil War have been avoided? Why has the earth's climate changed? Of course, Monday morning quarterbacks can always come up with some sort of an answer, but we can never be sure with certainty that any of their explanations is in fact on target. Sometimes, hindsight is twenty-fifty.

Throughout history, certain societies have achieved dominance and then faded into secondary importance; sometimes they have become irrelevant or even disappeared altogether. In a free market economy, the business cycle ebbs and flows constantly, with all expansions followed by contractions, and all bull markets followed by bear markets. Large, successful corporations routinely fail, and not simply because of financial fraud (Enron, WorldCom, etc.), but more often due to inertia and arrogance. Companies like Eastman Kodak, Howard Johnson, Polaroid, and Encyclopedia Britannica were in the end victims of change, but equally important was their inability to anticipate it or to adapt to it.

The conventional wisdom is that American industrial cities in the last third of the twentieth century all caught the same virus and developed a fatal illness. American manufacturers, it was said, were doomed. Their labor costs were too high, and their factories were too old. Multiple energy price shocks not only sucked money out of the economy, but they also whittled away at the self-confidence of the nation. The same could be said for the high interest rates of the 1970s and 1980s, which damaged the housing industry and kept a lid on discretionary consumer spending.

At the time, life seemed almost hopeless. Most people assumed that double-digit inflation was here to stay. Perpetually high interest rates would act as a permanent drag on the economy. In the early '80s, *Business Week* actually ran a cover story on "The Death of Equities," with a grave marker that read "NYSE—R.I.P." Ironically, the timing of this article marked the end of a bear market that had begun fifteen years earlier in 1968.

Many feared the United States would be pushed aside by new Japanese competitors. At one point in the early '80s, the United States and Japan entered into a trade agreement that limited the number of Japanese-made automobiles shipped into our country. I remember visiting a Toyota dealer at the time and being told that there would be a three-month wait for a new car, and that there were no cars available to test drive! To make matters worse, the dealer's selling price was set at a nonnegotiable premium over sticker.

American auto manufacturers had never adapted their production to smaller, more fuel-efficient cars after the price of gasoline spiked in the 1970s. They blamed their misfortune on unfair trade practices and cried out for government trade protection, which they temporarily received. When asked (rhetorically) what his company produced to compete with high-quality and competitively priced Japanese imports, GM's CEO Roger Smith replied, "A good two-year-old used Buick."

GM spent billions on poorly executed plans to automate production. Incredibly, their robots on one embarrassing occasion painted other robots and were also observed to have painted car doors shut. A cost-cutting plan to share body parts among different brands resulted in a loss of brand identity; from a distance, it was hard to tell a Chevy from a Buick or a Cadillac. There were massive and costly manufacturing reorganizations, which had no discernible effect on productivity; GM could have purchased Toyota with the money it squandered on capital spending in the 1980s. While the company made bad decision after bad decision, its factories were banging out large gas guzzlers and losing market share at a frightening rate. The answer seems simple today. Why not build a small, reliable fuel-efficient car that customers want rather than a large, costly, inefficient vehicle that they don't? It took another twenty years and a government bailout before GM got it.

The experience of the auto industry was not an aberration. Caterpillar was being severely pressured by Komatsu. Would this too be an end of an era? Japanese brands like Sony, Pioneer, Hitachi, and Toshiba quickly gained dominance in the consumer electronics market. Similar stories played out in the steel and textile industries.

Sadly, our biggest export was our wealth, for as Japanese-made goods flowed in, American dollars went out the back door. Japanese investors began buying up real estate around the world. Menus in the Canadian resort of Banff were written in two languages—English and Japanese—as a necessary acknowledgment of the influence of Japan's investment there. In January 1968, the Japanese (Nikkei 225) and the American (Dow Jones Industrial Average) stock market indexes were roughly comparable: 900 for the Nikkei and 1,200 for the Dow. By 1990, the Nikkei was at 38,000 (yes, 38,000), and the Dow was at 2,800. It appeared the United States was left in the dust.

At one time, it seemed there would be an inevitable changing of the guard, with Japan at least competing with and possibly supplanting the

United States as a preeminent global economic superpower. It never happened. In time Japan lost its labor cost advantage over the West, and its debt levels rose to unsustainable heights (during Japan's boom years, mortgages with hundred-year amortizations were not uncommon). Japanese banks, which financed the expansion, spent years writing off bad loans, and then they wrote off some more. They became known as "zombie banks." By 2015, both averages had nearly converged once again, with both indexes trading around 18,000; the Nikkei was down 60 percent, and the Dow was up 600 percent. No one could have foreseen a reversal of fortune of this magnitude.

With confidence shattered given the enormity of the Nikkei's decline, investors stopped investing and consumer spending atrophied. By 2013, Japan's trade surplus became a deficit. Economic power in Asia began to shift to China. Other nations, such as Korea, Thailand, Malaysia, and India, began to flourish as well. Nothing, it seems, stays the same very long.

Most surprising of all, manufacturing in the United States, instead of vaporizing, managed to bounce back when its recovery was least expected. A *Time* magazine cover story in April 2013 featured what was described as a renaissance in American manufacturing. US manufacturers added five hundred thousand jobs between 2010 and 2013—labor costs in other nations had begun to creep up, while union givebacks, painful as they were, did help to stem the tide of job losses. The shale oil boom created a new source of relatively cheap energy for US factories, a true game changer. Finally, newer technologically advanced and highly automated factories are far more productive than those they have replaced.

Apart from a relatively recent recovery in manufacturing, the national economy proved to be remarkably resilient after the difficult 1970s. American economic activity and personal wealth grew significantly in the '80s, '90s, and 2000s. Unfortunately, prosperity proved elusive in Allentown.

What does all this mean? Nothing is ever as simple as it may seem, and very little in this world is either predictable or inevitable. An undesirable outcome may occasionally be the result of bad luck, but more often, one can assign responsibility to a bad decision, a series of bad decisions, or no decision at all. In the end, many of the challenges and hardships experienced by the people in American industrial cities like Allentown could never have been avoided altogether, but I am certain they could have been mitigated, if only different responses were made to the given realities of the day.

The National Civic League is best known for bestowing the "all-American" moniker on ten cities that vie for this title in an annual competition. Think of it as a municipal bake-off or beauty contest. Allentown achieved this recognition in 1962 and 1974, but its attempt at a trifecta in 2001 met with disappointment, as its application for all-American status was denied.

The applications themselves are quite revealing. In 1962, each city was asked, "What major problems remain unresolved in your community?" Allentown cited a number of such "problems," but truthfully they were nothing more than luxury problems: provide $250,000 capital financing for a nearby ski area, expand a nine-hole municipal golf course to eighteen holes, build a new library, and raise $400,000 to lengthen a runway at the airport. There was an admission that the city had done very little in the area of public housing, and that a commission was looking into it. It was also noted that some of the sidewalks downtown had developed cracks that needed repair.

Allentown's All-America City Award Committee apparently didn't feel that the city was suffering in any material way, and in fact, it wasn't. It was booming. Crime was low, and the local economy hummed. The issue of race relations was not even the subject of conversation—the city was all white (99 percent English-speaking Caucasian). As many as fifteen thousand or more spectators watched Friday-night high school football, where sellouts were commonplace. Yes, life was one-dimensional and parochial, but there was a feeling of togetherness and a sense of community that have sadly faded away with the passage of time.

In 1974, Allentown achieved all-American status a second time. The years that had elapsed since 1962 were as turbulent as any in the nation's history. Civil rights legislation raised expectations of blacks in America, as did Lyndon Johnson's War on Poverty, but real change and measurable economic progress were slow to come. The war in Vietnam divided the country like no other and on many different levels. Student deferments tended to protect white, middle-class college students from the draft, and as a result, blacks served and died in the armed forces at a disproportionately high level. Their resentment was justifiable and real. Oddly enough, the antiwar protest movement of the '60s was largely inspired by white students, who for the most part were able to remain at home for the duration of the war.

The year 1968 was particularly chaotic. Robert Kennedy and Martin Luther King were assassinated. After King was killed, riots broke out in Newark, Detroit, and other major cities. Some black radicals openly espoused violence as a tool of revolution. Student protestors shut down operations at Berkeley, Columbia, and other universities. The Democratic Convention in Chicago was the site of near anarchy and police violence.

Culturally, massive changes were taking place. Unmarried couples began to cohabit (the phrase used then was "shacking up"), something considered scandalous a few years beforehand. Drug use proliferated and for the first time became commonplace in mainstream white America. If Vietnam weren't enough, the Watergate scandal helped to destroy what little confidence the average American had left in our government. In 1973 OPEC embargoed oil exports to the United States, causing a spike in gasoline prices, frequent shortages and long lines at gas stations, and ultimately, a severe recession. As these events played out, Allentown was again named an all-American city. It described itself as being a socially balanced, middle-income community. Its white population had been 99 percent in 1962; it was 98 percent in 1974. Apparently, socially balanced means different things to different people.

The 1974 application cited three key events for the Civic League to consider before deciding on all-American status:

1. The opening of the Hamilton Mall (a downtown pedestrian shopping mall project)

2. The construction of a large medical center on a hundred-acre site west of the city
3. The adoption of a mayor/council form of municipal government

One can charitably say that this is not much of a list. Rather than being a city in transition, 1974 Allentown turned out to be very much like 1962 Allentown, with a few gray hairs, but its residents were nonetheless proud to earn all-American honors once again. In a moment of honest reflection, the city admitted that there were obstacles to potential ongoing progress, which included a negative community attitude and resignation to a troubled future. In this respect, the mood of the people in Allentown was not much different than the rest of the country. During these years, Americans experienced all sorts of unimaginable happenings—recession, an oil embargo, street riots, political protests, Vietnam—and a general sense of discord and distrust. What had once been bright hope for the future—the elimination of poverty, the end of racial discrimination, peace, freedom, and prosperity—ended with Richard M. Nixon's election and landslide reelection.

Say what you wish about Nixon. The fact is he captured the spirit of the times. Nixon's presidency marked the first time we heard about the silent majority. There was widespread disgust with radicals, protestors, hippies, flag burners as well as bra burners, feminism in general, welfare cheats, and black Muslims. One could add to this list Eastern intellectuals, the *New York Times*, the US Supreme Court, and virtually any other person or institution whose world view did not embrace family values, religious conservatism, and patriotism. Many of Nixon's supporters simply would not or could not accept cultural changes that were taking place. In a sense, they were in denial. Nixon, ever the opportunist, rode these sentiments to the White House. In 1972 he was overwhelmingly reelected and carried swing state Pennsylvania with ease. The sentiments of this silent majority resonated deeply with the people of Allentown, Pennsylvania.

Times were hard throughout America in the 1970s and early '80s. The difficulties Allentown experienced as the years wore on were hardly unique. The so-called "stagflation" that typified this era—high inflation and unemployment, as well as seemingly chronic recession—was present everywhere. Throughout the country, especially in industrial cities, there was suffering, but there was also the hope, perhaps somewhat naïve, that in time the United States would get its mojo back. However, long-term recovery was to prove elusive. As foreign competition began to appear, at first slowly, and then as it heated up, American manufacturers cried foul, but they had no real game plan except to plead for trade protection.

Bethlehem Steel is a classic case study. Once one of the world's largest and most successful producers of structural steel, the company experienced its first losses and layoffs in the late 1970s and then struggled throughout the remainder of its operating history. After a massive $1.5 billion loss was reported in 1982, the company shuttered many unproductive operations and managed a brief return to profitability. In 1995, it shut down its huge plant in Bethlehem. Earlier, in 1993 it had exited its railroad car business, and by 1997 it was out of shipbuilding as well. Layoffs and closures were becoming commonplace events. The company filed for bankruptcy in 2001, and its remaining assets (a few plants) were purchased by International Steel Group several years later.

The failure of Bethlehem Steel was an economic catastrophe for Allentown and the Lehigh Valley, and its ignominious end was clearly a significant factor, though hardly the only one, behind the city's long-term decline. The steel company was the region's largest employer by far, and the ripple effect caused by its steady layoffs and furloughs quickly became obvious. Economic activity collapsed everywhere: department stores, supermarkets, restaurants, and virtually every other form of retail spending were hit immediately, and housing and construction entered into a protracted, painful tailspin. We shall take a closer look at Bethlehem Steel later, but suffice it to say, Allentown's economic troubles, which began in the 1970s, multiplied over time. The city never recovered with the rest of the nation in the 1980s, and the 1990s brought no relief.

In 2001, Allentown applied once more, this time unsuccessfully, to be recognized as an all-American city. By this time, the transformation of the city was complete. Billy Joel's hit song "Allentown" about the struggles and hardships the city experienced was released in 1982. Rather than marking a transitional point in history, like the Depression's "Brother, Can You Spare a Dime," Joel's song identified the beginning of what was to become an extended, long-term slide. By 2001, the city had become unrecognizable. Poverty, crime, drugs, gangs, dilapidated housing, and abandoned factories all became staple features of daily living.

The first request for information on the 2001 all-American city application was "Describe your community's most pressing challenges." The answer began, "Imagine a place where residents fear leaving their homes...a neighborhood with littered streets, graffitied walls, boarded-up businesses and gangs of loiterers...In the 1980s, increases in crime, declining rates of home ownership, and an overall lack of stability and pride in the city's neighborhoods had an adverse effect on the quality of life in Allentown." Clearly, the municipal government was well aware of what it was up against and went on to describe the plans it had in place to turn things around. Compared to the resources at Allentown's disposal, the challenges were overwhelming. For litter and graffiti, city officials suggested the formation of a "Clean and Green Committee" of residents and city employees. To address declining rates of home ownership, a $500,000 credit line would be provided by a local lender for short-term assistance to would-be homeowners who couldn't qualify for financing because of minor credit problems, inadequate savings, or lack of employment history. Realistically, how far could $500,000 go? Given the damage that had been done and the limited resources at the city's disposal in 2001, a quick and significant turnaround would have been next to impossible at that time.

It is easy to identify the reasons behind Allentown's early years of economic decline; the city was suffering from the same affliction as the rest of the country. What is not so obvious is why the decline became a death spiral, lasting thirty plus years. It may be safe to say the worst is over, but it will be a tough road back.

The judgment of history is clouded. Bethlehem Steel failed to be sure, but other steel companies didn't. Steel is still produced in the United States. One cannot even say that Bethlehem Steel's bankruptcy was inevitable; as we shall see, it was the result of a host of bad planning, worse decisions, and an almost obscene level of corporate arrogance. A number of textile manufacturers likewise folded, victims of foreign competition and onerous labor union contracts, but others survived and are still functioning today. True, many of them source materials and/or have transferred some production overseas, but the same can be said for Apple and Nike.

Allentown had the opportunity as early as 1960 to become active in urban renewal in an impactful way and build a connector from center city to the newly constructed I-178, which ran nearby. Nothing was done, and the city's infrastructure, even today, is virtually unchanged from the end of World War II.

When plans for the first suburban shopping centers were hatched after 1970, the city's response was to turn the Hamilton Street shopping area into a pedestrian shopping mall. The construction was lengthy and disruptive, and when it was finally finished, it quickly became obvious that this concept was not going to work. Within a few years, larger department stores and smaller specialty stores began to pull out. Today, for the first time in years, there is significant redevelopment taking place in the downtown area, but many of the old storefronts still feature pawn shops, check-cashing services, adult bookstores, and "For Lease" signs.

Equally damaging as the poor decisions that were then made were, for want of a better word, the "nondecisions." Inaction can sometimes be more damaging than a misguided act. Old brick factory buildings remained vacant; in other cities, they were redeveloped in commercial, residential, or mixed-use formats. The waterfront area of the Lehigh River was an eyesore, and it still is; it is interesting to compare what might have been with the likes of San Antonio's River Walk or Idaho Falls Greenbelt. Defeatism and a sense of resignation were commonplace; given this, it is not surprising there was little sense of mission or urgency to attract new and emerging high-tech businesses.

The Lehigh Valley is not home to a mega university. Lehigh University, located in Bethlehem, is the largest, with a total undergraduate and graduate enrollment of approximately seven thousand. There are several small private colleges, such as Muhlenberg, Cedar Crest, and Moravian. Penn State does operate a satellite campus nearby, but in spite of the critical role it could have played, this facility remained a fringe player for many years. Initially, the school offered a handful of courses and no degrees; its original role was to help prepare engineering students to attend Penn State University in State College, Pennsylvania. In 1970, Mohr Orchards donated forty acres of land in nearby Fogelsville for the school's first campus, but seven years elapsed before the initial build-out was completed. It was not until 1997 that the college, now called Penn State Lehigh Valley, began to offer four-year degrees (at that time, it moved to a new campus in semirural Center Valley, nearly ten miles from the heart of Allentown). One can only wonder how downtown Allentown could have taken a different direction, and how many lives could have been altered, if only the college was properly funded in the 1970s and conveniently located in the city itself—near the people it was meant to serve and who would benefit most from its mission.

As the economic decline progressed, many residents simply picked up and moved. Housing prices plunged, and for the first time Latinos and other minority groups, attracted by low rents, gravitated to the city. As this influx proceeded, many whites who had not already left town escaped to the suburbs. By 1990, nearly 25 percent of the population was Latino; within the next ten years, the amount approached 50 percent. Demographic changes like this are virtually unprecedented. Race relations in Allentown during this time can best be described as challenging and difficult; at its worst, the distrust between Latinos and a vocal minority of whites caused a near breakdown in civic life and paralysis in municipal government, where more time was spent finger-pointing and scapegoating than on addressing the problems that affected both groups.

In his book *The Time of our Lives*, Journalist Tom Brokaw recently asked, "What happened to the America I thought I knew?" His inquiry is far reaching, but clearly one thought he puts forth again and again is that as a nation and as a people we have become a house divided, lacking much of the common purpose and optimism that typified mid-twentieth-century America.

In Allentown in the 1980s and 1990s, this sense of alienation reached extreme levels. Many whites literally blamed every negative byproduct of the economic disaster—crime, drug use, gang violence, graffiti, as well as the collapse in housing prices—on Latinos; of course, many Latinos were terribly frustrated, feeling as if they were outcasts, unable to compete for decent jobs and a piece of the American dream.

Interestingly, most of the newcomers were Puerto Rican—they were American citizens with American passports. From their perspective, racism was very much alive in their world and responsible for many of their difficulties. As much as anything else, this polarization made it virtually impossible for the city to pull itself up and proactively address its unfortunate circumstances. Each side tended to blame the other for its misfortune, and as a result, collaboration was close to impossible.

Allentown's struggles in the late '70s and early '80s had a root cause and simple explanation: recession. What is much more difficult to pinpoint is why the illness became nearly terminal, and now, more than thirty years later, why it has not been entirely eradicated. Questions that begin with the word "why" are often very hard to answer. Change is often mysterious, and it was no different for Allentown, Pennsylvania—this place of my long-ago childhood.

In the course of my research, I learned about businesses that failed and those that survived. I saw government officials who made good decisions, bad decisions, and no decisions. Some folks were visionary, others reactionary. On certain occasions, citizens were able to collaborate, but more often they were adversarial. This divisiveness, in fact, often appeared to be embedded in local politics. Even when racial or ethnic issues were not involved, the inability of different interest groups to work together in a productive way was an ultimate game changer. Political debate, sadly, led only to stalemate and paralysis. It would take many years of toxic politics and endless frustration before the people of Allentown could begin to look to the future without being restrained by resentments of the past.

2

SEPTEMBER 1956

IT'S HARD TO write a memoir if you have a fuzzy memory. Over fifty-five years have passed since I stepped into my fourth-grade classroom on the first day of school in 1956. I have very vague recollections of what was taught or even who my classmates were. I know that every day began with the Lord's Prayer and the Pledge of Allegiance. Another "highlight" that comes to mind is that green Jell-O was served in the cafeteria during lunch, along with treats like fish sticks and creamed chipped beef.

Our teacher allowed us to blow off steam by supervising relay races that were held in our classroom while we attempted to balance erasers on our heads. At recess we played baseball—until one of my friends got hit in the head with a tossed bat, at which point, baseball season quickly ended. I recall that the subsequent transition from baseball to (I am sad to say) kickball was one of the great tragedies of my youth. A decent alternative was outdoor dodgeball, but neither kickball nor dodgeball could compare to Bombardment: an indoor team dodgeball-like game where the opposition would end up trapped against a wall before being pulverized at close distance. What fun!

We passed notes around our classroom all the time, or at least when our teacher's back was turned. I misbehaved often and was constantly corrected, but I found it difficult to toe the line. Some might say I was the class clown, but I was also a good student, so my report card was typically distinguished in some respects and deficient in others. English and math were mastered easily enough, but little things like social skills, helpfulness, humility, and the ability to listen and accept constructive criticism were apparently beyond my reach. In fact, I found it hard just to sit still. Fourth grade was a blur, every day was exciting, and my life was filled with high drama.

Being a child, of course, I had no ability to appreciate or understand my environment the way an adult might. In 1956, Allentown and the surrounding Lehigh Valley of Pennsylvania were booming. The population of the city had doubled since 1900. The area was a beehive of manufacturing. The city was not crime free, but the comparisons with today are striking. In 1956, the city reported 1,097 crime incidents, of which more than half (583) involved larceny of less than fifty dollars. There were no murders and only twenty reported robberies. In a recent year, there were nearly six thousand reported criminal incidents, including five hundred robberies, and on average, one murder per month. In 2010, the city's violent crime rate was 67 percent higher than the nation's and 84 percent higher than Pennsylvania's. Using one popular measure, Allentown's crime index is currently around 8, which means that 92 percent of American cities are deemed to be "safer" than Allentown. During the years I was growing up, we never latched the front door, and my parents never bothered to lock their cars.

The city of Allentown was (and still is) the third largest in Pennsylvania, and the population of the metropolitan area was substantial, over four hundred thousand according to the US census of 1960. Yet the flavor of life was clearly parochial, and the atmosphere was very small town. I thought my father was famous because it seemed everyone knew him by name, whether we were in a restaurant, walking downtown, or taking in a minor-league baseball game.

At least that was my recollection. What was life really like? One of the most obvious sources of information would likely be found in Allentown's daily newspaper, the *Morning Call*. The paper's owner, Call

Chronicle Publishing, was by far the dominant media outlet in the region. Allentown itself had no television stations in those years; all such broadcasts emanated from Philadelphia, about fifty miles to the south. The *Morning Call* had a daily circulation in excess of one hundred thousand and was the primary source of news and information to all of the city's residents.

The Allentown *Morning Call* is still published, and not surprisingly, it too has changed in the last fifty years. Once independently owned, Call-Chronicle Newspapers was sold to Times Mirror in 1984, which in turn, was acquired by the Chicago-based Tribune Company in 2000. The *Morning Call* had ceased publishing its evening edition, the *Call Chronicle*, in 1980.

I remember as a child taking a field trip to their offices and visiting what was called a morgue. This was a place that housed a collection of old newspaper clippings and articles, something we would now call an archive database. This morgue no longer exists, and its modern counterpart, a digitized library, is not maintained for use by the general public. As a result, management at the newspaper was incapable of giving me assistance in my research efforts, but fortunately the Allentown Public Library was able to provide me with access to some of the information I needed. Thankfully, the last twenty years or so of the paper's issues are available online, and this proved to be a lifesaver in terms of my research efforts. Some of my digging, though, had to be done the old-fashioned way.

I first visited the Allentown Public Library on a typically warm day in the summer of 2012, and I was struck by the crowd that had gathered inside. At first, I couldn't imagine a public library acting as a people magnet during such beautiful weather, especially considering that school was not in session. Sadly, it quickly became obvious that the real draw here was central air conditioning rather than the book collection or other library services.

Approximately one hundred years' worth of Allentown *Morning Call*s can be accessed through old microfilm readers. Searching on microfilm is a researcher's equivalent to panning for gold, but since I had set my sights on a specific point in time—September 1956—my search was fairly quick and relatively effective.

Entire pages were devoted to back-to-school coverage, town by town and school by school. There was good reason for this: the postwar baby boom. Most of my classmates, like myself, were born in 1947, year two of the boom. When we were old enough to go to school, there weren't enough schools, and after more classrooms were built, there weren't enough teachers.

Allentown's new construction that year was the Louis E. Dieruff School. Neighboring Hellertown had rented extra space in 1955 from the American Legion Home for high school classes; in 1956, the school board ended that experiment and opted for double sessions instead. Nearby, school districts in Stroudsburg, Tamaqua, Summit Hill, Kutztown, Berks County, and Red Hill were all in the midst of construction projects or had just completed them. Plans for expansion were being readied in Souderton, Longswamp and Rockland Townships, and Brandywine Heights. Bethlehem's Liberty High School added a new gymnasium.

The school I attended, Muhlenberg Elementary School, has just completed a major expansion project two years before; prior to this, the school department had authorized "doubling up" on a temporary basis, whereby two different grades were combined in the same classroom. Classroom deficits like this were common throughout the country. The US Office of Education estimated that in 1953, 60 percent of American classrooms were overcrowded, and an additional three hundred forty-five thousand classrooms were needed to restore balance.

Teacher shortages quickly became critical. In the 1950s, school-age population nationally increased from twenty-nine million to forty-one million, leaving the country with an immediate need for one hundred thousand additional teachers. Even with aggressive recruitment and funding efforts, a meaningful shortage still existed in 1960, year fourteen of the baby boom.

We often see a much different picture today. New school construction is often looked upon as an unaffordable luxury. Municipalities are generally pinched and frequently find themselves in contentious negotiations with teacher unions and other municipal unions as well. Extracurricular programs and athletics are routinely cut back, and layoffs are commonplace. Overcrowding is common in prisons, but not in schools.

Today, the Muhlenberg Elementary School, built in the 1920s with an addition constructed in 1953, stands physically unchanged from the time I attended. The Allentown School District's website currently lists policies on weapons, gangs, tobacco, controlled substances and drug paraphernalia, and pregnancy. The creeping old age of the school building and the school district's policies on student behavior are hardly unique to Allentown these days. I am afraid September 1956 was indeed a long time ago.

The guiding principles of elementary-school education were firmly rooted in the past. Corporal punishment was not uncommon. I know this for a fact because I got spanked, and I was not unique. Special education, as we know it today, did not exist. Schools were just beginning to identify students who were not able to learn effectively in a traditional classroom setting; they were called "slow learners," and these children were unilaterally assigned to a segregated classroom without any input or involvement by their parents.

In the 1950s, the role of women was far different from that of today. The *Morning Call* regularly published two sections, "Woman's" and "Society," although the two seemed virtually indistinguishable in subject matter. Apart from announcements of engagements and weddings, there was a vast amount of coverage devoted to mundane events and trivial happenings in the community at large. As an example:

> "Mr. and Mrs. George White left Allentown Thursday for Hermosa Beach, Calif., near Los Angeles, on a three-week visit with their daughter and family, Mr. and Mrs. Earl Behr and son,

> David. It's the Whites' first trip to the West Coast. The Behrs moved from Allentown a year ago."
>
> "Betty and John Durishin's hill-top house in Balletsville is a setting for houseguests this Labor Day weekend. Visitors are Betty's aunt and family, the Charles Sloans and children Susan and Charles of Kensington, Md. Mrs. Sloan, the former Helen Noble of Allentown, was head of physical education at Allentown High at one time and will be remembered as one of the prettiest girls in Allentown."

If this weren't enough, readers could get more local coverage in the "Here and There" section:

> "Mr. and Mrs. Clarence Knerr of Longswamp held a family picnic at their home on Labor Day."
>
> "Dr. Pauline Hinkle Wells, chiropodist of 719 Hamilton St, Allentown, will observe her birthday anniversary on Sunday."

The position of women was very clearly defined, with strict boundaries and limited expectations. It was more than amusing that Dr. Wells, a rarity of sorts as a female professional, had her birthday celebration—of all things—included in such announcements. From today's perspective, it is easy to ask rhetorically, "What was she (and the *Morning Call*) thinking?" Trivia like this isn't even printed today in small town weeklies, let alone a city daily with a paid circulation in excess of one hundred thousand issues.

What we would define today as "hard news" painted a very similar picture. A seven-paragraph news story described a fashion show that was held at the end of a sewing class given at the Singer Sewing Center on Hamilton Street. The show was described as a "grand finale" and featured the "pretty clothes the girls (all 16 and 17 years old) made during their lessons." There were three judges, all home economics teachers; they were identified using the first names of their husbands (Mrs. Ralph ——, Mrs. Henry ——, and Mrs. Theodore ——), as was common during this time. It would only be seven short years before the publication of Betty Friedan's groundbreaking *The Feminine Mystique*, and the women's liberation movement that followed would soon touch every corner of society. Within a few years of the book's release, 1956 would seem like a time warp.

It is truly amazing to look at the institution of dating through a 1956 lens. The *Morning Call* featured a then-current study that revealed among other things that "city girls apparently do not feel that necking is a must." This must have been because "in big towns or small, girls seem to agree that a goodnight kiss is about as far as they should go for the first three dates."

One thing both city and country girls could agree on was early marriage, although the definition of "early" was open to interpretation. In towns of less than fifty thousand, seventeen or eighteen seemed appropriate, whereas city girls preferred to wait until nineteen after putting in a year or so at college.

In Lehigh County, one in seven marriages ended in divorce in 1955; neighboring Northampton County experienced a one-in-five divorce rate. This represented a significant increase from the early 1900s, but the rate had remained relatively stable during the Great Depression, World War II, and beyond. Unmarried couples did not live together. "Relationships," as we know them today, did not exist. One was either engaged to be married, married, or single.

Somewhere in the midst of this seemingly prim, archaic society, burlesque flourished. It was a staple of Saturday-night entertainment at Allentown's Lyric Theater. Built in 1896 as the Central Market Hall and renamed the Lyric three years later, the venue was ultimately sold to the Allentown Symphony Association in the 1950s, and after several more years came to be known as Symphony Hall. Oddly, for some time after the symphony took up residence, burlesque remained a featured attraction and was the concert hall's major moneymaker well into the 1960s.

I remember Virginia "Ding Dong" Bell (how could one forget a name like that?) as the Lyric's most heavily hyped performer. Actually, I don't remember her, of course—just the newspaper ads detailing her physical attributes. Claiming to have a forty-eight-inch bust line, Bell was among the best-known and highly paid burlesque performers of her era. It is no mystery why an actress who couldn't act (or for that matter, a dancer who couldn't dance) was able to achieve such notoriety and success.

Ding Dong Bell notwithstanding, daily life had more than a hint of puritanical morality. In June 1956, police in Bethlehem raided a "gambling establishment" and arrested several patrons. Three men were actually prosecuted, convicted, and sentenced to the Northampton County jail for one year (eligible for parole after ninety days). Upon granting parole in September, Judge William Barthold noted that each of the men "has had time to consider the crime to which he has pleaded guilty." He had the offenders sign an affidavit pledging to "conduct (themselves) henceforth in a good and law-abiding manner." The judge concluded that "if we want to preserve our country and (its) freedoms...it (illegal gambling) has got to be stopped." While granting parole, Judge Barthold did quietly note that the ringleaders of the operation had yet to be caught. I am sure he would be surprised today to learn that what was formerly Bethlehem Steel's giant mill is now a casino run by the Las Vegas Sands Corporation.

Law enforcement was kept busy. A teenage gang called "The Wolfpack" was uncovered by Allentown police after receiving what was described as a "tip" from several residents. It was learned that the teenagers frequently gathered at an abandoned mine hole and drank beer during the summer months. An undisclosed number of the teenagers were arrested, presumably for being minors in possession of alcohol. Their cases were referred to juvenile court. The *Call* reported: "This gang did not resort to violence. They got their "kicks" drinking...The names and exact number of gang members were not divulged by police last night."

A twenty-year-old male was arrested for supplying the kids with beer. Not only was he charged with supplying alcohol to minors, but there was also a separate charge of corrupting the morals of minors. His bail was set at $1,000. It is worth noting that the average salary of full-time male workers in 1956 was less than $4,500, and for women, substantially less than that.

Allentown in 1956 was 99.6 percent white. I say this only because it is a fascinating fact, and it is true. I don't think there is a city in America today that resembles the city I grew up in. Strangely enough, racial prejudice was commonplace among locals, in spite of the fact that there was hardly a minority population against whom one could discriminate. Not only was my fourth-grade classroom all white, I do not remember ever attending class with a black, Hispanic, or Asian student. Sadly, though, I do recall hearing racial epithets uttered by both classmates and their parents—words that are now considered unprintable.

Though the 1950s were generally a time of optimism and prosperity, there was a dark side as well. The Cold War was a catalyst for a kind of mass paranoia among many Americans and spawned an irrational fear of communism and all things "Red." The McCarthy era represented a shameful episode in American history, in many ways similar to the Salem witch trials in the 1600s. Within Allentown, this manifested itself in a long-standing battle over fluoridated water, of all things. A significant number of opponents to fluoridating the municipal water supply believed that it was a communist plot designed to poison the population, make it more lethargic, and as a result become more susceptible to Communist domination. In the end, it took forty years for fluoridation to pass.

Of course, since I was a child, I paid no attention to this. During the 1950s, Roger Bannister broke the four-minute barrier for the mile, Sir Edmund Hillary climbed Mount Everest, and Rocky Marciano, the original Rocky, retired as undefeated heavyweight champion. George Reeves achieved both stardom and hero status when the *Adventures of Superman* made its television debut in 1952 and ran successfully for most of the decade. He was truly "The Man of Steel." Disneyland opened in 1955 and instantly achieved phenomenal success. Mickey Mantle! Marilyn Monroe! Elvis Presley! This was truly a time of wonder.

The Towne Theater had triple features on Saturdays—mostly monster movies—all for twenty-five cents. My friends and I would sit in the balcony and throw popcorn at those foolish enough to sit below. There was the Great Allentown Fair (still operating successfully today), and it was a very big deal indeed. In fact, several class days were actually eliminated from the school calendar during the fair's run.

I recall playing with a Slinky, especially Slinky Worm and Slinky Crazy Eyes, on those days when bad weather kept me indoors, but generally I found myself out in the fresh air, usually causing some minor mischief with friends who possessed the same endless reservoir of energy that I did. Sometimes at the end of the day, I would manage to settle down. Often I would listen to a radio in my bedroom, lying in bed with my eyes open, trying to pull in a station from New York or Philly, and hoping that somehow I could listen to some important news from either of these exotic, magnificent places. Once in a while, I would try to imagine what life would be like if I ever got to become an adult.

The mere thought of becoming a teenager was almost too much to process—entering adulthood, beyond comprehension. It seemed like I would remain nine years old forever. In time, though, I did grow up, and equally unimaginably, Allentown, Pennsylvania—this vibrant, flourishing, proud, small city—would begin to come apart at the seams.

3

August 2013

I collect social security. What little hair I have left is mostly gray. I have been blessed with good health but seemingly cursed with bad luck on the athletic field. Over the years, I have had to endure a number of injuries worthy of a professional football player, including surgeries on each meniscus, ACL, and rotator cuff. Recently, I underwent a spinal fusion, a procedure as grim as it sounds. Clearly I am not the man I used to be.

I suppose it is normal to become somewhat reflective as we get older. Ever since my visit to Allentown in 2010, my first time back in at least thirty years, my thoughts have repeatedly drifted back to my hometown. It is still hard for me to understand how a thriving city could have deteriorated to such a degree, literally within the space of a generation. The fact that American industrial cities like Allentown were hurt by a general decline in American-based manufacturing is common knowledge, but what amazed me was the degree of change that had occurred, the extent of the damage such change had caused, and the relative speed with which it happened.

I drove to Allentown from my home in Boston in a new automobile featuring satellite radio, voice-activated controls, GPS navigation, and power everything. I found myself comfortably ensconced in the lap of luxury. My sense of well-being and complacency ended suddenly shortly after I passed a city limit sign. I exited US Route 22 at MacArthur Road, which would lead me directly to the center of the city. Suddenly I felt as if I had entered a third-world country. I passed an industrial building that I remembered from my childhood. It had formerly been occupied by the Lehigh Valley Dairy. It is now in very rough shape and mostly vacant. I drove by dilapidated housing and abandoned buildings. There were a few pedestrians moving slowly or just hanging out on street corners. It was a sunlit summer day, and I experienced feelings of fear and dread. I locked my car door from the inside.

Route 22 is an east-west limited access road, two lanes in each direction, running a few miles north of the business districts in Allentown and nearby Bethlehem. During rush hour, it is choked with traffic, where the flow might average thirty to thirty-five miles per hour on a good day. Remarkably, when I had left the highway and headed down MacArthur that Wednesday morning, the streets were empty at 8 am. At the first traffic signal after the exit ramp, I observed two cars and one truck. There was just not a lot going on downtown. Unlike many cities that fill up with workers during the day, downtown Allentown was eerily quiet on that morning.

MacArthur Road turns into Seventh Street as it nears center city. I passed one restaurant that was clearly boarded up and closed; another could have been open for business, but it was hard to tell. Next I drove past a pawn shop. Six blocks from Hamilton Street, another building had most of its windows covered with sheet plywood. Soon a convenience store beckoned: “We accept food stamp EBTs.”

Hamilton Street itself told much the same story. Adult video, check cashing, and pawn shops abounded. I counted five pawns shops in center city. Several thrift shops were also within easy walking distance. The Salvation Army’s store is situated on Hamilton Street—formerly, the city’s high rent district for retail space.

Turning east on Hamilton, I came upon the remains of the Americus Hotel, a once-proud establishment that closed a number of years ago. As Allentown began to enter its death spiral in the late ’70s, business at the Americus worsened as well. In 1985 an aggressive twenty-nine-year-old,

Mark Mendelson, purchased the then-aging but mostly functional property for $1.25 million. At the time he promised the moon and a major retrofit, but after investing just a few hundred thousand dollars in largely cosmetic improvements, he began a nasty habit of not paying all of his bills. Over time the physical condition of the hotel began to deteriorate, and Allentown revoked Mendelson's occupancy permit in 2002. This came after the city's health department had cited the Americus for numerous violations, which in the end, were never addressed. Ultimately, Mendelson filed for bankruptcy in 2009, and the city of Allentown, sitting on a $600,000 tax lien, became owner of the property. Later that year, the city sold the Americus to Albert Abdouche for $676,000. Abdouche had ambitious plans to redevelop the site, but for a number of reasons that we shall examine later, he has been unable to do so. Sadly, the Americus sits as a grim reminder of what was—and perhaps of what might have been.

Several blocks from the Americus, however, I was witness to a massive construction site in the heart of downtown, as well as several smaller ones nearby. Posters and marketing materials trumpeted a huge urban redevelopment project encompassing retail space, commercial office buildings, apartments, hotels, an arena, and a conference center. The contrast between the run-down areas of the city and the scope and feel of this venture was stark. I felt as if I had passed through some sort of border crossing to get there.

It turns out this was the NIZ, or Neighborhood Improvement Zone, something that, as I was to learn, had the potential to jump-start a genuine turnaround in the local economy—the first in almost fifty years. The NIZ was given life by the Pennsylvania legislature a few years earlier and represents a public-private partnership that was created to promote investment and real estate redevelopment in Allentown's urban core. In 2013 NIZ was still largely a work in progress, and many people were highly skeptical about the project's chances of success. Nevertheless, I immediately realized that this endeavor was no half-baked scheme and would be something to watch closely in the months and years ahead.

Later that evening, I had dinner at *Bravo! Cucina Italiana* at the Lehigh Valley Mall, which is located five miles at most from the Americus. The mall is a howling success, owned and operated by Simon Properties. The names of its tenants (the usual suspects) are very familiar to Americans everywhere: Williams Sonoma, Pottery Barn, J Crew, L'Occitane, Abercrombie and Fitch, and Coach, to name a few. There are perhaps a half dozen other significant suburban malls in the Lehigh Valley. The difference between city and suburb was palpable and points to a growing disparity in the quality of life among local residents. There is a great gulf between the haves and the have-nots, and most people live in one of two worlds that has little if any connection with the other.

I had made plans to visit with a number of former classmates with whom I had no contact since grade school. First up was George Jenkins. I remembered him as a very congenial, easy-going boy, and that part of his personality had not changed one whit in over fifty years. He gave me the grand tour, zipping around town in a Jeep Wrangler. We stopped at a diner, and he graciously picked up our tab at lunch.

George grew up directly across the street from my grandparents. After they passed away, their property was sold, and the original lot was subsequently split. George purchased the second lot. Ironically, his home now sits on what used to be my grandparents' swimming pool, where I frolicked as a child. He attended Temple University and returned to Allentown after graduation. He taught in Allentown public schools for well over thirty-five years. Unlike some of his colleagues, he did not shift midcareer to a more affluent suburban school district. He didn't move to the suburbs either. His three children attended Allentown public schools all the way through.

As conditions began to change, he was challenged in the classroom. In the '80s and '90s, Allentown's Hispanic population swelled. Most of the new arrivals were Puerto Rican by heritage but came to Pennsylvania from New Jersey and New York. He explained that these new students had a completely different cultural background and were street tough in a way the locals were not. I felt compelled to ask him if there was racial tension between white and Hispanic students, and he said absolutely not. I was surprised to hear that because that was clearly not the case for some adults; there is also evidence as well that George's opinion about racial harmony in the schools was not universally shared by other teachers and administrators.

In any event, some of the Hispanic youth were raised in households with a single parent, and others, sadly, with no parents at all. George explained he and his colleagues worked hard, extremely hard, to educate these children and others, but that a perfect storm of sudden demographic changes, including suburban flight, classroom overcrowding, a suffering economy, and dwindling financial resources, made the task extraordinarily difficult.

Through it all, he was proud of the work he did and what his career stood for. He dismissed the oft-heard criticism of teacher unions—how they protect their turf through the tenure system, where critics say ineffective teachers with "no-cut" contracts predictably turn out poor students because they, the teachers, are accountable for nothing. He also believed that teachers in poor urban centers are playing against a stacked deck, and put forth the following challenge: try to switch the Allentown and affluent Parkland School District teachers for a year, keeping the kids in place, and (he said this almost defiantly) let's see if there is any sudden change in test scores, graduation rates, absenteeism, and the like.

At the end of our talk, he did quietly admit that he would not send his children to William Allen High School today. Conditions have worsened steadily since the 1980s, and in spite of a very visible police presence, it has become a very dangerous place indeed. Students there have been stabbed, raped, and shot. In terms of academic competency, scores have been declining for the last several years and are currently near historic lows: as recently as 2012, eleventh graders achieved only 34 percent proficiency in reading and 25 percent in math. The only metric I could see that has been on the rise is the number of students qualifying for a free lunch.

When I left his home, I drove west on aptly named Greenleaf Street, which runs through a quiet, welcoming residential area that appeared just as I remembered it many years ago, except for one thing: it was deserted. Every so often, I would see an older man or woman working in the yard or chatting with a neighbor, but rarely if ever did I spot school-age children at play. This seemed particularly odd given that I was there in early August, and school, of course, was not in session. Later someone explained that this was part of the great suburban exodus of the '80s and '90s. During that time, many affluent families living in the West End of Allentown scrambled to the suburbs simply to avoid sending their kids to the Allentown public schools. The neighborhood was now largely populated by young couples with no children, who typically leave town when their kids start attending local schools, or empty nesters. One can only speculate what will happen when the older residents move on.

Next up was Rich Kershner. We met for breakfast at the Parkland Restaurant, one of many such establishments still popular in Pennsylvania, where locals congregate as if on some sort of schedule to socialize and check in. The menu includes shoofly pie and scrapple, two dishes entirely unknown to most Americans, but practically the foundation of the food pyramid to area residents. Most pastries are homemade, and the Parkland unabashedly promotes itself as a purveyor of "comfort food." I loosened my belt and settled in. I was home.

I hadn't seen Rich since I was twelve, but there was an instantaneous sense of déjà vu when we shook hands. His mouth naturally still had the pleasant upturned shape to it that I remembered—it reminded me vaguely of a leprechaun—with an eerie likeness to his fourth-grade picture. When he began to speak, I recognized the distinctive cadence to his voice that I hadn't heard for so many years. It was somewhat haunting.

Rich's life has been the model of stability. He served in the US Navy during the Vietnam War, received an engineering degree, and was hired by Bell Laboratories immediately upon graduation from college. Bell Labs, the former research arm of AT&T, had several iterations since the breakup of AT&T in the early '80s: first Lucent, then Agere, and now (via acquisition) LSI Corporation. Rich is very talented, and he was recognized as a Distinguished Fellow upon his retirement a few years ago.

Nevertheless, the AT&T reorganization and its aftermath hurt him financially, as stock option after stock option expired worthless. He explained this to me matter of factly, with no sense of bitterness or regret.

He married in his twenties. He and his wife are still married, and their two children both live close by. As a young couple, the Kershners moved to the suburbs north of Allentown and have remained there ever since. His career saw him work in several different facilities in the area, and as time went on, he had to travel rather heavily to meet with clients, but he never left the Lehigh Valley.

In recent years, Rich and his family have gotten active in drag racing of all things, traveling about the countryside to compete. One never really knows the turns that life can take—it amuses me to contemplate how a young engineering student can go through life and end up behind the wheel of a dragster after becoming a grandfather and a social security recipient.

We had a long, thoughtful discussion about the fate of Allentown. The deeper I dived into this with him, the more it became obvious that there were a multitude of factors that contributed to the city's long and painful slide, but front and center was the collapse in local housing prices and the destruction of wealth that accompanied it. The national recession in the late 1970s hit Allentown hard, and the city began to lose population as manufacturing jobs started to dry up. It was very important to many of the city's political leaders, most especially former four-term Mayor Joseph Daddona, to keep the population of the city proper from falling below one hundred thousand. Bad optics, as they say today.

Daddona supported the idea of having single-family homes rezoned as multifamily dwellings. To his way of thinking, this represented an easy way to stabilize or even boost the population. Most of the homes in question—row homes with no yards, attached on either side to a neighbor's house—were built in the early 1900s; they were rather small and, by today's standards, minimalist. The houses typically had electrical and plumbing issues to begin with, and these problems obviously did not improve with the passage of time. Daddona felt that by converting this housing stock to multifamily, the original owners could stay in place and also rent out a newly created unit or two in their existing buildings. His vision was simple and optimistic. You would have owner-occupants maintaining their homes as usual and functioning as responsible resident landlords. All the while, new and inexpensive housing units would be able to attract residents from New York and New Jersey, where housing was far more expensive.

Suffice it to say that these theories proved disastrous when applied in the real world. First, many original owners did not stay on—most either moved to the suburbs or out of the area altogether. Titles passed to nonresident landlords. Modest row homes morphed into slums almost overnight. A typical housing unit that may have been home to one family now supported three times as many people. Living conditions deteriorated, and many of the ills that we think of as being the special province of large urban centers—drugs, crime, graffiti, and gang violence—began to appear in Allentown for the first time. The more that transplants arrived, the faster whites moved out.

This demographic transformation created new challenges in the public schools. I asked Rich Kershner, as I had George Jenkins, about racial prejudice. His response was very similar—Rich described himself as "race agnostic." He did not feel that there was an undercurrent of racism among area whites either. There was ample evidence to suggest, however, that this view was not universally shared—especially among the people that counted: the Latinos.

He saw no connection between the deterioration in public education and the increase in minority students, but he did point out, as had George before him, that many of these students did not have two-parent homes as we did as children. Rev. Margie Maldonado, executive director of Allentown's Casa Guadalupe Center, recently wrote that by the year 2000, one-fourth of the four thousand families living in the first and sixth wards were single-parent households.

Rich spoke very sincerely about the importance of the family unit in child rearing and mentoring and expressed a sense of despair about some of the cultural values that all Americans (whites included) seem to have cast aside in recent years. I couldn't agree more. Although I may not have been outwardly thankful for the guidance and discipline my parents provided when I was a child, I certainly am today.

Later that day I visited Ron and Megan Skinner, both of whom were in my class in fourth grade. Megan explained that they were not high school sweethearts but "re-met" each other after college and married shortly thereafter. Whatever the case, I still found it amusing to look at our old class picture, seeing them next to each other as ten year olds, while the three of us, all senior citizens, chatted in their living room. They went to the trouble of handing me a copy of the group picture with the name of every student handwritten underneath each head shot. I can only imagine how much time and effort was spent on this task.

Following graduation from college, Ron from Lehigh and Megan from Hobart and William Smith, the two returned home. Ron was a lifelong employee at Air Products and Chemicals, a Fortune 500 company headquartered in Allentown. He retired a few years ago. After earning an MBA, Megan worked in commercial banking and later as an independent CPA. Today they live in a lovely home in Allentown's West End, surrounded by an impeccably cared for garden.

In a sense, they were unaffected by the economic troubles that Allentown experienced. Like me and millions of other middle-class baby boomers, they studied hard, graduated from college, and worked as professionals in long and productive careers. Luckily, the Skinners were not directly influenced when major area businesses like Bethlehem Steel failed or when Western Electric (formerly AT&T's equipment supplier) closed. True, they were firsthand witnesses to the changes that took place and to the subsequent decay in the city's core. After all, they live only five miles from city hall. But the fact remains that their education and career choices virtually immunized them from financial harm. In that respect, their experience wasn't much different from mine. We both watched the debacle play itself out. The only difference was that they had ringside seats.

Nonetheless, Ron and Megan were, and still are, very much committed to Allentown's well-being. They were extremely well informed about local issues and the responses of city and state government to them, and both held strong opinions. In fact, Ron served twenty years on the school board, including terms as finance committee chair and president. This seemed particularly remarkable to me since the Skinners had no children and, one could argue, had no tangible stake in Allentown's public schools. Obviously, they saw things differently and wanted to make a difference.

I later met with another Muhlenberg classmate, Elena Pascal, at a restaurant near the Fairgrounds. Strangely, the site of the Great Allentown Fair (all forty-six acres of it) is located virtually in the geographic center of the city—probably not the best example of urban planning. We dined at Wert's Café and feasted on their incomparable, oversized Wertsburgers and onion rings. We were offered dessert but passed on the coconut cream pie, much to our waitress's disappointment and disbelief.

I last saw Elena when I was about fourteen. I remember her as being somewhat quiet, mature beyond her years, well spoken, polite—clearly, we had nothing in common back then. She was not hesitant to remind me of my past behavior ("shenanigans" I believe was the word) but was quick to accept my most sincere apologies. We got along famously.

Elena attended college in Washington, DC, and graduated with a major in business. She was married shortly thereafter. After her husband completed medical school and his residency in urology, they moved back to Allentown. Elena had started a promising career at RCA but for a number of years gave up working full-time to raise her children. Throughout this period, she was very active in various civic and charitable activities.

She got involved in her own business, oddly enough, through medical society meetings. Most of us think of the AMA as the only medical society, but in fact, every state has its own such association, and within each, there are active regions and districts. Elena, who always had an interest in business, started a fledgling retail business by bringing her show on the road, offering a potpourri of merchandise for sale at regional medical conferences, and donating a significant amount of her revenue to each sponsoring group.

Over the years, she became extremely busy. She sourced goods in New York City every so often and had to travel frequently. Each event was a logistical challenge: loading up a van or truck with merchandise, setting up displays, and breaking down and packing up at the end. Volume ramped up, and she began to attract a healthy following in the region. One day it dawned upon her that it might make more sense to have her customers come to her rather than running after them. She suggested to her husband that she would like to open a brick and mortar retail store in Allentown. He thought it was a poor idea. Any married man will not be surprised to learn that the store nevertheless opened shortly thereafter. Elena had a vision, and she was adamant that the store would be located in the city, not in the suburban malls. She always felt connected to the city.

She agreed to lease space in what is called the "West End Theater District," a newly spiffed-up area of boutiques, restaurants, an arts cinema, community theatre, and the like. Revealing a pleasant ambiance, it contains a few city blocks located roughly in the geographic center of Allentown—a DMZ of sorts between center city and the more affluent, residential West End. Truthfully, this was probably the only location where her fledgling business would have a ghost of a chance.

Boutique2Go opened in 2007. In hindsight, Elena could not have picked a worse time to start it. Within two years, the United States was mired in recession, by most metrics the worst since the Great Depression of the 1930s. Surprisingly, in spite of dreadful economic conditions, her business gained traction and in the end flourished. It's easy to see why. She had experience and some preexisting customer relationships. Additionally, she is passionate about her work and has labored long and hard to build upon the glue that connects her to her customers. She currently has plans to expand and introduce a distinct line of goods for children and toddlers, and she may take the venture online as well.

We talked at some length about the state of public education. Understanding how this works in Pennsylvania requires patience.

Virtually all states in the United States contain counties and cities, but in addition to these forms of municipal government, Pennsylvania has townships and boroughs. Not to stop there, there are two levels of townships: first class and second class. Some townships have just a few hundred people, while others have more than fifty thousand. What is especially interesting is that roughly half of the population doesn't even have a township to call home!

Confused? Of course! Only Rubik's Cube masters could figure this out. Allentown is surrounded by four townships: South Whitehall, Whitehall, Hanover, and Salisbury. You can have an Allentown address and also live in any of these townships or none of them. If you live in Allentown proper, your children attend Allentown schools. If you live on the periphery of the city, your children cycle through one of several different school districts. For example, Salisbury High School serves Salisbury Township. That makes sense, but North and South Whitehall are combined to form the Parkland School District. The more heavily populated areas of Allentown are served by the Allentown School District; townships simply don't exist within the urban core.

Elena lives in Allentown *and* in Salisbury Township. Her children are grown, but if they were school age, they would attend Salisbury Township schools. Schooldigger.com ranks Salisbury High 76th out of 676 schools statewide, putting it close to the top 10 percent; William Allen High scrapes the bottom at 615th. She stated she would never send her children to William Allen High. Like everyone who lives in the Valley, she is all too aware of its shortcomings. She echoed the same thought that was put forth by every individual I had a chance to speak with; namely, that the citizens of Allentown have a huge social problem on their hands, and that the breakdown of the family and many traditional values have been key factors behind it.

I met another old friend, Marc Nissenbaum, for breakfast at Perkins on Cedar Crest Boulevard. Perkins is a Memphis-based chain of family restaurants, but its menu is tailor-made for Allentown—eight varieties of home-baked pies, for example, to tempt customers who may have room for just a little bit more after a dinner of chicken-fried steak, gravy, several side dishes, and dinner rolls.

Marc went to Penn State and after graduation taught for a few years in Brooklyn's Bedford-Stuyvesant neighborhood, a very challenging environment indeed. He returned to Allentown and then worked in municipal government, specifically the Office of Economic Development. In the mid-1970s he joined his brother in a family-owned textile business, Berkeley Manufacturing, and remained active in it until the 1990s, when the business was closed and Marc retired. He and his wife always lived in Allentown proper, and their children all cycled through public schools there. The youngest graduated from William Allen High about twenty years ago. (He quickly mentioned that he wouldn't send them to William Allen today.)

His story is so familiar—college, job, marriage, children, and retirement. In his family, like mine, and seemingly everyone else's, college was not an option, but rather a nonnegotiable pathway in life. I found this amazing. Some of the kids I went to school with were raised in wealth, most somewhere in the middle, others in very modest environments. Yet everyone I spoke with pursued advanced education and worked in a professional capacity. Today, well over a third of the students who enroll at William Allen High drop out before they even have a chance to graduate. Like my other classmates, Marc lamented the current state of affairs and appeared almost bewildered by the changes that had taken place before his eyes.

Of course, my contemporaries were not immune from loss and tragedy, and it was no different for this group from Allentown. A number of them have already passed away. Several lost battles with cancer, and a few others suffered heart attacks. The Vietnam War, the scourge of my generation, claimed others.

Some of the stories were arresting. One of my best childhood friends, I learned, had died as a result of a one-car accident about twenty years ago. He spent months in a coma before his death, and his parents were reportedly at odds over removing him from life support. Many months elapsed before that painful decision was made. One can scarcely imagine the struggle that took place within his family. Another couple—both students at Muhlenberg Elementary School who also married—lost a child in a horrific automobile crash when their daughter's car was struck by a large truck. Her fiancé, who was riding with her at the time, also lost his life. Incredibly, the truck was owned and operated by the mother's employer. Mom, who was in my third-grade class, told me the story while we were having lunch near a new suburban Wegman's. As I listened to her, I felt like I couldn't breathe. Equally chilling, yet another classmate, an old friend who had lived just a few blocks up the road from me, was murdered by his mistress in Philadelphia after she discovered he was simultaneously carrying on an affair with yet *another* woman. After the murder, she then took her own life, leaving a suicide note that revealed the whole sordid tale.

It was very hard for me to absorb these stories, with no forewarning, having come in like a time traveler from afar. Every so often, I look back at my fourth-grade class picture, a smile etched on each face. I took it with me on my trip in 2013. On this visit, old friend George Jenkins was kind enough to pull out his Allentown High School yearbook for me, and I was able to see many of the same individuals as they looked at eighteen. The girls were impeccably groomed, and the boys wore white shirts and ties. This was 1965, just as the Vietnam War was becoming front page news in America and before flower children and hippies became generational symbols. When I graduated from fourth grade, I had no deep thoughts and certainly no long-term plans—just being finished with school for a few months was about all I could handle. When I graduated from high school, however, I took a long, slow breath, realizing that a new chapter in my life was opening up, but not quite knowing exactly where it would take me and how it would play out. Looking back, my life has had a minimum of bumps and detours. I was one of the lucky ones.

I continued to wander around and take it all in. The difference between 2013 and 2010 was clear. There was genuine evidence that the city may have seen its bottom and could very well have been in the early stages of a transformation and recovery. For the first time in many years, money was flowing into Allentown, and shovels were in the ground. Much of the activity consisted of the large-scale area of development in center city that I had witnessed when I first arrived, namely the Neighborhood Improvement Zone (NIZ).

The NIZ scheme is a complex piece of financial engineering. Legislation for the NIZ was written by State Senator Pat Browne and signed into law in two separate installments: Act 50 in 2009 and Act 26 in 2011. The zone itself covers roughly 128 acres of land in downtown Allentown as well as the western shore of the nearby Lehigh River. The NIZ was created to spur development in downtown Allentown and help revitalize the city.

Sara Hailstone, the city's director of community and economic development who arrived in Allentown in 2010, is intimately involved with this project and unofficially the spokesperson of the NIZ. She was kind enough to explain to me how the NIZ works. Business taxes (generated within the NIZ) paid to the Commonwealth of Pennsylvania are recycled back from the state to a local public authority, which in turn uses the funds to subsidize debt service (mortgages) on newly constructed buildings within the zone. Additionally, and somewhat amazingly, personal state income taxes (payroll taxes) withheld by employers who operate within the NIZ receive the very same preferential treatment.

The authority in question is called the Allentown Neighborhood Improvement Zone Development Authority, or ANIZDA. Because of ANIZDA's payments, real estate developers get a huge break, and as a result, they are able to offer prospective tenants very attractive, below-market rents. In a sense, this is corporate welfare—tax money supports commercial real estate development and in effect subsidizes rents for business tenants—but in the end, if the project is successful and downtown experiences a rebirth, not many would argue with the steps that were taken to get there.

The centerpiece of the plan is a sports arena that will be home to the Lehigh Valley Phantoms, a minor-league affiliate of the National Hockey League's Philadelphia Flyers. The arena will seat eight thousand five hundred for hockey and ten thousand for concerts. City officials envisioned a project of fairly massive proportion—one that would include office space, hotel, residential, mixed use, and retail in addition to the arena project. The downtown hockey arena project, by itself, involved over $230 million in municipal financing. In 2013 it was believed possible that an additional $700 million, perhaps more, would be raised to bring the project to fruition. Optimism may not have been embraced by everyone, but it was clearly present. I even saw a picture of Taylor Swift on one of ANIZDA's promotional websites, even though construction of the arena was at least a year away from completion at the time, and no concert dates had been announced.

It doesn't stop with hockey. Minor-league baseball had last been seen in Allentown in 1960, when the Allentown Red Sox (a single-A farm team of the Boston Red Sox) were relocated to Johnstown, Pennsylvania. The team's venue, a dreary ballpark called Breadon Field, contributed to the abysmal attendance numbers. Paid admissions of over one thousand were extremely rare. When the team moved, the stadium sat abandoned for a number of years and was then torn down. Ultimately, the Lehigh Valley Mall was built on the site.

It seemed both surprising and ironic to learn that professional baseball had returned in a big way—in 2008, no less—as the credit crisis roiled the financial markets and a severe recession was unfolding. In that year one of minor-league baseball's priciest stadiums ($50 million) opened as the home field for the Lehigh Valley IronPigs, the AAA affiliate of the Philadelphia Phillies. The ballpark was built with public funds: $20 million from Pennsylvania and the remainder from a Lehigh County bond issue. Interest on the bonds is covered by rent from the team, approximately

$1.3 million annually. It is a tight squeeze, but so far all payments have been made on time and without incident.

In fact, it is fair to say that the team has been a howling success. The IronPigs field, Coca Cola Park, is situated in East Allentown, on land once occupied by Western Electric. The surrounding area is—I am being charitable here—both dingy and depressing, but a combination of good marketing, a first-rate stadium, and reasonable prices have enabled the IronPigs to achieve the highest-paid attendance in minor-league baseball, over six hundred thousand for the past several seasons. It is plausible to think that the ambitious NIZ project would never have been able to gain traction were it not for the prior success of the IronPigs.

Of course, there are skeptics and cynics. Can a luxury hotel and pricey restaurants survive in the center of a high-crime city? Can professional hockey draw fans from a population with such a high percentage of poor Hispanics? Most importantly, will the lives of the inner-city residents be transformed in any material way? If they can't, what is really changing here, apart from the age and size of the buildings that lie within the NIZ?

There is a real possibility that after all the construction is completed, Allentown will someday become a place where white suburbanites simply commute to work and then return home at the end of the day. There may be a few new bagel shops and cafés serving the needs of downtown office workers, but this can hardly be considered an effective means of "revitalizing" the city's commercial center. In the end, unless the residents themselves are able to improve their job skills, they will never be able to compete successfully for the positions they so desperately want. Without the proper training, dead-end, low-paying jobs become the norm, and true careers remain a pipe dream.

To this point, Hailstone described loosely formed plans to enlist the private sector in what she sees as a potential renaissance of manufacturing within the city. She spoke about the possibility of retrofitting old, abandoned factories and creating incentives for employers to establish new operations there. The logistics are huge—many of the buildings are situated in contaminated brownfield sites. Obviously, redevelopment would require costly and time-consuming remediation. Beyond that, Hailstone described a somewhat Utopian vision where many of the new factory jobs would be taken by local workers, and by local, she meant city residents who could now walk to work. One can't argue with her vision, but it was difficult to see how these workers could suddenly acquire the skills to make them employable. Perhaps the new businesses would be able to offer them some sort of career pathway via entry-level job training. Anything is possible, but given the environmental challenges and financial constraints, success is far from assured.

In any event, the city was actively promoting the NIZ and the urban renaissance it could help create. A number of construction projects are presently underway, and more than a few businesses have made commitments to establish local operations. An NIZ brochure proudly claimed, "Allentown is quickly becoming a center of excellence for employment, commerce, entertainment, culture and more!" Not many neutral observers would agree with that Pollyanna assessment, at least in 2013, but it seemed clear at that moment that the city was at a critical inflection point in its evolution, and for the first time in many years, there was at least tangible evidence that its future might be brighter than its inglorious recent past.

4

FORTITUDE

BILLY JOEL'S "ALLENTOWN" gave the city an odd and undesirable iconic status. His lyrics suggested failure and permanent loss. Even today, conventional wisdom suggests that when the economy tanked, factories began to close, and conditions in the city began to deteriorate, misfortune and hardship became unavoidable. There was nothing that could have been done to change the outcome. Allentown was destined to circle the drain.

There is evidence to suggest that this was not entirely the case. Exceptions did exist. One that comes to mind is a company called Schiff Silk and Ribbon, which was established in Allentown during the depths of the Great Depression in the early 1930s. It survived those difficult times and grew opportunistically in the years that followed. Three generations of Schiffs shepherded the company through obstacles and challenges for more than eighty years. It did more than survive; it prospered. Its success illustrates all too clearly that well-run manufacturing businesses could indeed make it in Allentown. To believe that they were all doomed to fail is a myth.

Lawrence Schiff was born in Brooklyn, New York, at the turn of the twentieth century. He was first-generation American, his parents having come to the United States in the great wave of immigration that brought millions to our shores in the 1880s and 1890s. His family was from Poland, or more accurately, an area that we now know as Poland. Poland as a political entity did not exist; its western areas, especially Silesia, were controlled by Germany, and the remaining land was ruled by czarist Russia.

Immigrants, of course, did not as a matter of practice come to the United States highly educated and financially secure. Theirs was a hard lot. Some men who began their trek in Eastern Europe actually began by walking across the continent to the seaports in the West, trudging alongside horse-drawn wagons that held women and children. Most, however, were able to take trains. Some ports, like Bremen in Germany, were configured with train station platforms located immediately adjacent to loading docks, so passengers could literally walk off a train and board a ship to America.

Most immigrants in the late 1800s traveled in steerage class. The living conditions were deplorable. The steerage cabin was located in the bowels of the ship, near the engine room, where as many as four hundred people would bunk together, barracks style. Typically, this area was designed for cargo, but on these steamships "cargo" meant people. Burlap sacks stuffed with hay were used for mattresses, and life preservers doubled as pillows. Ventilation was virtually nonexistent. There was a very small area on the deck where passengers could get some fresh air, but during stormy weather, of course, this would have been impossible. There was hardly enough room for someone in an upper bunk to sit up in bed. There was no separate dining area. Passengers were given metal utensils, went through a chow line, and brought their food back to their bunks to eat.

Prepaid tickets cost about twenty-five dollars, standby tickets less. The amount seems laughably small today, but in those years, it represented several weeks of wages for one worker. More often than not, a family would sell off some belongings to raise cash, and one family member would then purchase a ticket and complete the voyage by himself. Over time, the others would join him.

The conditions the immigrants left in Eastern Europe were extremely difficult. In many areas, and this of course included Russian-controlled Poland, absolute monarchies ruled, and rarely was this rule enlightened or benign. Economic, political, and religious freedom—the basic building blocks of American democracy—simply did not exist. The United States of America, this amazing social experiment conceived in 1776, became a magnet for millions seeking both freedom of expression and financial opportunity.

Life for the Schiffs and many other immigrant families in New York City was hard as well. The tenements that housed them were dingy and crowded. Sometimes running water was only available from an outdoor pump, which would often freeze in the winter. Coal stoves were used for cooking and heating. If there was running water inside, it was always cold and would have to be heated for bathing. Frequently, bathtubs were shared among several families. Ventilation was poor. All apartments were stifling in summer and frigid in winter. There were rarely lights in the hallways. Indoor toilets were not required until the New York State Tenement Act mandated them in 1901.

Mice and cockroaches were everywhere. Rents could range anywhere from three to four dollars per month to as much as fifteen. The least expensive apartments were in the attic, and tenants would generally have to climb five or more flights of stairs to gain access. Some tenements featured a live-in manager who was given free rent in turn for providing maintenance, basic cleaning, and upkeep. When compared with the worst buildings, they would have been considered highly desirable, but in truth, we are really just talking about degrees of suffering. Everyone wanted out, and tenants often moved several times a year just to get a little more living space or a very modest improvement in "amenities."

Making it in America didn't come easily. These new Americans worked and sacrificed without letup. They rarely complained and almost never returned to the "old country" to live. They could count on very little when they first sailed to the United States. Freedom of expression, religious freedom, and the separation of Church and State were, of course, constitutional guarantees, but financial success was not. That was dependent upon one's resourcefulness, enthusiasm, and hard work. At the turn of the century, the United States offered unique opportunities for risk takers and would-be entrepreneurs. There was no other place like it on earth.

Lawrence Schiff left school at fourteen, which was mandatory until that age. Like many of his peers, he gravitated to the textile industry and took a job with J.H. Lamport in Manhattan. Lamport operated one of thousands of small businesses in what was then a growing and vibrant industry. Lawrence immediately proved to be eager and ambitious and went to work every day with his eyes wide open. His first tasks, of course, were rather menial: stocking, counting, sorting, sweeping, moving, and lifting. He was anxious to learn, however, and created an excellent impression with his boss.

He was also very curious about the business and acquired a great deal of valuable knowledge as time went on. At seventeen, he made his move, and he became what is known as a jobber. Jobbers are brokers or middle men, individuals who buy raw goods from a textile manufacturer and sell those goods to a finisher. Lawrence began to put such a transaction together, but he had one problem: he had no money. He spoke with Lamport, who then agreed to serve as Lawrence's "bank"; that is, he would provide him with the credit necessary to purchase the raw goods that he would subsequently sell. His first transaction was for four cases of fabric, each case containing perhaps four or more bolts. The total price was $320. Lawrence Schiff was in business.

The 1920s brought many changes. Lawrence married Gertrude Isaacs and started a family. He broke the cord with Lamport after his fledgling business was able to operate independently. His three brothers soon joined him in business, and his Aunt Minnie lent him the money to establish an office in Manhattan. Over time he became a "convertor," contracting with looms to produce finished goods that could be sold directly to apparel manufacturers. Schiff had no looms of his own; in today's parlance, we would say he outsourced this production.

He became interested in the stock market and all forms of investing, a passion that would remain with him for the rest of his life. As the bull market during the Roaring Twenties gained steam, he began to accumulate an investment portfolio. Apart from common stocks, he also invested in rare stamps and coins and in gold bullion. Some of these stamps are still held by his descendants. After the stock market began to shudder in the early summer of 1929, Schiff had his first real epiphany and sold every share of every stock that he owned. Whether he was clairvoyant or lucky, he avoided the carnage that ensued when the market crashed in September.

The crash of 1929 was truly the mother of all crashes. During the next four years, stocks declined over 90 percent from their bull market highs. It took another twenty years for the market to crawl back and recover the ground it had lost. In the interim, the nation would endure its greatest economic crisis ever, the Great Depression, and simultaneously suffer its most damaging environmental disaster, a multiyear drought that enveloped vast areas of the Great Plains. The phrase "dust bowl" says it all.

Schiff had some money in the bank and ambition to spare. In 1931, he made the decision to enter direct manufacturing. Only one of his three brothers was willing to join him in this venture. There was good reason—the economy had collapsed. Besides, all manufacturers have to make a significant upfront investment to acquire real estate and production facilities, and in addition, they have large, regular payrolls to meet. Lawrence considered his options and decided his potential upside justified the risks he was about to take. His first factory was located at the junction of Fountain and Utica Streets in Allentown, Pennsylvania. It was a two-story building of perhaps fifteen thousand to twenty thousand square feet. Allentown was situated a good ninety miles from New York City, Lawrence's home, but close enough to make the round trip in a day, at least occasionally.

Allentown, which was known as the silk city, also had a number of attractive features. By 1930 there were one hundred forty active textile and silk mills that operated in the Lehigh Valley. This gave Schiff a ready-made supply of skilled labor that he would need to staff his operation and run his looms. As the economy worsened and other mills began to lay off workers or close entirely, Schiff was able to gobble up these displaced workers. Besides that, real estate values were falling dramatically, and he was also able to acquire the factory building for a song. His prescient stock sale in 1929 was serving him well.

Commercial weavers in 1930 did not weave. They were skilled workers who monitored the machines (looms) that did the weaving, maintained them for optimum performance, and repaired them when they broke down. Schiff's first factory started out with eight looms, which he was able to acquire at a substantial discount given the pervasive weakness in the economy. Allentown-based Kalmbach and Stevens, then one of the largest ribbon companies in the country, had been plagued by poor labor union relations, and its workers had gone out on strike. The agreement that followed proved onerous for management, and as a result, the company was forced to lay off some workers after the strike was settled. Some of those laid off were experienced weavers, and the best of them were hired by Schiff.

At this time, Schiff also modified his looms so that they had an "auto stop" feature; in other words, they would shut down automatically if something went amiss, such as a broken part, overheating, or fouled strands of silk. Before this safety feature, every loom in the factory had been monitored by a different weaver. With auto stop, each weaver could handle four looms. A small innovation like this enabled Schiff to obtain an obvious competitive cost advantage. This was something that he was able to do for his entire working life.

He was a good man, and he treated his workers with exceptional kindness. At the end of 1932, with the nation's unemployment at 25 percent and the economy in free fall, Schiff gave every one of his workers a generous and totally unexpected Christmas bonus. One weaver, who admitted he had been told as a child that Jews had horns like the devil, began to cry openly, so overcome with emotion he could not express his gratitude. On a number of occasions, Lawrence would fill up the trunk of his car with eggs, bread, and other foodstuffs and drive to the office to hand out to his employees.

Largely as a result of his honesty and kindness, his workers never certified a union to represent them, with one exception. Many years later in 1960, Schiff bought a union shop, and when he was threatened with a strike after failing to negotiate a new collective bargaining agreement, he ended up closing the facility altogether. This was one business deal that clearly didn't pan out. He had opened his books during the negotiations and tried to be as forthcoming as possible in terms of what the business could and could not afford. He was never a pushover, but the hostility that bubbled up during this struggle disheartened him as much if not more than the financial losses he suffered when this particular facility was shut down.

Schiff's business grew throughout the 1930s. There are not many businesses that could lay claim to that, especially manufacturing businesses in Allentown, Pennsylvania. In 1938, he rented more space in nearby Quakertown to expand his manufacturing base. Here, seam bindings (used in hems for skirts and dresses) were made. Later, the facility produced specialty products for footwear manufacturers. Over the years, he introduced rayon and then nylon to his stable of products. By the end of the 1930s, Schiff was selling nationally. He had started with just eight looms, but by now, Allentown was running thirty-two, and Quakertown forty-three more.

International tensions grew steadily after Adolf Hitler took power in 1933. Schiff became convinced that war would break out in Europe and that the United States would be drawn into it. When Hitler invaded Poland in 1939, Schiff bought silk futures. He had never speculated in the commodity markets before. In fact, it is fair to say he never speculated—he invested. This time was no different. Unlike commodity traders who buy futures with the hope of selling them at a profit, Schiff held the contracts until expiration and took physical delivery of the silk. His decision was prescient. If, in fact, the United States were to be drawn into a European war, he believed shortages of many raw materials would develop (he was right), and that they would be particularly acute in silk (he was right again). Silk, of course, was used in the manufacturing of parachutes, and military demand for silk pushed commercial inventories down and prices up. Lawrence's intuition had served him well once more.

The company continued to flourish after World War II. Another production facility was established in Carlisle, Pennsylvania, in 1947. About that time, Lawrence's son, Mortimer, joined the business after graduating from the University of Virginia. He was handed nothing except opportunity. His first job was in sales, and he became the first in his family to move to Allentown.

At its peak, the company employed about three hundred people, with four production facilities in Pennsylvania and a sales office in New York. As time went on, it became increasingly difficult for manufacturers like this to hang on. Labor costs in the Northeast were high, factories were old, and companies were often offered tax incentives to relocate to another state. Schiff considered moving south but stayed in Pennsylvania. He received unsolicited offers to sell the company and resisted.

During Richard Nixon's presidency, Congress passed the Care in Labeling Act. This required apparel companies to identify the fabrics that were woven together and the percentages of each. The law also required manufacturers to include cleaning instructions on each label. The garment industry looked upon this as an unnecessary intrusion and a money waster to boot. Schiff, as he so often had done before, just thought about the opportunity, and he created an adhesive label tape that could withstand the rigors of commercial washers and dry cleaning. In an instant, he created a viable business with national reach.

By this time, Lawrence's health began to fail him, and Mortimer began to assume an increasingly important role in running the company. Lawrence, however, was able to remain reasonably active in his company's affairs until his death in 1979. His real legacy can be found in his character and generosity. He and his brother Sidney, who joined him in business back in the 1930s, became active philanthropists early in life. Mortimer continued this tradition, and his own family foundation has funded a number of worthy causes in the Lehigh Valley. Mortimer's son, Richard, who joined the company after college and became president in 1990 when his father passed away, has sustained this culture of philanthropy.

Schiff Silk Mills stopped weaving silk altogether in the 1960s, when its production shifted 100 percent to synthetics. When other textile manufacturers in Allentown and throughout the United States folded, they survived. When competitors moved south to save money, they stayed where they were. Certainly, increasing globalization hurt the company. Its peak employment was achieved long ago in 1970. Richard Schiff was ultimately forced to move some production overseas, a choice that was especially hard for him given the close and caring relationship his grandfather, his father, and now he alone had built with so many employees.

Richard, I might add, was a close childhood friend of mine. We both attended Muhlenberg Elementary School and hung out together constantly. We lost touch with each other at the age of fifteen or so, not to reunite for another fifty years. Our wives were both incredulous to hear us describe ourselves as mischief-makers and class clowns, but that is exactly what we were. It was wonderful to reconnect with him. He is a good man and has lived a full, purposeful life.

Richard ultimately sold the business to a private equity firm in 2012. He had just turned sixty-five, and there were no other family members waiting in the wings to take control. He took great pains to share his business values with the new ownership. He openly admits that he probably had been too generous to his long-term employees, and his staffing was nowhere as lean as it could have been. Nonetheless, after the sale closed, over 90 percent of the existing workers were kept on by the new management. Schiff insisted upon it, even though he knew full well that the willingness of the buyers to comply directly with these terms affected what they were able to pay for control of the company.

Given the hand the company was dealt, one would think that Schiff Silk and Ribbon had no chance of surviving into the twenty-first century, but it did. There was no secret formula. At the outset, Lawrence was willing to take a large but measured risk, namely, to start a manufacturing company from scratch in the middle of the Great Depression. He was fearless. I suppose all successful entrepreneurs are. But beyond that, in the years that followed, three generations of Schiffs shared a common ethos. They were able to innovate and adapt to change when necessary. They built a well-earned reputation for integrity with suppliers and customers. Most importantly, they treated their employees as their most treasured asset. These characteristics are what defined the company and are responsible for its legacy.

Lawrence Schiff's singular success was not an isolated occurrence. As we shall soon see, several other manufacturing businesses were able, against all odds, to take root in Allentown and endure the most difficult of times. They may have been the exception rather than the rule, but their survival—and success—speaks for itself. These entrepreneurs had both vision and common sense, but most importantly, they had an indomitable spirit and will to win. A little perseverance can go a long way.

5

IMPOSSIBLE

THE SUCCESS OF Schiff Silk and Ribbon was not an isolated incident. Other traditional manufacturers managed to stay the course, and they remain viable and competitive to this day. In every such instance I came across, there was a common thread. Ownership was totally committed to quality and customer service, remained unreasonably positive regardless of the environment, and always demonstrated a deep and sincere appreciation for their employees.

The early years of the Industrial Revolution were hardly distinguished by such benign and enlightened management. During the late 1800s, many aspects of what we call "work" in our society were entirely transformed, and nowhere was this more apparent than in the textile industry, where thousands toiled under deplorable working conditions. By 1900, textile manufacturing had emerged as one of the key drivers of our economy. The industry's growth was made possible by a fortuitous combination of circumstances and events. Technological advances that had been made in looms, dyeing equipment, and sewing machines were obviously critical, but without the steady flow of immigrants with established relevant skills, the industry would never have been able to grow as quickly as it did. Millions of immigrants came to the United States at this time; many of them, especially Italians as well as Jews from Eastern Europe, were able to find work easily upon settling in America. Initially, manufacturing was concentrated in the Northeast. In fact, at one point nearly 60 percent of all US-made apparel was cut and stitched in New York City itself.

The industry flourished for another sixty years. At first, the expansion was limited to New England and the Mid-Atlantic states, and then it moved to the South. Most of these businesses were initially established by first-generation Americans, the children of poor immigrants who came to our shores with high hopes, raw ambition, and no capital. Typically, their businesses started on a very small scale. Owner/entrepreneurs often never graduated from high school and would obtain menial, entry-level positions to get started. Then with the help of family and friends, they would cobble together a bit of money and with a great leap of faith go out on their own.

By the mid-1960s, over 95 percent of the clothing purchased by Americans was made in the United States. Today, more than 95 percent of the clothing purchased by Americans is made overseas. Many of the old brick factories and mills have been converted to other uses: office lofts, condominiums, light industrial, shopping centers, or antique malls. Some of these buildings still sit vacant, scary-looking hulks with broken windows and graffiti.

At the end of World War II, the United States had the largest and most productive textile manufacturing operation in the world. The industry's most powerful labor union, the International Ladies Garment Workers Union (ILGWU) saw its membership peak at four hundred fifty thousand in 1969. In 1995, with membership having declined precipitously, the ILGWU merged with the Amalgamated Clothing and Textile Workers Union. This new entity became known as UNITE (Union of Needle Trades, Industrial, and Textile Employees). UNITE's total membership fell to two hundred fifty thousand workers *after* the merger.

In 2004 UNITE merged in turn with the Hotel Employees and Restaurant Employees Union (HERE), creating UNITE HERE. In the years since, it has continued to struggle. Its current membership is only two hundred sixty-five thousand, down over 40 percent from the

ILGWU's peak fifty years ago, a fact even more astonishing since UNITE HERE represents the combination of three formerly separate unions. A small minority of the workers remain active in the textile industry, as most work in hotels, food service, or commercial laundries. While UNITE HERE has become especially powerful in the hospitality industry in Las Vegas, the old ILGWU has all but disappeared. It is not much more than a historical footnote or an answer to a trivia question.

I was most surprised to learn, then, that a company called Anda Industries, a textile finishing company, is alive and well in Allentown, Pennsylvania. Anda operates from what it describes as "the oldest continuously operated textile mill in the United States." From the first moment I heard about Anda, I was inspired to learn more about it. How did it get started, and once it did, how was it able to survive when most of its competitors could not?

Anda Industries is located in East Allentown, next to a canal that parallels the Lehigh River. The factory is difficult to find, and the neighborhood nearby has a dangerous, troubling feel to it. Armed robberies, shootings, and assaults may not be everyday occurrences, but they do occur often enough. Emily Opilo reported in the *Morning Call* on March 20, 2014, that during a city council meeting concerning the renewal of a liquor license in East Allentown, a resident was moved "to compare prospects in East Allentown to the Taliban resurgence in Afghanistan."

David Buechele is the president of Anda Industries, and he drives to work through the streets of East Allentown every day. He is a type A, high-energy individual who holds back nothing. Like many small business owners, he is unhappy with what he believes to be government's hostile attitude toward business and would be more than happy to share his feelings with anyone within shouting distance. He is also filled with a reservoir of positive energy, and he is totally committed to Anda's success.

Anda's history and roots are atypical. The company was established in the 1970s, not the 1870s, by David's father, Heinz. The Buechele name has French roots, but the Buecheles are German. Heinz spent his youth in southern Germany near the Swiss border and then studied at the highly regarded RWTH Aachen University, several hundred miles to the north near Cologne. RWTH Aachen is the German equivalent of Cal Tech or MIT. Upon graduation, Heinz was hired at Ciba AG, then a large and successful Swiss conglomerate with a significant presence in chemicals and pharmaceuticals. Since then Ciba grew through a series of mergers—from Ciba to Ciba-Geigy, then Sandoz, and finally Novartis, today the second-largest pharmaceutical company in the world.

Heinz's first assignment was in Canada, where he developed an expertise in dye houses, the factories used to produce finished textile products. In 1964 he was married, and he and his wife (a native German) settled in Canada together. He moved to the United States shortly thereafter, where he was to remain for the rest of his life. Heinz worked in Rhode Island, then later in Pennsylvania, as a GM/plant manager for several different textile manufacturing companies. One of these companies was Sunbury Mills, which interestingly enough is still operating today in Sunbury, Pennsylvania, a small town in the center of the state. There Heinz met a teenager named Harry Douglas, and the two of them formed an unusual business connection that was destined to endure for a lifetime.

Heinz caught the entrepreneurial bug in his early thirties. He began to moonlight, locating buyers for finished goods, but since he had no manufacturing capability of his own, he was forced to outsource all of his production. Then, in 1972, he made the decision to strike out on his own. At this time his son David was still in diapers. I find this especially interesting. Heinz had an educational pedigree that earlier entrepreneurs may have lacked, but he showed the same independent spirit and ability to take on risk—just as they did more than half a century earlier.

He went "all in" and purchased a large building at 15 South Albert Street in East Allentown and began business operations as HAB Industries. HAB and later Anda Industries have produced finished goods there ever since. The facility had been in use since 1909, originally as the National Silk Dyeing Company and later as Allentown Converting. David founded Anda in 2004, wanting to differentiate the company since it used different equipment to produce higher-end fabrics.

HAB Industries functioned as a textile converter. Converters take unfinished goods— those that are neither dyed, bleached, nor prepped in any way— and convert them to a finished state. Converters will do this by either dyeing or printing unprepared fabric. Converting fabric is a highly exact, detailed, and technical process. There is no margin for error. New automobiles, for example, may have defective parts, but they can be easily replaced. Finished fabrics with a crooked stripe, the wrong pigment, or a mismatched print cannot.

From the very beginning, Heinz invested in modern, highly efficient equipment. He was keenly aware the only way he would be able to compete effectively with foreign converters was by keeping his costs of production down without sacrificing quality or speed in the manufacturing process.

Harry Douglas followed Heinz to Allentown where he was hired as the company's dye master. His skills were a perfect complement to Heinz's industry contacts and plant management experience. Business was strong through the mid-1980s, and while growth slowed after that, HAB Industries remained consistently profitable.

David followed his father into the business. He had always demonstrated an interest in its technical side, from buying chemicals to overseeing and monitoring the manufacturing process. He attended the Philadelphia College of Textiles and Science, now known as Philadelphia University. Today, the school offers a wide variety of courses typical of modern universities. Students can earn both undergraduate and graduate degrees in areas such as architecture, liberal arts, engineering, and finance, and like many universities, it maintains a School of Continuing and Professional Studies for working adults. Learning is available online or in a traditional classroom setting.

In its earlier days, however, the school provided training for textile professionals and little else. As the US textile industry declined, so did enrollment at the college. Unless the school had been able to reinvent itself and broaden its appeal, it would have been unable to survive. Excellent programs in textile engineering and textile design still exist, but they attract a distinct minority of enrolled students.

David joined his father at HAB Industries immediately after completing his studies. He brought with him a reasonable amount of technical knowledge and the enthusiasm of youth. Heinz stayed on for a few years to mentor him and then retired in 1996. Dye master Harry Douglas, who had worked for Heinz from HAB's first days, also remained, and he is still active at the company today. While the guidance of these individuals was clearly essential, the fact remains that David took over full responsibility for HAB when he was only in his mid-twenties. At this time the economy was limping out of a recession, and the domestic textile industry was being pulverized by foreign competition, particularly from China.

The mere mention of the words "foreign made" can agitate David. I expected him to complain about the lack of government support for our textile industry, as well as the excessive number of costly government regulations—and he did not disappoint. His thoughts are echoed by many industry and trade groups that have spoken out against unfair foreign competition, especially direct state subsidies and currency manipulation. He also explained that great numbers of foreign workers toil for extraordinarily poor wages in substandard conditions, and many of the factories they work in are among the world's worst polluters. Workplace safety and environmental safeguards are looked upon as dubious luxuries in many emerging economies. In Bangladesh, the second-largest textile producer in the world, workers are paid an average of thirty-eight dollars per month. Over eleven hundred workers died there in 2013 when a factory collapsed. The year before, more than one hundred lost their lives in a fire. It is hard for David to understand how US trade policy can be so friendly toward nations where the treatment of workers would be considered criminal activity if it took place here. He is not alone in that opinion.

I called on David Buechele for a very simple reason: to find out how his company managed to survive when most others like his could not. It seemed impossible. How could a textile converter based in Allentown,

Pennsylvania, compete successfully with low-cost producers in Asia? Did Buechele possess some magic formula?

From the outside, it certainly didn't seem like it. Anda's factory is very old and has not aged well. The building is enormous, easily fifty thousand square feet on one level, perhaps more. It was surprisingly hard to find, being tucked away in a relatively inaccessible part of East Allentown. I couldn't even find a sign on the building's exterior. In spite of its urban location, Anda exudes a feeling of quiet isolation.

Anda produces three to four million pounds of finished fabric each year, which by my calculation works out to approximately ten thousand pounds daily. This output is achieved because Beuchele has invested, and continues to invest, in modern, high-capacity, energy-efficient equipment—really his only choice since local labor rates here are so much higher than in Asia. His workforce, by necessity, is small. It is also very productive and extremely loyal.

The first pieces of equipment I saw on my tour of the floor were two enormous boilers that are used to produce the steam that is essential in the dyeing process. When fabric is dyed and later dried, it needs to be exposed to very high heat for extended periods of time, typically ten to fifteen hours. Anda's boilers are running almost continuously, and the company's gas bill averages $20,000 per month.

The other need is water. Anda's water supply comes directly from the Lehigh Canal, and unlike town water, it is exceptionally pure. Municipal water is typically chlorinated, and Allentown's is no exception. If Anda were dependent upon town water, it would have to filter out the chlorine first—an expensive process that could very well endanger the company's ability to survive.

The dye room is Harry Douglas's domain. Anda purchases various dyes (mostly European) in powdered form. The dye master's job is to ascertain how to mix these dyes to create a finished fabric that has the exact tint and color each customer has specified. Harry first hand mixes small batches and uses specialized software on his computer to end up with the perfect formula. There is no wiggle room here, no margin for error, no "do-overs." It has to be done right the first time.

The equipment Anda uses is expensive and highly specialized. To those unfamiliar with the process, dyeing (and printing) fabric would seem like a pretty pedestrian undertaking, but it requires a substantial capital investment in both technology and machinery. On its website Anda identifies twenty-two different kinds of machines that it uses in its factory. Most of these are completely unrecognizable to the layman. Among them are an eight-color Stork RD4 printer, a Gaston County 4-port Millennium jet, and a twenty-four-cut knitting machine. Even the manufacturer's description sheds very little light on the subject. For example, Gaston County writes of its Millennium jet dye machine: "Individually adjusted reel speed control permits fine-tuning to achieve lot-to-lot shade reproductions, tube-to-tube shade uniformity, and isolation of any cloth circulation problems that may occur." Indeed!

In addition to being expensive, most of Anda's machines are made in Europe, and because of their sheer size and weight, shipping them to the United States adds materially to their cost. Beuchele explained that having state-of-the-art equipment is critical to his company's survival; dependability, energy efficiency, reduced water consumption, quick turnaround time, and high quality can go a long way in offsetting lower labor costs enjoyed by foreign competitors. David has never lost sight of this. In fact, one day when I called him he was on his way from New Jersey to Allentown—hauling equipment on a flatbed truck. He never stopped believing in his company or in himself. In hard times, he put his own savings at risk, once remortgaging his own home to obtain additional equity capital. He always recognized that his greatest resource was a core of skilled and dependable employees; he consistently treated them well and was rewarded by minimal turnover and high productivity. Additionally, he has never rested on his laurels. He persuaded his most important supplier of unfinished fabric, Triumph Knitting, to relocate from another state to Allentown; at the same time, he rebranded Anda as Diamond Dye and

Finishing. This rather unorthodox joint venture served to benefit both companies because it shortened Anda's turnaround time for producing finished goods by two to three days. A competitive advantage like this, Buechele reasoned, should result in more business for both firms, and he was right.

Anda is hardly the only exception to the prevailing opinion that American manufacturing was caught hopelessly in a death spiral. Aetna Felt, an Allentown-based manufacturer of felt products, has managed to operate profitably for many years without succumbing to the numerous obstacles most US-based manufacturers face today. Jim Weppler is currently president of Aetna Felt and speaks of his company with great pride and sincerity. The company has been family owned and operated since its origin in 1929, when his great uncle, Howard Dederich, started up a small operation in New York City. Dederich Felt and Textile struggled through the Depression but managed to survive it. After World War II, Jim's father Wilfred went to work for Dederich as a sales representative, beginning a career that was to become a lifelong passion. There was nothing in Wilfred's life history that suggested that he would thrive in the felt business or in any business. He never attended college, instead opting for the merchant marine, where he completed two voyages around the world.

In 1946 Dederich moved the company to Weehawken, New Jersey. Business had improved from the dark days of the 1930s, and the company needed more room. Space was so tight in Manhattan that occasionally rolls of fabric were placed on an elevator, taken out on the sidewalk, and cut to a customer's specifications because there wasn't enough room to complete this work indoors. Dederich made a few small acquisitions over the years, typically from aging owners. To be honest, his company was not optimally managed, and while profitable, growth was slow and hard to achieve.

Wilfred bought the company from his uncle in 1971 and renamed it Mechanical Felt and Textile. Five years later, he acquired Aetna Felt and Textile from a former partner of Dederich, consolidated the two companies, and rebranded them as Aetna Felt. In 1980, needing more space, he moved his company to Union, New Jersey. In 1986 Wilfred purchased Fidelity Felt of Philadelphia, and in the following year, Continental Felt of New York City.

Shortly thereafter, Wilfred found himself in Allentown to source some shelving he needed to put in his factory. By the late 1980s, Allentown was already ten years into its misery, and real estate prices had already begun to erode. Specifically, commercial real estate, especially the type of property zoned for manufacturing, was available at fire sale prices. Local manufacturers of course had been struggling for some time. Many had moved production elsewhere or simply liquidated. "For Sale" signs had cropped up everywhere.

Aetna Felt (and its predecessor companies) had always rented manufacturing space. This time Wilfred broke the pattern and bought a building. He was taking a big risk and making an even bigger investment, but Wilfred figured that he would realize long-term cost savings and also have the flexibility to grow in future years without having to relocate yet another time. He ended up moving Aetna Felt to Allentown literally overnight, without losing one day in factory production. I still marvel at the irony of it all—moving a factory to Allentown, Pennsylvania, of all places in 1988. Central America or Asia one could understand, but Allentown, Pennsylvania??

By this time, Wilfred was already in his sixties, a stage in life when many business owners are thinking about retirement, golf, spoiling their grandchildren, and other like-minded pursuits. Wilfred just kept working. He was active on a daily basis well into his eighties, and he continued to take an active interest in Aetna Felt's affairs in his nineties.

Wilfred's son Jim had also been involved with Aetna Felt, but mostly on an ad hoc or part-time basis. Much of his life was spent farming commercially in Lebanon, New Jersey, a tiny town of thirteen hundred located a few miles east of the Pennsylvania line. The farm was his boyhood home, and he always maintained a close connection with it. He still lives there. As time passed, Jim became progressively more active, especially as his father's age began to restrict his activities. The transition occurred smoothly. Jim had earned a business degree in college and was very familiar with Aetna itself when the time came for him to assume control of the company.

In the world of business, knowledge and experience are valuable commodities to be sure, but they do not necessarily guarantee successful results. Aetna Felt's survival (against long odds) and its subsequent sustained profitability would not have been possible without a shared sense of pride, commitment, and integrity. These intangibles have functioned like glue, helping to connect management with rank-and-file workers as if they were members on the same team.

Jim Weppler described the company as a family. There are a number of production workers who moved to Allentown from Union, New Jersey, in 1988 that are still active employees. Turnover is virtually nonexistent. The Wepplers have on more than one occasion helped out employees in a time of need. There are no labor unions. Some years ago, during the company's only union election, workers voted unanimously against unionization.

There have also been no layoffs. During the Great Recession of 2008–2010, Aetna was forced to reduce its work week to three days and then to four, but no one on the payroll was ever pink-slipped. This is something Weppler speaks about with understandable pride. This paternalism is rewarded in spades; Aetna Felt's workers are not job hoppers. Typically, the byproduct of a stable work force is higher productivity.

There is nothing sexy about the felt business, and while some production steps have been influenced by modern technology, particularly CAD-CAM software, many of the machines on the company's factory floor haven't changed much in forty years or more. While Weppler spares no expense in terms of the ongoing maintenance of Aetna's machinery, he realizes it is naïve to think that Aetna Felt can create a magic formula that will enable it to separate itself from its competitors. Additionally, some markets for domestic felt producers, like appliances, simply disappeared when productions of such items went overseas. Fortunately, Aetna was able to replace this lost business with different products for munitions and ordnance suppliers by contracting with the Department of Defense. A strategic shift like this can buy a mediocre company some time, but it can't ensure its long-term viability.

What he does believe is that the company's success is based upon an unwavering commitment to reliability and quality. Of course, this sounds like a cliché, but the fact remains that if you ship late or ship low-quality merchandise (or both), you are not going to do very well. This passion for excellence and customer service was established early on by Wilfred Weppler, and the tradition is carried on by Jim today.

It's no mystery why Aetna Felt survived and was able to achieve the impossible. As we have seen, ownership rightly placed the interests of its customers ahead of its own and, as a result, was able to achieve their long-term goodwill and loyalty. The company was also willing to take measured risks to grow, acquiring a few competitors along the way and then consolidating all of their operations in Pennsylvania. The initial cost was significant, but it paid off in the end. The move gave the company a larger, more modern space that offered room to expand.

In addition, because of its relatively small size, Aetna's owners found it was easy for them to get close to their employees and stay connected. The importance of this can't be overstated. Large manufacturing firms, particularly in older industries, tend to be heavily unionized, and collective bargaining, almost by definition, creates an adversarial environment that typically separates labor and management into two unfriendly camps. Trench warfare almost always follows. In these kinds of wars, there are occasional cease-fires. At best, a tolerable period of coexistence may follow, but often there will appear an undercurrent of resentment and hostility. This can prove toxic to any organization, especially during difficult times that call for compromise and fairness. Just ask Bethlehem Steel.

6

BESSIE

THE ENDING WAS neither happy nor pretty. When Bethlehem Steel declared bankruptcy in 2001, the company employed only fourteen thousand workers and was paying pensions and other benefits to over one hundred thousand retirees. These numbers don't explain the whole story behind the company's failure, but they do reveal why there was no way out. If Bethlehem Steel had been able to fabricate gold instead of structural steel, it might have had a chance.

Without a monumental government bailout, it could never have emerged from bankruptcy and hoped to conduct business as usual. After 2001 it did manage to temporarily continue operations (in locations other than Bethlehem) for a few more years, but in the end, its remaining assets were sold to International Steel Group in a court-supervised bankruptcy proceeding. In 2006, ISG was in turn acquired by Arcelor Mittal, currently the world's largest steel producer. Bethlehem Steel has disappeared.

Robert S. (Steve) Miller was Bethlehem Steel's last CEO. He had earned a stellar reputation as a turnaround expert, most prominently at Chrysler in 1980, where he was instrumental in obtaining federal loan guarantees for the floundering automaker. This time he wasn't able to work his magic. The government was not willing to fully and unconditionally rescue Bethlehem Steel's pension plan, and it was equally disinclined to backstop health-care coverage for retirees. Bethlehem Steel was once the seventh-largest company in America. When ISG acquired the company for $1.6 billion in 2003, it wouldn't have made the top one thousand.

Bethlehem Steel was for many years one of the largest and most successful corporations in the world. Dubbed "the Steel" by locals and Bessie by Wall Street brokers, the company once employed in excess of three hundred thousand people, over thirty thousand in Bethlehem alone. It produced much of the structural steel for Manhattan's skyline. A vast number of ships commissioned by the US Navy in World War II were built in Bethlehem Steel's shipyards. According to a *Business Week* survey, at one point in the 1950s, nine out of the twelve most highly compensated corporate executives in the country worked for Bethlehem Steel.

Many of the postmortems describing Bethlehem Steel's collapse place much of the blame upon its labor unions. It was said the unions were intransigent and greedy, that the steelworkers were overpaid, and that they collected hefty pensions and other extravagant benefits as retirees. Some of this may be true, but clearly the compensation earned by Bethlehem Steel's executives served to set the bar when the time came for collective bargaining. Both sides would have done well to give a little more and take a little less.

Eugene Grace was president of Bethlehem Steel from 1916 to 1945 and served another twelve years beyond that as chairman of the board. He was of course the highest-paid individual within his own company; for many years, he was also the highest-paid executive in the nation. He was a Bethlehem Steel lifer, joining the company immediately upon graduating from Lehigh University in 1899. He had become president before he turned forty.

Grace's reign coincided with Bethlehem Steel's years of greatest financial success and dominance. As a child, I remember seeing smoke billowing out of the enormous stacks in South Bethlehem. There was no talk then about acid rain, pollution, or greenhouse gases. The stacks were a symbol of success and industrial might. In an oft-repeated story, when Grace (while golfing) was notified that Hitler had ordered the invasion of Poland in 1939, he instinctively realized that it would not be long before the United States was drawn into war. The first words he said were, "We're going to make a lot of money." He was right.

The contrast between 1939 and today is stark. Currently a venue called SteelStacks, a center for arts and culture, is located on the same land where steel was produced just a generation ago. Here former Bethlehem Steel buildings have been preserved like museum pieces and can be viewed as part of a historic walking tour. In 2009, the Las Vegas Sands Corporation opened a huge casino-resort on land at the east end of the giant mill. Meanwhile residents are still waiting for the National Museum of Industrial History to open. The museum was conceptualized in 1997, shortly after steelmaking operations in Bethlehem came to a halt. After $19 million worth of fundraising and one grand jury investigation, ground has yet to be broken, but when and if the museum ever opens its doors, it will represent the chief link connecting the present with the company's glorious past.

Bethlehem, Pennsylvania, sits next to Allentown, sharing a common border that runs several miles. Were it not for the ubiquitous "Welcome" signs posted on the boundaries of each city, visitors would have no way of knowing if they were in Allentown or Bethlehem. The cities are joined at the hip, like Minneapolis-St. Paul or Tampa-St. Petersburg. One could not suffer a catastrophe without the other feeling it. The failure of Bethlehem Steel was such a catastrophe. The Lehigh Valley lost tens of thousands of jobs in a twenty-year period beginning in the 1970s. While many of the losses were suffered by smaller companies, there were a number of occurrences that were headline grabbers. Black and Decker, Mack Trucks, Downeyflake Waffles, Lehigh Structural Steel, and AT&T's Western Electric division represented just a few of the region's major employers who announced significant layoffs during this time. Similarly the Lehigh Valley's cement industry experienced a number of plant closures. None of this, however, compared with what happened at the Steel. Layoffs started there in the 1970s and continued almost without letup until the bitter end. There were short periods of stability and occasional worker recalls, which provided optimists with hope—hope that proved to be illusory.

Bethlehem Steel laid off more than seven thousand workers (in Bethlehem) in the 1980s alone. Keep in mind that the company had already chopped thousands of jobs in the '70s. In early 1989, after much of the damage had already been done, Marvin Peters, an official of the United Steelworkers of America, appeared to look forward to the future with a sense of resignation if not outright doom. He predicted several thousand more workers were likely to lose their jobs soon because the mills in Bethlehem were "too old to compete, and too costly to modernize."

Bethlehem Steel's earlier success created a culture of entitlement that went beyond the normal boundaries of pride—the sense of satisfaction one has in a job well done. From the outset, there was a feeling of privilege that permeated the executive ranks. In time, this smugness turned into arrogance, and then, in the last decades of the company's existence, as profits turned into losses, arrogance morphed into denial. Going back many years, poor strategic decisions and a seemingly endless war of attrition with the USW combined to seal the fate of the company. Ultimately, it was left with no flexibility to adapt to changes that had already taken place within the industry.

I had a nebulous connection with Bethlehem Steel, having attended a private school in Bethlehem for a few years while I was in my early teens. Many of my classmates were children of steel company executives. One of them, Malcolm Briggs, had been on my mind for many years since I overreacted to an apparent slight (a one-fingered salute delivered just before algebra class in eighth grade) and punched him in the face a few times to show my disapproval. We sat in class for the next forty-five minutes, my erstwhile friend bleeding without letup into his handkerchief. As the cloth began to turn crimson, I became convinced I would be expelled from school within minutes. For some reason, I escaped without a warning. I always felt bad about this incident and knew I owed Mac amends.

Briggs still maintains a home in Bethlehem, and he was easy enough to reach. I hadn't spoken with him for perhaps fifty years. Not surprisingly, the first subject that came up in conversation was our classroom scuffle, and he was very gracious in accepting my apology. The talk quickly moved back in time to the old days of Bethlehem Steel. He proved to be a treasure trove of information.

His father was a Bethlehem Steel executive and worked there for thirty-nine years before he retired. The company hired him as soon as he graduated from MIT, where he earned a degree in metallurgical studies. He was selected to join Bethlehem Steel's highly coveted management training program, called the Looper because its participants were reassigned to new jobs several times a year to gain familiarity with different facets of the business. He rose quickly through the ranks, and near the end of his career, he was named head of commercial research and later VP of planning. For a time he was considered a potential CEO candidate. In the end, he was not chosen for the job and subsequently retired in 1981. Mac believes that as the '80s progressed, his dad's disappointment may have turned to gratitude because he never had to lay off large numbers of the people he had worked with during his lifetime.

Mac graduated from one of New England's elite boarding schools (Northfield Mt. Hermon) in 1965 and earned a BA degree from Harvard University in 1969. Like me, he obtained a liberal arts degree with a major in history. I could also identify with him when he said upon graduating he had no clear career objectives or specific technical skills. I chose Wall Street; he opted for steel. Mac was hired by Bethlehem Steel and joined the same Looper program that his father had completed years earlier. He described his decision to join the company as a "default" decision. He had no other option that intrigued him, and it seemed like the sensible thing to do at the time. His father was fine with his joining the company, and his mother was extremely pleased as well.

He stayed with the Steel for three years, working mostly at a huge mill in Sparrows Point, Maryland. Sparrows Point, apart from being recognized as the place where Bethlehem Steel used to produce steel, is probably best known for the magnificent Sparrows Point Country Club. The club was built in the early 1950s by the steel company (of course), specifically for its top executives who worked locally. This followed the pattern in Bethlehem itself, where the Saucon Valley Country Club was established in 1920. When Eugene Grace was president, it was not uncommon to have a Bethlehem Police Department motorcade lead the way from his office to the golf course when he wanted to get in a round of golf. Golf at Bethlehem Steel maintained a rigid caste system; there were clubs for top management, others for middle management, and still others for union workers.

At Sparrows Point, Mac worked in labor relations. While he had hoped to be assigned to sales and wasn't, he tried not to let this disappointment affect his attitude at work. He had a sense of idealism that was very common among young people in the 1960s. His job at Sparrows Point was to investigate grievances in the plant. In time he became somewhat disillusioned to discover that labor-management negotiations represented little more than horse trading, rather than a fully transparent process that after a period of discussion and compromise could lead both parties to a just resolution.

He did not warm to life at Sparrows Point. His starting salary was only $735 a month *before* taxes. He remembers having to punch in and out every day—a rather odd requirement for a salaried employee and one which Mac found demeaning. He was bored to tears. When he wasn't working for the steel company, he was a weekend warrior with the US Army Reserve. A girl he was dating at the time lived three hours away in Allentown. Nothing seemed to be working. He remembers listening to Peggy Lee's recording "Is That All There Is?" and ruminating on the possibility that he could be spending the rest of his life at Sparrows Point, collecting a paycheck and banking two weeks of paid vacation a year. At twenty-five, he experienced a midlife crisis.

Feeling somewhat rootless and in need of direction, he spoke with his mother. She was a deeply religious woman and suggested that he read the Gospel of John. Mac said, "I was desperate enough, and I did it." The Gospel of John is more concerned with spiritual themes than historical events, and many parts of it contain instructions on how to live one's life according to God's will. This led Briggs to a spiritual awakening and the ability to look at life through an entirely different lens. He no longer felt a sense of impending doom in which he envisioned himself enduring a lifetime of drudgery at Bethlehem Steel. He made a decision to leave the company and follow his heart. He soon joined a very small insurance company in Allentown, much to the shock and horror of his mother. This was not the sort of spiritual awakening she had in mind.

Dad was a bit more understanding: "It's clear you're not on fire here; I hope you catch fire where you're going." He did just that. Over time, he moved this company aggressively into the corporate executive benefits market, particularly in the emerging field of corporate-owned life insurance, and after a number of years, bought out his erstwhile partner. Now known as Andesa Strategies, this firm has grown dramatically in both size and reputation. He has done well and is justifiably proud of all he has accomplished. He worked long and hard. It only took him forty years to become an overnight success.

He has some clear thoughts on Bethlehem Steel. The culture was extraordinarily insular. Questioning the status quo was not welcome. Even though he was hired with very high expectations, in his opinion it would have taken him at least ten years to rise to a position of reasonable authority. In itself, this was a very depressing thought. He was quick to pick up on a feeling of arrogance that went deep into the organization. When he resigned to join the aforementioned fledgling insurance company in Allentown, most of his colleagues thought he had gone completely off the rails. Unlike today, small businesses in general and entrepreneurs in particular were looked upon with a level of derision and amusement, especially at companies like Bethlehem Steel.

Why? Simply put, the company had been extraordinarily successful and made a great deal of money. Unfortunately, success sometimes breeds complacency. Bethlehem Steel's management was far more likely to continue doing business as usual rather than anticipate change and adapt to it. In labor negotiations it always seemed to give in to the USW, confident future cost increases could be passed on to customers. When foreign imports began to take market share in the '70s, the company's response was to plead with Congress for trade protection. When domestic minimills took more sales away from the company in the 1980s, the Steel stood still. Mac looked upon the company as a dinosaur long before it finally became extinct. He mentioned a book recently written by former Intel CEO Andrew Grove, entitled *Only the Paranoid Survive*. He says that it was the opposite at Bethlehem Steel, where smugness and complacency ruled.

Briggs left Bethlehem Steel in 1972, and at the time the firm was still riding high. In fact, it was only two years later that it posted record earnings of $342 million. The subsequent downturn in the company's fortunes came with unexpected suddenness. A weak economy and the appearance of foreign competition were a lethal one-two combination, and fairly quickly the company began to struggle for its very survival. For many years, nonetheless, it remained in denial, firm in the belief that if only Congress would step in to protect the American steel industry, the company's fortunes would recover as soon as the general economy did.

On Friday September 30, 1977, Bethlehem Steel laid off twenty-five hundred white-collar workers, including eight hundred fifty who were located at the company's headquarters in the city of Bethlehem. Most of those worked at the newly built, twenty-one-story Martin Tower. The building was a symbol of opulence and excess. Design features included executive offices with handwoven rugs and door knobs engraved with the Steel's logo.

After the company finally went bankrupt, the Martin Tower was abandoned and sat vacant for years; developers were scared off by its omnipresent asbestos and the lack of an adequate sprinkler system. Even though the building was relatively young, having been constructed in 1972, it was oddly enough named to the Register of National Historic Landmarks. For some time it appeared that the Martin Tower was destined to become some sort of tourist attraction, perhaps the centerpiece of exhibits in a ghost town. Fortunately in 2013, the city of Bethlehem was able to win a coveted special tax zone designation from the Commonwealth of Pennsylvania, spurring redevelopment at long last.

The September 30th layoffs represented the first time in its history that Bethlehem Steel had ever dismissed white-collar employees. The Allentown *Morning Call* referred to Black Friday as "the day the Bethlehem Steel gravy train jumped the tracks." The Steel could never have anticipated that in the winter of 1977 a horrific blizzard would force a shutdown of its plant in Lackawanna, New York, marooning its workers on the shores of Lake Erie; the same could be said for a legendary rainstorm and flood that badly damaged the mill in Johnstown, Pennsylvania, and was responsible for seventy-eight deaths in the area in July. Similarly, no one could have predicted that later that year in December, two of its supertankers would collide—with each other, no less—and be put out of commission for many months. Executives learned of this misadventure just before a black-tie Christmas party was about to begin at the Saucon Valley Country Club. This truly was a perfect storm of disasters, both natural and man-made. At the same time, the company faced a national recession and relentless foreign competition made worse by a strong dollar, which benefitted companies that sold into the US market. Bethlehem Steel had run out of bullets.

Many of the dynamics at work within Bethlehem Steel in the 1970s were present throughout the industry. Arch Kunkle, a recent acquaintance, is now happily retired in semirural Hellertown, Pennsylvania, a small village just south of Bethlehem. Back then he worked for Luria Brothers, at the time the largest reseller of scrap steel in the country. Luria had a number of facilities scattered throughout Pennsylvania, including Bethlehem.

Kunkle was responsible for sales to commercial and industrial customers, and he was able to witness firsthand how dysfunctional many participants in the industry had become. It was almost as if they were able to mimic many of Bethlehem Steel's worst practices. The relationship of Luria Brothers with the USW Local was lukewarm at best. Once, during an eleventh-hour negotiation with the USW, management opened its books to show workers what it thought was (and was not) possible. The Local wouldn't budge. In the end, management caved, being desperate to complete a very large, half-finished order, but warned the USW Local that in all probability would not be able to operate profitably under this contract. This was no bluff. As Luria had feared, profits turned into losses, and within a year, the company closed its area operations. Labor felt this was done spitefully; management defended its actions as a financial necessity. It really didn't matter because at the end of the day, everyone lost.

Kunkle had a bird's eye view of the Steel in action. He observed that the company didn't take competition from the newer minimills seriously, never utilized continuous casting, and failed to produce smaller, more specialized pieces of fabricated steel. Also, the company rarely made steel for its own use, period. The practice was to produce only what was needed to fill a customer's order. Assuming there was a run of one hundred tons and the company could have used five tons for its own needs, it would nevertheless buy what it needed from a competitor, even if it meant (as it always did) costing more money in the end and incensing its union workers to boot. It's just the way they did things. Some traditions die hard.

The Allentown *Morning Call* has published a highly readable history of Bethlehem Steel called "Forging America," and of course most of the material is focused on the company's long slide into bankruptcy. Black Friday was identified as a jumping-off point. "For Bethlehem Steel, there would be years when profits would return, and there would the occasional signs of hope. But overall, Black Friday signaled the start of a quarter century decline in which jobs were lost, dreams were shattered, and an industrial icon plodded toward a slow, agonizing death."

In 1977 Donald Trautlein joined Bethlehem Steel as comptroller, and within three years he was named CEO. He had handled the company's account while he was with Price Waterhouse. Trautlein was the first CEO brought in from the outside. In his first formal comments to company executives, he dramatically said, "We are not in the business of making steel. We are in the business of making money." He tried, but he didn't have much luck.

While conditions had temporarily stabilized after Black Friday, by the early 1980s, the entire industry was in free fall. The company had to deal with intensifying competition, poor demand, and the loss of some market share to plastics and aluminum. To make matters worse, the US dollar went on a tear, rising steadily between 1980 and 1984. One might intuitively think that strong is good and weak is bad. In currency, however, weak can be a blessing if you are selling goods into another country's market—you'll end up with more money in your bank account that way. During the early '80s, it became more and more profitable for foreign steel producers to sell into the US market. They had the ability to keep their US dollar prices low and still make very good money.

The dollar skyrocketed for many reasons: one of the most important being that interest rates were at extraordinarily high levels here in the United States. In January 1982, the ten-year US Treasury yielded 14 percent; today, it returns less than 2.5 percent. To buy Treasury bonds, you need US dollars, and if you didn't already own them, you would need to acquire them. All things being equal, as long as interest rates were high, the dollar would remain strong—an untimely curse on a struggling industry.

Trautlein immediately embarked on a series of cost-saving measures. Some were relatively benign—reductions in advertising, curtailment of executive perks, or cutbacks in community outreach and charitable giving. Others, of course, were far more dramatic, and within a matter of months, he initiated what soon became a seemingly endless series of worker layoffs and plant closures.

On December 26, 1982, Billy Joel performed at a sold-out Stabler Arena at Lehigh University. Lehigh is located in Bethlehem and within sniffing distance of the mill, perhaps a twenty-minute walk. He opened and closed his show with "Allentown." The Associated Press, which was covering the concert, interestingly labeled this as a recession-rock song.

Allentown Mayor Joe Daddona was present, hoping to somehow turn a negative into a positive. He gave Joel an Allentown all-American T-shirt, a key to the city, and a certificate of honorary citizenship. Joel and Daddona made quite an odd pair and reminded me of the meeting between Richard Nixon and Elvis Presley at the White House. Daddona waxed poetically at the key ceremony, saying "We hope this key will lock securely the bonds of friendship between Billy Joel and the citizens of Allentown." He continued on, praising the song as "a gritty song for a gritty city." Throughout the day, the mayor gave interviews to TV and newspaper reporters, but Joel was a little less forthcoming. "I didn't want to make such a big deal about it. I just wanted to do the gig."

Joel grew up in Hicksville, New York, near Levittown, and his song was originally composed with Levittown in mind. Apparently he had trouble creating dynamic lyrics or a memorable narrative about his old haunts. Levittown, of course, is looked upon as the original modern-day suburb, created from scratch by New York developer Levitt and Co. It was, and is, a quiet bedroom community. A chance visit to Allentown gave him sudden inspiration and an entirely new topic about which to write.

"Allentown" was somewhat controversial when it was released, especially for Allentonians. Over time, however, many wore it like a badge of honor. In the same way that some people in the path of a hurricane refuse to evacuate their homes, many local residents felt connected to their community and decided to tough it out no matter how difficult the circumstances. When Joel sang "Allentown" to close his show (it was his third and last encore), he told the audience, "Don't take any shit from anybody." He got a standing ovation that lasted five minutes.

Two days after Billy Joel's concert, ten thousand more workers were let go by Bethlehem Steel. The company announced it would be permanently closing its ancient integrated steel plant in Lackawanna, New York, putting seventy-three hundred employees out of work. The remainder was to occur in Johnstown, Pennsylvania. The write-offs associated with this restructuring, coupled with operating losses that occurred throughout the year, caused Bethlehem Steel to finish 1982 with a loss of approximately \$1.5 billion.

The company dispatched its chief spokesperson, Bruce Davis, to Lackawanna to deliver the grim news to a shell-shocked staff. This is akin to the president of the United States having his press secretary speak to the nation after a national tragedy. Davis was understandably uncomfortable in this role and left the company several years later to pursue a law career.

Bethlehem Steel had actually already embarked on aggressive layoffs and closures long before these Lackawanna and Johnstown actions. In 1981, within the city of Bethlehem itself, the company had let go twenty-one hundred workers, and over six thousand others were forced to accept salary cuts. In two years, between 1980 and 1982, the Steel furloughed approximately thirty thousand workers across the nation. The bloodletting continued for several more years. Collective bargaining at Bethlehem Steel devolved into tactical warfare. Trautlein was regarded with contempt by the rank and file, and management saw the unions as intransigent and defiant. The sad fact was simply that there was little room for either side to "bargain" without selling out their constituents—the shareholders on one hand, the USW on the other. With deep-seated resentments on both sides, there was no wiggle room. Even though the operation was completely "upside down," there was never a cooperative effort made to fix it. Plants were old and inefficient, and wages were among the highest in the world.

Trautlein was able to appeal somewhat successfully to the Reagan administration about foreign competition. Ultimately he won some relief in the form of import restraints and quotas. This legislation helped to stanch the flow of red ink, as did a recovering economy, the closure of several inefficient plants, a now-falling US dollar, and the opening of several low-cost continuous casting mills. Trautlein stepped down in 1986, and for a few years more, business stabilized and actually improved. Soon afterward, however, as the national economic recovery stalled, the Steel continued on its road to oblivion.

Before long, the subject of pension security began to crop up. As early as 1983, an ominous event occurred: the number of retirees receiving pensions exceeded the number of workers employed by the company. With each succeeding round of layoffs and plant closures, the company's unfunded liability increased, and its financial condition became even more seriously impaired.

There were two issues at first here, each equally hair-raising. The first concerned long-term workers, now middle aged, who were not yet vested in their pension plan, but awfully close. What if such individuals were put out on the street a year, or even a week, before being able to secure their retirement benefit? The pension they were counting on would go up in smoke. To make matters worse, there were no other jobs in the steel industry for the suddenly unemployed, either for managers or USW members. The situation for rank-and-file workers was particularly acute; these people were typically high school graduates, semiskilled, and middle aged. Their American dream became a nightmare. Those that were able to find alternative employment did so at a fraction of their former wages.

Similar issues haunted the retirees. Was their pension plan safe? Could they count on it? What would happen if the company was simply unable to meet its obligations? These questions were answered in 2003, just a year after the company declared bankruptcy. At this time the pension plan, which had been underfunded by $3.9 billion, was taken over by the US government's Pension Benefit Guarantee Corporation (PBGC). The "average" retired worker in the end did receive about 90 percent of what he had expected; however, most workers were not average. Some got 100 percent, and others got much less. The PBGC had a statutory limit of $42,954 per year for a fully vested, sixty-five-year-old retiree choosing a single life payout (i.e., no spousal survivor benefit); there were some workers with a larger promised benefit, and these retirees simply didn't receive it. Others who were laid off before becoming vested in the plan got nothing.

Worse yet was a clawback provision from individuals who had already lost their jobs through plant closings or early retirement. In a prior contract, these workers had secured an additional $400 per month as a supplement to their pension checks. The PBGC announced that in the future, these supplemental payments would cease, and worse yet, what they termed "overpayments" would have to be paid back by the recipients. The fact that the PBGC's actions were clearly defined and proscribed by law was simply irrelevant to workers who suddenly realized they were never going to receive the benefits that they had been promised. They felt conned and betrayed. Dan Shope of the Allentown *Morning Call* spoke with a disheartened retiree, Joe Jancsavics, who said "I feel like a dog, but I am going to try and live off what they give me."

The loss of company health care and life insurance benefits was another punch in the stomach, and for early retirees not yet eligible for Medicare, this was particularly devastating. Like many of America's well-established industrial companies, Bethlehem Steel promised retirees virtually free health care—with premiums as low as six dollars per month. After the company filed for bankruptcy, this coverage was abandoned, as was retiree life insurance.

Long-term steelworkers were not a healthy lot. The AP reported that eighty-one-year-old Joe Pancoe, who had worked for the Steel for over thirty years, was suffering from asthma, a chronic cough, and other maladies that required a number of medications. Mill workers were routinely exposed to toxic substances—paint, smoke, asbestos, and more. Pancoe observed, "We old timers were part of the industrial revolution. Now we are part of the medical revolution. We have the emphysemas, we have the cancers. We have everything." Medicare's drug benefit did not come into being until 2005. Even for people like Pancoe, who had been covered by Medicare for years, the loss of the company's retiree health-care package was a significant blow.

In 2007, Billy Joel gave a rare interview to the *Morning Call.* It had been twenty-five years since the song "Allentown" was released. He had performed in the area a number of times since his first concert in 1982. He reminisced, "We had actually seen—I don't wanna call it a decline—but over the years of playing in the Lehigh Valley there did seem to be not a sense of futility, but there was a kind of wearing on the area from what had happened in the steel industry. There wasn't a sense of growth anymore. There was a sense of wanting to go somewhere else, but they were going to stay…which is something I wrote about in the song. I wanted to end on an optimistic note—'It's getting very hard to stay, we're living here in Allentown.' We're staying. We're here."

The story of Bethlehem Steel is perhaps more dramatic than most, but in no way unique. The company's collapse was due to a combination of arrogance, inertia, and denial. In the end it was simply unable to adapt successfully to a changing global economy. I suppose the same could be said for countless other manufacturing firms based in the Lehigh Valley.

Billy Joel is an exceptional composer and performer, and perhaps his song did inspire a few souls to stay on and gut it out. The plain truth, though, is that thousands upon thousands of people were put out of work permanently, and many of them were forced to uproot themselves and relocate. Not all of them were steelworkers. Unemployment did not discriminate. The pain was universal.

7

Rags To Rags

Many financial success stories of the early 1900s had very unlikely origins. Great waves of immigrants—largely poor, almost always lacking a formal education, and often not able to speak English—set out to forge a new future for themselves in America. My great grandmother was told that the streets in New York were lined with gold, and when she saw that they weren't, she started crying and told her husband she wanted to return to the Ukraine. He talked her out of it, and they built a new life for themselves here in the United States. Now my own grandchildren are sixth-generation Americans. They live a life of comfort and affluence, far removed from the constant struggle and suffering that was endured by those that came before. If I told them the full narrative of *Rags to Rags*, the story behind the story of Phoenix Clothes in Allentown, they would regard it with a mixture of curiosity and disbelief.

We are a nation of immigrants. The very first immigrants, of course, were English. They were followed by Irish, Dutch, Germans, and Portuguese. Then came millions more from Italy, Greece, the Balkans, Poland, and Russia, where life was especially hard. The great wave of immigration from Eastern Europe began in the late 1800s and persisted until early in the twentieth century. The journey of these would-be Americans across Europe, and later overseas, was arduous, and it was made more difficult by poor sanitary conditions and disease. Finally, at Ellis Island, many were turned away, often for poor reasons or no reason at all; occasionally individual family members were refused admittance and sent back to Europe, leaving the entire family anxious and vulnerable.

Many of these immigrants from Eastern Europe were Jewish, especially from Poland, Ukraine, and Belarus, all of which were controlled by czarist Russia. Life for Jews under the reign of Alexander II (Alexander the Liberator) was fairly promising until he was assassinated in 1881. Alexander II had been rightly regarded as a reformer. He encouraged the establishment of parliamentary government and a more tolerant, open society. Under his rule, Jews were able to attend universities, establish businesses, and own property without restriction.

The so-called "May Laws" were issued in 1882 by Alexander III, Alexander the Liberator's successor. These regulations were issued as temporary measures but stayed in force for approximately thirty years. The May Laws institutionalized anti-Semitism in Russia. Jews were not permitted to relocate to the country unless it was in a "Jewish agricultural colony." They could not obtain mortgages on agricultural lands either. Clearly, the intent was to eliminate Jews from independent farming. Later, quotas were placed on the percentage of Jews that could attend high schools and universities. In the early 1900s, approximately twenty thousand Jews were summarily expelled from Moscow.

And then there were the pogroms, best defined as violent mob attacks directed against Jewish citizens. These attacks were not specifically ordered by Alexander III or his minions, but whenever they occurred, they were conveniently ignored by officials. Homes were burned, women raped, and countless innocents maimed and murdered. Participants in pogroms were never prosecuted criminally. It was this environment of official repression and unofficial mayhem that was the catalyst behind the great wave of Jewish immigration to the United States in the 1880s and 1890s. By 1910 the foreign-born population of New York City numbered two million. Immigrants and their children (first-generation Americans) made up over half the population of America's largest city.

By the late 1800s, the American textile industry had already undergone dramatic transformation. Isaac Singer introduced the first commercially viable sewing machine in the early 1850s, and within twenty years' time, sales were approaching three hundred thousand machines annually. Even with the limitations of a foot-powered treadle, these machines had a capacity of nine hundred stitches per minute. The modern American garment industry was thus born, and by the turn of the century, nearly half of the clothing that was worn had been manufactured "ready to wear." Clothing was sold either in smaller retail stores or in catalogs such as Sears and Montgomery Ward. When the US Postal Service instituted rural free delivery service in the 1890s, the potential market for mail-order catalog companies increased dramatically.

It was almost serendipitous that the waves of immigrants from Eastern Europe began to arrive in the United States at a time when the American textile and garment industries were entering a period of explosive growth. Many of these people brought with them skills as seamstresses and tailors. Journalist Malcolm Gladwell likened this to showing up in Silicon Valley in the 1980s with ten thousand hours of computer programming under one's belt. That may be a bit of a stretch, since late nineteenth-century factory workers were poorly paid and toiled under extremely difficult and often unsafe conditions. They did not receive signing bonuses and stock options. Nonetheless, their skills gave them the ability to gain entrance to a rapidly growing segment of the economy, and through a combination of guile, hard work, and opportunism, some were able as time went on to successfully establish small businesses themselves. Virtually all of these early entrepreneurs lacked college degrees, and many did not graduate high school.

This is a far cry indeed from today's entrepreneurial pathway, which involves earning both an undergraduate and graduate degree, and the ability to create a business plan compelling enough to attract outside investors. The lion's share of the seed capital is typically provided by private equity firms, not by the founders themselves. Finally, founders and the investors both share a common exit strategy, which means if the business proves to be viable and begins to flourish, the company will be sold or go public (and the sooner the better). This is euphemistically called a "liquidity event."

Phoenix Clothes opened shop in Allentown in 1939. I have more than a passing interest in the company because my paternal grandfather was one of the three cofounders. On the surface, the Phoenix story seems completely unremarkable, something which could be told in thirty seconds. My grandfather Nat Berkwits and his two partners, Jack Warsaw and Al Lerner, had started the company in Philadelphia and then purchased a red brick factory building in downtown Allentown. Phoenix Clothes was a success from the beginning. After a period of consistent profitability and growth, the company was sold to Nashville-based Genesco Corp. in 1964. Genesco ran Phoenix as an independent brand for a number of years and then in 1983 merged it with another apparel manufacturing subsidiary, Greif Corp. In the 1990s, Genesco fell upon hard times and ended up exiting the apparel business altogether. Finding no buyers for Phoenix/Greif, they simply liquidated everything, closed their factories, and put several thousand people out of work. My grandfather did not live long enough to see the business he helped to create enter into its death spiral, but his two partners did.

Of course the actual history is more complex than that. Nat Berkwits was born on the Lower East Side of New York City in the 1890s. His parents were from Eastern Europe (Hungarian Jews) who came to the United States to build a life that would have been impossible in the Old World. He was one of eight children and had little formal schooling. His father laid down the law: boys left school after eighth grade and went to work. They lived at home until they were married, and during this time, they had to turn their weekly paychecks over to their father. It is probably not surprising that many of his brothers got married very early in life. So did he.

Two older brothers, Max and Lou, had started small millinery businesses and were successful from the outset. In time, both were to become multimillionaires. They gave advice to Nat and helped him procure work in the industry. He did a little of everything, from manual labor to modeling, and like many others, learned about the business by osmosis. As a young man, he wanted to get involved in manufacturing apparel, where finished goods are physically cut and sewn into ready-to-wear garments. His brothers wanted no part of that, but they helped to set him up. He started on a very small scale in Passaic, New Jersey, then Poughkeepsie, New York, and finally Philadelphia. Along the way he met his future partners, Warsaw and Lerner, and in the 1930s, they established Phoenix Clothes. Warsaw possessed financial acumen and money as well; Lerner, who was a little younger, oversaw sales; Berkwits ran the factory and was responsible for dealing with labor unions.

Labor union relationships were particularly contentious in the 1930s. How could they not be? The country was in the midst of the Great Depression. Although legislation in the early 1900s helped to eliminate the most egregious of unfair labor practices and occupational safety concerns, factory work during the '30s was long, hard, unforgiving, and most importantly, terribly uncertain. Labor unions provided a much-needed psychological safety net and rallying point for their membership.

The relationship that many companies had with labor unions was made more complex by a strange and sinister connection some unions had with organized crime. This was especially true in the garment industry, where Louis "Lepke" Buchalter used labor unions to build a "business" based upon threat and coercion. Ultimately, his business model evolved into a massive protection racket. Through the unions, Buchalter repeatedly threatened business owners with strikes, sabotage, or even personal harm. As a reward for the deals he was able to "negotiate," Buchalter skimmed money from union coffers with impunity.

Buchalter's racketeering actually represented the soft side of the man. His buddies included Meyer Lansky, Bugsy Siegel, and Albert Anastasia. He was the founding father of "Murder Inc." and is credited for inventing what became known as the contract hit. Buchalter, in fact, is the only well-known mobster of his era to be put to death in prison. He was clearly a fearsome individual.

In any event, Nat Berkwits's early business adventures were challenging. At least part of the reason he moved his young businesses from Passaic to Poughkeepsie to Philadelphia was union trouble. Legend has it that he experienced the kind of pressure and intimidation that only Buchalter or one of his cronies could provide. Whether Lepke Buchalter himself was involved is uncertain, but it was no secret that union strong-arm tactics served as the principal force behind this constant movement.

Upon arriving in Philadelphia, as the Depression deepened, he experienced extreme financial stress. In the early 1930s, his house burned to the ground, and he moved his wife and four children into a small apartment. Yet he struggled on, and during this time he established and then solidified his relationship with Lerner and Warsaw. Soon Phoenix Clothes was born.

From the middle years of the Depression leading up to World War II, Phoenix produced men's clothing, mostly trendy suits and slacks, and sold them to specialty men's stores and some larger department stores, usually under private label. These were hard times, so the decision was made to produce a suit that came with two pairs of pants. The expansion to Allentown represented a huge financial commitment on the part of the owners and an even bigger gamble on the ability of the country to pull itself out of the Depression.

World War II represented one of the greatest catastrophes in human history, but in a very narrow sense, this conflict gave the American economy a shot in the arm, and it proved to be a boon for Phoenix Clothes. The company was able to secure military business and in short order was turning out dress uniforms and Eisenhower jackets for the US Army. Since the vast majority of Phoenix's factory workers were women, it experienced no labor shortages during wartime. The company grew and prospered. For Phoenix, the Depression ended abruptly on December 7, 1941.

After the Allies' victory and our sudden return to a peacetime economy, there was a period of adjustment. Over ten million GI's were being released from active duty, and it was difficult for the nation to adapt to this sudden change. Inflation spiked, the job market softened, and ultimately the economy slid into recession in 1948. Before long, however, the United States was to enter the so called "Golden Years," the 1950s. This was a time of American dominance, of peace and prosperity, and of an unshakeable feeling of self-confidence and pride.

The stars were aligned perfectly for Phoenix. Their designs received a strong reception in the marketplace. Also noteworthy was the unusually good relationship that management was able to build with labor unions. There was only one work stoppage (more of an informal sit-down strike, in truth) that ended up lasting for a matter of minutes. Workers had planned on reporting to their jobs, taking their seats, and doing little or no work. Management welcomed the workers but had quietly removed all the chairs from the factory floor before they reported to work. The sit-in became a stand-up. Both sides quickly made peace.

Company social events like picnics and barbeques were attended by both management and rank and file, and union bosses attended regularly. By the time the company was sold in 1964, approximately one thousand people were working for the company. No one was ever laid off.

It wasn't completely obvious at that time, or even five or ten years later, that changes were beginning to take place that would ultimately have a devastating impact on the textile industry in the United States. As we have seen, almost all of the clothing sold in the United States in 1964 was made here—well over 95 percent. Since then, we have seen a complete reversal, with over 95 percent of sales attributed to imports. The domestic textile industry has practically disappeared. The once-powerful ILGWU (International Ladies Garment Workers Union) once boasted four hundred fifty thousand members. As time went on, it became irrelevant, merged with other unions two times, and no longer exists as a separate entity.

The first warning sign of change to come was the development of a high-speed loom using "water jet" technology. This didn't directly affect manufacturers like Phoenix, which took finished fabrics and turned them into ready-to-wear garments—at least not at first. In time, however, water jet looms came to be recognized as the first shot across the bow, the seminal event that led to the long-term decline in American textile manufacturing.

A little research into the mechanics of looms was enough to convince me that what seemed to be a very simple matter, namely weaving, is technology of the highest order. Textile weaving has a distinctive terminology; weaving is accomplished by intersecting threads called warps and wefts. Things called healds raise the warp yarns and create a space, called a shed. A device called a shuttle brings the filling yarn into this space and moves back and forth at a very high speed, allowing the fabrics to be woven together and ultimately producing a finished product.

Water jet weaving machines were created in Europe but made their first splash in Japan in the 1960s. They were wider than shuttle looms, had fewer moving parts, and were 30 percent faster. Most importantly, these looms used no oil or grease. Conventional shuttle looms used both, and grease and dirt were often embedded in the woven fabric. As a result, the standard contract for "greige (pronounced like the color gray) goods," the plain, white fabric created in the first step of textile manufacturing, was written 80 percent white, 15 percent dark, and 5 percent seconds (irregular) at 5 percent off. Clearly, it was expected that at least 20 percent of a given run would produce imperfect goods. When goods were graded like this, it affected the price that the manufacturer could obtain.

The same goods produced by water jet looms were virtually perfect. One industry veteran I interviewed remembers the first time he saw goods produced by water jet looms in Japan. He turned to a colleague and said, "We're out of business." Apart from producing higher-quality goods more efficiently, the Japanese possessed another huge advantage: cheap labor. At the time, wage rates in Japan were a fraction of those in the United States.

Along with the production of greige goods (unfinished fabric), there are several other steps necessary in the production of finished clothing, and all of these processes remained in the United States for some time. Unfinished fabric is sent to converters, who are basically designers who have the fabric printed or dyed to their specifications. Converters can do their own work, but they typically subcontract their work out to a finishing plant. Once this is done, they will show their fabrics to manufacturers like Ralph Lauren or Ann Taylor. These companies, in turn, will actually cut the fabric and produce articles of clothing, or just like the converters, they can also subcontract the production of the clothing that finally finds its way into department stores and specialty shops.

The decline in the American textile industry was relatively slow at first. Initially most American textile factories were in the Northeast. An exodus by the producers of greige goods to the southern United States began slowly, as there was a shortage of skilled labor there, as well as a need to build factories. Nonetheless, the movement of production from north to south gained momentum as time went along. This was the American response to Japanese water jet factories—labor costs in the South were lower, and new factories could be operated more efficiently than the creaky old ones that they replaced. Besides, water jets were used primarily for synthetics, not wool or cotton. American producers thought they had a chance.

Ultimately, water jets were followed by air jets and other technological advances. Additional refinements allowed Asian manufacturing of unfinished goods to expand from synthetics to more traditional materials. Over the years, as cheap Japanese labor became more expensive, production moved to Indonesia, Thailand, China, even Vietnam. Once it became possible to produce unfinished goods on a massive scale in Asia, it would follow that the converters and end users would establish manufacturing facilities there as well. The only companies that were able to make it in America had deep pockets, advanced logistics, state-of-the-art factories, and good labor relations.

None of this, however, was common knowledge in 1964. The buyer of Phoenix Clothes, Genesco, was a large, diversified company whose shares were traded on the New York Stock Exchange. They were a "strategic" buyer and expected to own and operate Phoenix for the long term. They had no interest in uprooting managers, slashing overhead, or making dramatic changes like all "financial" acquirers do today. They didn't buy Phoenix to dress it up and sell it; they liked it just the way it was. For some time, Phoenix kept its name and brand identity and operated as a subsidiary of Genesco.

History is seen by most as a pretty dry subject, and the history of American corporations especially so, but the narrative of Genesco could be the basis for a Hollywood screenplay. The company was founded in Nashville, Tennessee, by James Franklin Jarman and was incorporated in 1924 as Jarman Shoes. Walton Maxey Jarman, the founder's son, dropped out of MIT and returned home to join his father's business. In 1933, in the depths of the Depression, he was named president at the age of twenty-nine. With obvious skill and an entrepreneurial streak, he built the company brick by brick. He was so successful at it that he was able to take the firm (soon to be known as General Shoe) public in a stock offering in 1939.

After World War II, Maxey Jarman went on an acquisition spree unlike anything that Wall Street had experienced in the past. The company, now known as Genesco, became so dominant in the shoe trade that the US Department of Justice took the company to court for antitrust violations. Part of the settlement was that they could not buy another shoe company for nearly a year and would have to obtain government approval on any further acquisitions within the next five years. Jarman couldn't sit still. He began to make acquisitions in the apparel industry and in other fields as well.

Genesco in short order purchased Greif Manufacturing and then acquired the high-end retailer Henri Bendel. The company bought a 65 percent interest in the Hoving Corporation, which in turn had controlling interests in Tiffany's and seven Bonwit Teller department stores. The largest of his purchases, an ill-fated one at that, was S.H. Kress, a national chain of variety stores. By the late '60s, Jarman's empire was impressive indeed, and Genesco's annual revenue hit $1 billion for the first time.

After Maxey Jarman's retirement, Genesco performed erratically, and on several occasions, it was questionable whether or not it would be able to continue as a viable concern. The company had grown much too fast and had assumed significant debt to complete most of its acquisitions. A number of the acquisitions were financed by offering the sellers a special series of preferred stock. Periodically, Genesco was unable to pay dividends on these preferreds, and the company on several occasions was sued as a result.

Not only were there angry shareholders, there were angrier labor unions. The US economy struggled for most of the 1970s and early 1980s, an especially hostile environment for a consumer products company. To make matters worse, the company occasionally made some huge and expensive blunders. The Kress acquisition was bad enough, yet a few years after the last Kress store was shuttered, Genesco had to write off $38 million after realizing it had grossly misjudged the market for western wear, especially western boots.

Occasionally there were periods of recovery and hope. At one time, Genesco was able to collaborate with Hughes Aircraft, and the joint venture created a highly efficient laser-operated cutting machine, which provided both savings and efficiency. Nevertheless, an occasional innovation like this could in no way save Phoenix-Greif from the inevitable. After a number of boom-bust cycles, the company decided to exit the apparel business altogether in the early '90s and return to its roots as a shoe manufacturer and retailer.

Business at Phoenix, however, was initially quite stable, and the company was profitable well into the 1970s. Executives realized that the plant in Allentown was old, inefficient, and in the eyes of some, a firetrap. After much debate, a decision to proceed with construction of a new factory was made. Shortly after 1980, these new digs were ready—a huge, state-of-the-art building located in the suburbs of Allentown, just a few miles from center city.

Business for Phoenix began to worsen dramatically just as they moved into these new facilities. The country had been in and out of recession almost continuously. Unemployment was up, and for the first time, foreign competitors were able to wrest significant market share from domestic manufacturers, not just in textiles, but also in autos, steel, construction equipment, and other vital industries. Many once-thriving cities suffered, as factories closed and residents moved out of the region. The Rust Belt was born.

Larry Shelton was a Genesco lifer who joined the company out of college in 1956 and worked there until his retirement in the 1990s. The first half of his career was spent mostly in the home office. He held a variety of executive positions, ultimately leading to his appointment as CFO. When business conditions worsened in the late '70s and early '80s, Shelton was named president of Genesco's apparel division, with the obvious challenge of being able to bring it back from the dead. By this time, apparel represented more than 50 percent of Genesco's total revenue, and its success was critical to Genesco's survival.

Shelton made the decision to consolidate most of the operations of Baltimore-based Greif and Phoenix in the newly built facility in Pennsylvania, and in 1983, he moved from Nashville to Allentown, where he lived for the next four years. It was at this time that the Phoenix name disappeared and the combined operations were renamed Greif.

Within five years Shelton engineered an impressive turnaround. The division, which had reported a $5 million loss in 1983, came in with a $5 million profit in 1988. By this time, Greif's headcount approached one thousand employees in the Allentown area alone. Greif continued to produce the higher-end, private label men's specialty clothing that had been Phoenix's hallmark. Additionally, they turned out a more traditional and diverse line of apparel under license to well-known designers, such as Perry Ellis, Lanvin, and Ralph Lauren. The consolidation in Allentown went smoothly during Shelton's watch; being a fair and skillful negotiator, he was also able to preserve a healthy working relationship with Greif's unions.

Greif's turnaround was also aided by the contributions of Norman Fryman, a highly regarded sales executive who had strong relationships throughout the industry, especially with regional and national retailers. He joined Genesco in 1986 and worked closely under Shelton for the next several years. Shelton continued to run the division from his offices in Allentown, and Fryman was named president of Greif. They were a formidable team. Ultimately, Shelton was rewarded for his efforts and was named president and COO of Genesco in 1988. When Shelton returned to Nashville, Fryman succeeded him as apparel division president.

Suddenly, it all came apart. Even with the benefit of hindsight, it is hard to understand precisely what happened, who was to blame, or when the tipping point was reached. This much is indisputable: the national economy, which had rallied brilliantly since the early '80s, began to stall and entered recession. Interest rates, while down from historic levels, remained stubbornly high—well above the growth rate in the economy. Casual dress began to become more common in the workplace. More and more manufacturing processes in the apparel industry were being moved overseas. The smaller men's specialty store, which had been a fixture in virtually every town or small city in the country, began to disappear. Perhaps if the company had been able to sell into different channels—off-price retailers like T. J. Maxx, catalogs, and later the Internet—they may have been able to make it, but they did not. During this time, Genesco also began to experience worsening relationships with its labor unions. The Greif division's future may have been saved if its parent had been able to engage with the unions in a more productive way, or if it had adapted more rapidly to the changes that had taken place in menswear fashion.

In addition, Genesco had other issues to deal with. Douglas Grindstaff was recruited from Proctor and Gamble in 1992, became CEO in 1993, and resigned in 1994. His was a brief and forgettable reign. Grindstaff was a highly regarded marketing executive, but he had no experience in either apparel or footwear and, as a result, found it difficult to establish credibility with his management team. According to some, he personally created a very strained relationship with Genesco's labor unions, one of which actually orchestrated a national boycott of Genesco footwear in the early 1990s. Prior to this, Grindstaff's tactics included buying a non-union shop in Carrolton, Georgia, with the intention of gradually moving manufacturing there from Allentown. The union fought back, and the active picketing outside Genesco-owned stores around the country forced Grindstaff to back down.

To make matters worse, it was during this time that Norman Fryman left the company, and his departure meant the loss of some very important accounts, such as Ralph Lauren. His leadership and extraordinarily strong rolodex of customers and industry contacts proved next to impossible to replace.

Sometime in 1993, after reporting yet another operating loss, company spokesperson Teresa Mangelsdorf explained it this way: "Some weeks are up in retail, and some are down." Securities analyst Gary Dennis of J.C. Bradford put it more succinctly: "Basically, they are not going to make any money this year." Genesco's back was against the wall, and the company took the humiliating step to announce it was getting out of the apparel business altogether. There were no buyers for the Greif division. The only alternative was liquidation. This is a polite term for fire sale. Oddly enough, Larry Shelton was dispatched back to Allentown to oversee the piecemeal dismemberment of the division he had helped to rescue just a few short years before. He retired from the company shortly thereafter.

A year or so later, another Allentown-based textile company, Surefit, moved into Greif's old factory. Surefit was a leading producer of furniture coverings, especially slip covers. It still is. The company began operations in 1914 and has operated successfully in Pennsylvania throughout its history. At the same time that Genesco was trying to find a buyer for Greif and failed, Surefit was purchased by Fieldcrest Cannon. It is beyond ironic that their paths crossed in this manner.

It was painful for Shelton to look back at the closure of Phoenix-Greif. "I spent four years in Allentown and was part of a successful turnaround. During this time I developed great respect and admiration for Greif employees—both union and nonunion. It was heart breaking to see what the closing did to so many lives…(but) I was glad I was the one selected to do the job, and I believe I did it with compassion for the employees."

Just a few months before Greif ended operations, Ron Devlin penned a moving feature story for the *Morning Call*. He wrote about a middle-aged couple that had worked for Greif for twenty-seven years since they were married in 1967. The husband, Stanley Wisneski, was let go first. With an eleventh-grade education, he subsequently had a great deal of trouble getting another job. Like many unskilled or semiskilled, middle-aged factory workers, he typified the displaced American worker of that era. He also suffered from poor circulation in his legs and had large medical bills and minimal health insurance; his medical condition alone made him virtually unemployable. His wife Violet worked on for a while, and then Greif announced it would close the factory. She said, "I don't want to lose my job, and I don't want anyone to lose theirs. I thought we (Greif's workers) would never go out."

The story of the rise and fall of Phoenix Clothes (and Bethlehem Steel, for that matter) could be a business school case study of errors and omissions, just like the stories of Schiff Silk & Ribbon, Anda Industries, or Aetna Felt can be seen as blueprints for survival and success. Economic conditions impacted all of these companies equally, but the companies themselves had divergent destinies. Looking back, it seems fairly obvious why some businesses made it and others failed. For the Wisneskis and countless others, however, this was a moot point.

Muhlenberg Elementary School in 2014. When I stopped to take a picture of the building, a security guard politely asked me to move on after I was done. Times have changed.

This is the class picture that was part of the inspiration behind My Bittersweet Homecoming. The author is bottom row, second from left.

The Americus Hotel, still a vacant eyesore after decades of neglect. Notice the ground floor windows covered over with brown paper. The Americus sits only a block or two from City Hall.

Coca Cola Park, the first class home of the Lehigh Valley IronPigs. The team has been a huge success, and has set attendance records.

The old Phoenix Clothes factory building as it stood in 2015. A fitness center was once situated at the far end of the building, and a pet store at the behind the covered walkway entrance in the foreground. Today it is entirely vacant, and has been for years.

The rolling hills behind my boyhood home have been replaced by a parking lot for Muhlenberg College. If you use the no parking sign as a rangefinder, you can see my house.

The centerpiece of Allentown's recent redevelopment, the PPL Center is home to minor league hockey as well as concerts and other events. To the right is the Marriott Renaissance, and to the left a new commercial office building.

An aerial shot of Anda Industries, now Diamond Dye and Finishing. It is the oldest continuously operated textile mill in the country—still very much active today.

8

Hess Brothers

In 1996 Hess's Department Store, an iconic fixture in local business for nearly a hundred years and an acknowledged jewel among American retailers, ceased business operations and closed its doors. After decades of rapid growth in the early twentieth century, Hess's (originally known as Hess Brothers) achieved national notoriety in the 1950s and continued to flourish for some time afterward—even after the exceptionally creative and bold Max Hess Jr. sold the business in 1968. At its peak, Hess's enjoyed a 40 percent share of all retail sales in the city of Allentown, and its sales per square foot were among the highest in the world.

I bought my first record at Hess Brothers, a 45 rpm single of Guy Mitchell's "Singing the Blues." It was released in 1956, when I was nine years old. In those years, Hess Brothers' massive store sold everything under the sun: shoes, sporting goods, books and records, jewelry, fine china and crystal, mass-market and designer clothing, small and large appliances, and furniture. Even gold bullion was put on sale after the practice was made legal by Congress in 1974.

Over time, however, Hess's morphed from an entirely unique, standalone department store into a very ordinary regional chain, at its high point operating approximately eighty stores. Ultimately it became a victim of hard times, questionable strategic decisions, and changing consumer tastes; finally, in 1996 Hess's then-current owner, the Bon Ton Stores, shut it down just two years after buying it. Afterward, the flagship store on Hamilton Street sat vacant for some time. It was very old and in need of major rehab and retrofitting. The city of Allentown ended up buying the Hess's site and later sold it to PPL Corporation, originally known as Pennsylvania Power and Light.

The demolition of Hess's occurred in piecemeal fashion, and once it began, the process took approximately one year. The store had been built in stages, the way some hospitals are constructed—patchwork fashion, wing by wing. Since the building was really an amalgam of separate structures, there was no way it could be easily or swiftly demolished. To make matters worse, asbestos and other toxic substances were present throughout the store and its adjacent warehouse, and the time-consuming process of disposing of these hazardous materials brought added complexity to the task.

The last vestige of Hess's fell to a wrecking ball in the fall of 2001, five years after Bon Ton locked the doors. The failure of Hess's represented a crushing psychological blow to the residents of Allentown, and the demolition of the store moved many to tears. Hess's importance, not just to the local economy but also as a symbol of civic pride, cannot be underestimated. Allentown is not Paris, and Hess's is not the Eiffel Tower, but the analogy is accurate enough.

The Allentown Economic Development Corporation (AEDC) was involved with all aspects of the property's demolition and the transfer of ownership to PPL. Kurt Zwikl was at that time the AEDC's director, and on the day before the last pieces of Hess's came down, Zwikl led an AEDC contingent throughout the building. His connection with Hess's was unique. His father, William, worked at Hess's for many years as the company's photographer, and Kurt himself had taken summer jobs there while he was still in school. In 1975, as a twenty-six-year-old Pennsylvania state representative, he had the opportunity to meet future President Jimmy Carter during a campaign stop in Allentown; the meeting naturally enough took place at Hess's. Much later, he coauthored a book with former *Morning Call* reporter Frank Whelan about Hess's early history, which included a number of fascinating pictures from his father's private collection.

Hess's last day was a media event. *Morning Call* columnist Bob Wittman accompanied the AEDC crew. At one point, Zwikl paused next to a freight elevator's steel doors and said to Wittman, "I can remember carrying rolls of carpet through here and loading them on to the freight elevator. Looking back, I can still hear that door closing." He was hearing an echo that endured for forty years.

The beginnings of Hess's in Allentown were not too dissimilar from many other businesses that were established at the turn of the twentieth century. Max and Charles Hess were brothers who operated a small retail store in Perth Amboy, New Jersey. The family was Jewish, originally from Germany, and immigrated to the United States to seek out both personal freedom and economic opportunity.

Perth Amboy was small, with a population at that time of approximately ten thousand people, and the brothers quickly realized that in order to grow, they would have to establish a second location. In 1896, while visiting nearby Easton, Pennsylvania, Max made a chance stop in Allentown and returned to Perth Amboy highly enthusiastic about his discovery. Charles was not immediately won over, as he had his own eye on Atlantic City, but in time he agreed to go along with Max.

The brothers signed a lease for approximately six thousand square feet of retail space on Hamilton Street, taking over a vacant storefront adjacent to the Grand Hotel. The cost of the lease was $1,200 per year, or $0.20 per sq. ft. The amount at first glance seems laughably low. In today's dollars, this translates to $35,000 a year, or $6 per sq. ft.—still a bargain by any standard.

The risk that the brothers took was not so much in the lease per se, but rather in the location. The Grand was located on the periphery of the shopping district in Allentown. The only other retail establishment on the block was a hardware store. Imagine locating a single storefront across the street from an enclosed shopping mall; it could work, but it would be a very long shot. When the Hess brothers took the plunge in 1897, Max Hess was thirty-three. He had been counseled to back off by family and friends, who felt the risk was too great. Like many young entrepreneurs, he rejected their well-meaning advice.

Hess Brothers opened with a splash on Hamilton Street in the summer of 1897. Hess spared no expense, hiring a marching band to celebrate the grand opening, and then began what was to be a long-term tradition of advertising heavily in the *Morning Call*. For decades, Hess's was the paper's largest advertiser by far. On opening day, Hess had already hired twenty-three employees, a huge leap of faith for a brand new store with such a small footprint.

Success was immediate. Within a few months, a dozen more people were hired, and adjacent space was leased as soon as it became available. Within five years, the brothers closed their store in Perth Amboy, consolidated operations in Allentown, and bought the entire building. The Grand Hotel was no longer a hotel. It was now Hess Brothers.

Business was sensational. From the beginning, Hess Brothers had a unique strategy of offering expensive European imports (from haute couture to fine crystal and china) while at the same time promoting rock-bottom pricing on other merchandise by way of periodic, soon-to-become legendary sales. This strategy persisted for many decades—well into the latter part of the twentieth century.

Charles was largely responsible for what retailers call merchandising—he made the call on what goods ended up on the selling floor. From time to time, he would travel to Paris on buying trips. Max, in addition to being the strategist and visionary entrepreneur, also functioned like a chief operating officer, running the store's day-to-day operations. The brothers made a great team.

Hess Brothers grew almost exponentially in its early years. By the time Charles passed away in 1929 (Max had died seven years earlier), the store measured two hundred thousand square feet, slightly larger than the average "Super Walmart." Even then, the company had achieved iconic status and served as a benchmark against which other retailers could measure their own performance.

The stock market crashed a few months after Charles's death, and the country soon fell into the Great Depression. Unlike the normal expansions and contractions that are part of a typical business cycle, with recessions typically measured in months, the Great Depression lasted many years. The decline in its first four years was horrifying. By 1933, national unemployment stood at 25 percent. In those years our government did not offer the safety nets such as Social Security, Medicare, Medicaid, and food stamps that are commonplace today. If you fell, you fell hard.

There were over twenty-five thousand banks operating in the United States in 1929; within four years, ten thousand of them had failed. Bank deposits were uninsured. If you had a bank account and your bank closed, you were no better off than if you had lost your wallet. The same was true for brokerage firms; for many investors, this indeed was the final wipeout. If you maintained an account with a Wall Street firm and that firm went out of business, your account disappeared with it.

It is not surprising, then, that business at Hess Brothers soured after 1929. The country, after all, was in survival mode, and within a few years, consumer spending nationally would drop nearly 50 percent from its prior peak. To be truthful, even before the Depression had taken hold, some observers felt that Hess Brothers had become somewhat tired and predictable in its approach, and that change would be both welcome and beneficial. As the Great Depression deepened, it became a necessity.

Max Hess Jr. dropped out of Muhlenberg College on his twenty-first birthday in 1932 and went to work for Hess Brothers. He became president before he turned twenty-five. From the very beginning, he brought both chutzpah and marketing genius to the table. All entrepreneurs are risk takers, but not all of them are successful. Hess was bold, energetic, and charismatic, but more importantly, he had an intuitive understanding of retailing. He was a born innovator, and Hess's ultimate success sprang from Max's commitment to make Hess Brothers totally unique.

Even in the dark days of the 1930s, Hess redesigned the storefront as well as the window displays to impart a more modern look (something we would now call art deco). Merchandise in the store was upgraded as well. Yet Hess never went so far upstream that he forsook the bargain hunter, and his heavily promoted, periodic sales events often drew such crowds that lackadaisical customers could find themselves in danger of getting trampled.

The Patio Room, which first opened in the 1930s, operated as a high-end restaurant within the store itself and offered fatigued shoppers a welcome respite as well as friendly service and an inviting menu. In time, the Patio would offer a menu of over one hundred items, with a number of specialties flown in. The pièce de résistance was home-baked strawberry pie, piled high and deep with strawberries and whipped cream. One pie weighed ten pounds out of the oven.

Max Hess never made money on the Patio, and he didn't care. He used it as a loss leader. Never one to let a selling opportunity pass by, Hess began to stage fashion shows in the restaurant proper—he knew he had a captive audience there and decided to take full advantage of it.

Once in a while, my mother would take me along if she went shopping at Hess's, and I remember the Patio well. There I sat, nine or ten years old, eating a bowl of ice cream and minding my own business, while trying mightily to avoid paying any attention to a steady stream of beautifully coiffed, sexy models passing by our table. While the scene I have painted may seem comical, it was validation to Max Hess Jr. of what seems to be a fairly obvious proposition—shoppers can only spend money when they are in the store. The Patio was enough of a draw that it attracted entire families to make shopping at Hess Brothers a special event.

After World War II ended, Hess Brothers entered its golden era. Always the promoter, Max Hess Jr. began to bring A-list Hollywood celebrities to attract attention and, of course, shoppers. In the 1950s through the '60s, Sophia Loren, James Garner, Rock Hudson, and Zsa Zsa Gabor were among those that made appearances at Hess's, as did George Reeves (television's Superman) and Barbara Walters. Max enjoyed his connection to Hollywood. In 1967, Sonny and Cher (she was then only twenty-one) flew to Allentown to perform at his New Year's Eve party and ended up spending the night as guests at his home.

He innovated constantly, and virtually everything he tried set Hess Brothers apart. The French Room offered exquisite designer goods from Paris. He sponsored a week-long flower show that attracted shoppers from afar. Christmas is, of course, prime time for all retailers, but Hess took things to another level entirely, with elaborate decorations, giant toy soldiers, and a Christmas-themed professional puppet show, "Pip the Mouse." The show actually ran until the early 1990s, and today a video of it can be found on YouTube.

After avant garde designer Rudi Gernreich introduced a topless bathing suit in 1964, future CEO Irwin Greenberg, then a young buyer, immediately snapped up a dozen copies for the store. Gernreich dubbed his creation the "monokini," and, if nothing else, it created instant excitement and publicity. (Gernreich remains a legendary figure in the fashion world largely because of the monokini, which few women bought and even fewer wore.) Seeing the opportunity for the kind of publicity that no amount of money could buy, Hess Brothers promoted the monokini heavily in the press and featured it on mannequins in its Hamilton Street window. It turned out the store never sold a single copy, something that Greenberg admitted with a shrug more than thirty years later. Yet both Hess and Greenberg viewed the episode as an unqualified success—the buzz that surrounded the monokini quickly drove traffic (and sales) measurably higher.

"The Teen Trip of a Lifetime" was another Max Hess original. It represented the grand prize of a heavily hyped drawing. Teenage girls entering the contest would, among other things, have to write essays on subjects like fashion and grooming. The trip itself was a fully chaperoned, multicity, two-week tour of Europe with few if any expenses spared—first-class air travel, four-star hotels, along with VIP visits to fashion houses, including Hess's locations in France and Italy. Hess naturally sent a film crew along to take full advantage of the promotional possibilities. In fact, when the lucky winner was first notified, Hess always sent a team to that person's home to convey the good news, and a photographer was part of the group. Many photos that were subsequently published showed the winner in joyful tears. The pictures were touched up with glycerin to create a more dramatic effect.

Business was conducted on a predominantly cash basis. Credit cards did not exist prior to World War II. Diners Club cards were launched in 1950, but they had very limited circulation and acceptance. It was nearly ten more years before American Express was to issue a card bearing its name. Initially, the card was made from paper. MasterCharge (MasterCard) and BankAmericard (Visa) followed a few years later. Noncash transactions at Hess Brothers were handled either by check or a charge account that the store maintained for its better customers. In both cases, it took about five minutes to check out at the register. A salesclerk would write up an order by hand on a small receipt pad, verify the customer's name and address, and then call within Hess's for approval either to accept the check or process the charge. If everything passed muster, the customer received a carbon copy of the handwritten receipt, and the original was retained by the store. These sales receipts were an integral part of the store's accounting and financial recordkeeping; there was no other way to save or store data.

Apart from the topless bikini, the world of Hess Brothers seems pretty quaint: strawberry pie, Santa, Pip the Mouse, flower shows, celebrity sightings, and handwritten order slips with carbon copies. All of this seems quite archaic by today's standards, but it worked. As time progressed, in spite of the enormous social and cultural changes that had taken place in the 1960s, Hess Brothers chugged along, growing year by year, and producing annual sales of nearly $50 million. In today's dollars, that's nearly $350 million, approximately five times the revenue of an average Walmart supercenter. Max Hess Jr. never opened a second store; Hess Brothers on Hamilton Street was truly one of a kind.

Yet Max Hess was concerned about the future. Postwar prosperity created unexpected problems. One of the biggest was the result of upwardly mobile, largely white families moving to newly developed suburban locations, leaving a vacuum of sorts in older urban areas. Population growth in many such northeastern cities stagnated and, in some cases, actually declined. At the same time, poorer minority populations within many urban cores surged. There was a visible increase in crime, drugs, drop-out rates, teenage pregnancy, and one-parent families. In West Philadelphia, over 70 percent of the residents in 1950 were white; that number stood at 20 percent by 2000. All this happened while West Philly's total population declined every decade from 1950 to 2000, and the population loss was huge—over one hundred thousand. "Urban blight" was a phrase used more and more often to describe the physical manifestation of a variety of complex events that were having a profound impact on our society. Martin Luther King's assassination in 1968 was the catalyst for spontaneous riots in a number of American cities, but in truth, poverty had existed in them for a very long time, and resentments had smoldered for many years.

Years before in 1958, Max Hess purchased Breadon Field, a minor-league ballpark that was then home to the Allentown Red Sox. Hess, not surprisingly, renamed it Max Hess Stadium. His promotional magic did not extend to baseball. In 1960, the team drew only fifty-one thousand fans—well under one thousand attendees per game. After the team left Allentown, Hess was unable to attract another minor-league team, and his stadium sat vacant for several years.

It had been thought that the only reason Hess bought the site to begin with was to develop a shopping center that would feature a suburban Hess Brothers as its anchor tenant. That may well have been his agenda, but for years he hesitated to act. Apparently, he would have had to go all in, borrow money, or both in order to take on a project of this magnitude, and he was unwilling to take the financial risk; in the end, he sold the land in 1967. The ultimate irony is that a few years later, the Lehigh Valley Mall was built on that very site and competed successfully against Hess's from the very first day it opened.

Within a year, Max Hess Jr. sold Hess Brothers itself to Philip Berman, a local industrialist and personal friend. The announcement of the sale came without warning, and Hess himself was circumspect as to his motivation. Berman paid $17 million for the store, and incredibly, the transfer was literally an all-cash transaction. Hess insisted upon this. It took the Philadelphia Federal Reserve Bank several days to come up with the currency. At the closing, money was piled everywhere, and Hess took it away in trunks.

Berman ran the store for eleven years. Over that time, Hess's opened a few smaller stores in other locations, first in the Lehigh Valley, then elsewhere in eastern Pennsylvania. Max Hess's senior management team stayed on under Berman, and apart from this expansion, there were no dramatic shifts made in Hess's long-term strategy and customer focus. In 1979, when he was in his early sixties, Berman sold out to a privately held shopping mall developer, Crown America. The price was $35 million. Berman spent most of the rest of his life involved in philanthropy, including a number of years as chairman of the Philadelphia Museum of Art.

Crown America and its founder and CEO, Frank Pasquerilla, picked a challenging time to get into the retail business in Pennsylvania. The deindustrialization of America had already begun, and cities like Allentown were feeling the pain. The country had recently emerged from recession, but it was experiencing a feeble recovery. The economy remained weak throughout Jimmy Carter's administration, with recessions appearing, fading, and reappearing with numbing regularity. Inflation remained high, and mortgage rates hovered near 13 percent. Millions of manufacturing jobs were lost, and most of them never came back when the economy recovered. The Iranian Revolution in the fall of 1979 and a subsequent spike in oil prices sent the economy into yet another recession within months. The economy continued to struggle until1982. That was the year Billy Joel released the song "Allentown."

Well we're living here in Allentown
And they're closing all the factories down
Out in Bethlehem they're killing time
Filling out forms
Standing in line.

Pasquerilla himself had no prior experience in retailing. Obviously, he thought there would be a natural synergy between his company and Hess's. After a few years, this relationship became somewhat incestuous. At one point in the 1980s, Crown America operated thirty shopping malls, and Hess's was the anchor tenant in twenty-six of them.

For a while, the company continued to perform profitably, especially as the general economy began to improve after 1982. Hess's became a regional chain, expanding into New York, New Jersey, Maryland, and then south into Virginia, Tennessee, and Kentucky. Store openings accelerated in the late 1980s, and at its peak, the chain was composed of approximately eighty stores. By this time, the fate of Hess's was obviously no longer tied exclusively to Allentown's economy, but local residents nevertheless continued to look upon the store with an enormous amount of pride.

For some time, Pasquerilla kept Hess's management team in place. Irwin Greenberg, a Hess's lifer, followed Philip Berman as CEO. (Berman stayed on for several years after Hess's was sold to Crown America.) As he was about to step into his new role in 1985, he said, "I'm not a workaholic, but probably a Hess-aholic, if there is such a thing. I eat it; I sleep it; if I didn't I wouldn't be here as long as I have, or done the things (and) accomplished the things that I have."

As more stores were added, the Hess brand understandably became less and less unique. Hess seemed to occupy an odd middle ground, being a somewhat ordinary higher-end store in midsize, colorless shopping malls. Because Hess's was privately held, it was, and is, difficult to get detailed information about its sales performance and financial operations. There is enough circumstantial evidence, however, to strongly suggest that the company did not invest enough in logistical support or additional management resources, given the pace of its expansion and the scope of its operations. It wasn't just a case of growing "too fast," but also that Crown America was unwilling to invest in people and technology to manage its growth.

Crown America embarked on an extremely ambitious expansion plan in the mid-1980s. Prior to this, Hess's grew conservatively. For example, it had opened a number of smaller suburban stores outside Allentown, where its brand was well known and respected and management could provide good operational and logistical support. Hess's then expanded into New York and was quite successful there as well. Utica and Schenectady were especially profitable.

Pasquerilla had big dreams. He took Hess's to Tennessee, acquiring several Miller's stores in that state. In Kentucky, more stores were purchased—the sellers being Ben Snyder and L. S. Ayres. Most of these stores were weak performers, but Pasquerilla was determined to pursue a southern expansion.

As we have seen, virtually every Pasquerilla-owned mall was anchored by a Hess's store. I am not sure how one can describe this as a "business strategy," but it is a factually accurate statement. This was obviously not the result of sheer coincidence. Some have speculated, and it appears to me reasonable enough, that without Pasquerilla's involvement, Hess's management would not have taken on many of the leases that it did. The arrangement seemed a classic case of the tail wagging the dog. There seems to be little doubt that it caused friction between Hess executives and Crown America.

The flagship Allentown store began to see its sales plateau for a variety of reasons, chief among them being the deteriorating condition of the downtown shopping area and competition from suburban malls. As the '80s wore on, Hess's on Hamilton Street began to lose some of its panache, and a number of the events and promotions that had made the store unique began to disappear.

Irwin Greenberg retired as CEO of Hess's in August of 1990. His departure was "effective immediately." It was also completely unexpected. "My leaving is amicable," he said. "I have worked successively for three owners and helped build the company from only one store to 75. That takes something out of you. Besides, it's time for a change." Years later in 2004, the *Morning Call* caught up with him and reported that "he stayed on with Crown America for 10 years, but left, as he said he would, when the fun was gone. He said that the company had seemingly become less interested in retailing...and his replacement did not seem to grasp the magic that made Hess's what it was." After his retirement, he visited the store and old friends several times but stopped because he believed it was poor for morale—including his.

The Gulf War began the same month that Greenberg retired, and very quickly the US economy faltered. It had been stumbling anyway, but skyrocketing oil prices and war anxiety pushed the country into recession in 1991. Almost immediately, Hess's began to struggle, each year becoming more difficult and more challenging than the last. Changes in retailing impacted as well. The appearance of big box stores like Costco, off-price retailers like TJX, and huge national chains like Macy's and Target put stores like Hess's in a bind. If this competition were not enough, there was Walmart, the thousand-pound gorilla. Traditional, midmarket regional department stores like Hess's were crushed; they were simply unable to compete effectively, either on the basis of price or selection.

In 1992, Pasquerilla said, "Last year was a really difficult year." At the same time, he claimed that the chain was worth $100 million, three times what he had paid for it. When Hess's new CEO, Robert O'Connell, was asked about problematic leases, he admitted that there were a few bad ones, but he was quick to point out that there were good ones too. "It all evens out," he said confidently. Some might question his analysis. When asked if a Hess's store would or could leave a Crown America property, he said, "The question hasn't come up."

Pasquerilla began to retrench. The stores by now were selling apparel and cosmetics almost exclusively. Once known for its uniqueness, Hess's now became virtually indistinguishable from many of its competitors. In time, some vendors began to express concern over Hess's liquidity. Initially there were selected layoffs; then a number of store closings followed.

Crown America sold most of the remaining Hess's stores in 1994 for $65 million to Bon Ton, a retailer based in York, Pennsylvania. A few others went to May Department Stores, which itself was later acquired by Macy's. Proffitt's of Tennessee acquired the rest.

After paying off all of the debt that Hess's had taken on over the years, Pasquerilla realized nothing from the sale. CEO Robert O'Connell, however, profited handsomely. Even though the company closed more than half of its stores and lost money every year during his tenure, O'Connell received a $2 million severance payment when the Bon Ton deal was closed. His employment contract contained a "golden parachute," which was triggered by a change in control (the sale of the company). It was a bitter pill to swallow for many of Hess's employees who lost their jobs during this difficult period.

It was clear from the outset that Bon Ton had no sentimental feelings about Hess Brothers or its legacy. After the Hess chain was acquired, its name disappeared, and Hess stores were rebranded as Bon Ton. Before the purchase was completed, Bon Ton announced that the jobs of two hundred home office workers would be protected temporarily; in fact, they were eliminated within six months' time. When Bon Ton took control in 1994, management said it was totally committed to keeping the flagship store in Allentown operating. Within a year, it admitted this pledge was under review.

Bon Ton was struggling in the mid-1990s, as were many traditional department store chains, but conditions in downtown Allentown were eroding with frightening speed. Sales were declining significantly, sometimes by double digits. This was partly the result of very trying economic conditions in the area; the Lehigh Valley ended up losing over 40 percent of its manufacturing jobs in the last third of the twentieth century. Apart from that, Hess's had opened several suburban stores, and these obviously siphoned off shoppers from downtown, which had become increasingly run-down and unappealing. Some residents avoided the area altogether as the rate in violent crime rose ominously.

In July 1995, Executive Vice President Michael Gleim claimed Bon Ton did not have an accurate understanding of the performance of Hess's downtown store before it completed its purchase in the prior year. He said, "It is difficult for us to tell if the store ever made money in the past, but I doubt that it did in the recent past." This was but one of several somewhat vague allusions Bon Ton management made concerning the accounting practices of Hess's under its prior owner, Crown America. In November 1995, Bon Ton reported a quarterly loss of $3.2 million and announced it was going to close the downtown Allentown store. This location was responsible for nearly two-thirds of the chain's entire loss.

Kurt Zwikl, the director of the Allentown Economic Development Corporation, was in the middle of this. In a recent conversation, he told me that early on, "everyone felt they might close the store." By the time he actually began his tenure at AEDC, the store in fact was no longer operating. What was idle speculation a year or so before—"What is going to replace Hess's?"—now became a rather urgent matter. He quickly discovered that the building itself would have to be totally gutted to attract a new tenant. Many of the interior floors were on slightly different levels, connected by steps or ramps. Asbestos would need to be removed. Furthermore, there was no central heating system. Incredible as it seems, Hess's employees would enter the store before 4:00 a.m. daily and turn on all of the overhead lights as a way of raising the temperature inside. I suppose body heat did the rest.

Zwikl and the AEDC were concerned they would be unable to attract a suitable tenant, and they were afraid that what had been Allentown's defining landmark structure would soon become a humiliating eyesore. The city bought the building from Bon Ton in 1998 for $1.5 million and began discussions with Lucent Technologies, the AT&T spinoff, about relocating its operations there. When it operated as a subsidiary of AT&T, Lucent was known as Western Electric and had a large presence in Allentown for many years. Negotiations ultimately proved unsuccessful, and Lucent, realizing how difficult it would be to retrofit the building to meet its needs, chose to consolidate its operations at a suburban site along US Route 22.

Zwikl looked at several other ideas, but it was a proposed sports arena project to which he devoted most of his time and attention. Local investors Dan Schantz, Terry Bender, Jeffrey Trainer, and David Stortz approached the city with a proposal to build an arena on the 9th and Hamilton site, but after several years of failed negotiations, the project was abandoned. Zwikl told me that the investment group was never able to get a firm commitment from the minor-league hockey team it had been courting. The team, the Lehigh Valley Xtreme, was in fact nothing more than a concept—an expansion team that hadn't begun to operate. Absent a lease, long-term financing was hard to find; even the most optimistic assumptions regarding trade shows, conventions, and concerts projected that the new arena would lose money without a strong anchor tenant. The project blew hot and cold for several years, but in the end, nothing happened. Things got so dicey at the end that the investor group ended up suing the city in order to block alternative development proposals.

The problem all along was financing. Near the end, one of the AEDC members intoned in frustration, "Show us the money!" The money never came through. This particular arena project was history in 2001; another one was to resurface successfully a decade later.

While this drama was playing out, the last vestige of Hess's, its warehouse, was demolished in 2001. The store itself had come down a year earlier. By the time the site was ultimately sold to PPL for $2 million, all of the necessary environmental work had been completed. PPL constructed additional office space there, directly across the street from its own corporate headquarters.

Hess's closure in downtown Allentown was inevitable given the long-term economic difficulties of the city, the physical decay that had taken place there, and the loss of customer traffic to suburban shopping malls.

The failure of Hess's as a business entity was another matter entirely. Crown America expanded the Hess chain much too quickly, especially in areas where Hess's was unknown. In the process, it lost the financial flexibility to change its strategy and reformat the stores to meet changing consumer tastes. A few old-school retailers did just that; Zayre reinvented itself as TJX, and Dayton Hudson as Target. Sadly, though, these were exceptions, as many traditional department stores began to stagnate and ultimately disappeared.

On August 18, 2012, more than one hundred former Hess workers gathered together for a reunion in nearby Emmaus. It had been sixteen years since Hess's (Bon Ton) closed its doors, but memories were still vivid. Seventy-nine-year old Steve Saganowich, who had worked as a tailor at Hess's for forty-seven years, told Matt Assad, a *Morning Call* reporter, "See, lots of big stars came to Allentown to appear at Hess's. Hess's put Allentown on the map." Assad opined, "The dividing line between downtown Allentown's heyday and today's economic struggles was January 16, 1996"—the day Hess's closed.

In truth, the city had been struggling for nearly twenty years against a perfect storm of overwhelming force. No one was surprised that Hess's finally folded its tent in Allentown or that the building was demolished a few years later. There was, however, a widespread feeling of sadness, if not actual grief, when the end came. Change, of course, is part of life, but even after the passage of many years, some changes are hard to swallow.

9

EMMA

ONE DICTIONARY OF slang expressions defines the word "character" simply as an interesting person, but real characters are a lot more interesting than that. Characters are unique, quirky, and memorable. They are not afraid of being different—they revel in it. Russian President Vladimir Putin and Microsoft founder Bill Gates are both extraordinarily powerful and influential, but they are not "characters." Ross Perot, Donald Trump, and Muhammad Ali are.

It is rare to find true characters in American politics. Ours is a two-party system that features Republicans and Democrats; if one party holds power, the other covets it. Our politicians typically need to appeal to a broad base of voters—ordinarily 50.1 percent or more—to hold office. They are usually unusually careful and circumspect when they speak for fear of offending current or potential supporters. It is commonplace for them to sidestep or evade difficult questions and issues. They are, no pun intended, politically correct by necessity. Yet every now and then, true characters emerge within the political arena. They are generally fringe players and third-party candidates, but occasionally even mainstream politicians whose personas are extraordinarily unusual may qualify. These individuals often become marginalized in terms of genuine power and influence, but through the force of their personalities, they are able to attract and maintain a devoted and highly vocal number of adherents and true believers.

We like to think of these folks as being upbeat and good humored, and they usually are. Sometimes, however, this description doesn't fit. The late Alabama Governor George Wallace is a perfect example of this. He was a segregationist who opportunistically disavowed segregation, and after this "epiphany," ran for president of the United States as a law-and-order candidate in 1968. He railed against the "pointy-headed intellectuals" in Washington, as well as hippies and welfare cheats. He called for a total victory in Vietnam; to reinforce the point, he chose Gen. Curtis E. LeMay as his running mate. Wallace won five states and got ten million votes, and many say his candidacy cost Hubert Humphrey the presidency. Although he didn't win the grand prize, he certainly had a significant impact upon the 1968 presidential election, and in a larger sense, the times he lived in—all because of the force of his personality.

Emma Tropiano, character though she was, had neither Wallace's mean streak nor blind political ambition. She was respected by her foes and eulogized by many of them upon her death. She didn't even enter the political fray until she was in her fifties and had no desire to perpetually seek higher office as many career politicians do. At one point in the 1970s, Emma had an awakening. Like many of her friends she didn't like what she saw happening to her neighborhood and in the city of Allentown. Then, through a strange set of occurrences, she ended up in politics, propelled there almost by accident.

She was born in Allentown in 1930 and raised there during the Great Depression. She was first-generation American, the daughter of Anthony and Antoinette Minutolo, who had come to the United States several years earlier from Italy. Her husband, Rosario "Sal" Tropiano, was himself first generation, and after marrying, the couple settled in a working-class neighborhood of the city. Emma and Sal lived at 416 Ninth Street, and it was there that they raised their only child, Victor. Emma's sister Edda lived at 418 and her parents at 419.

Antoinette was a seamstress at Phoenix Clothes. The Phoenix factory was about a fifteen-minute walk from her home, and even then, it was dingy and in poor condition. The factory floor was noisy, and there was no modern ventilation system, let alone air conditioning. It was not a welcoming place to work. Anthony spent many years working in Mack Trucks' assembly plant in Allentown. In those years, Mack was a large, very successful, privately held company that was a major player in the heavy-duty truck market. Now owned by Volvo, it still is both large and successful, but much has changed. Mack, which at the time was Allentown's largest employer, closed a sixty-year-old factory there in the late 1980s, and as a result, eighteen hundred workers lost their jobs. Mack then moved these assembly operations to South Carolina. Later, it relocated its world headquarters from Allentown to Greensboro, North Carolina. Mack still maintains some corporate functions in Allentown and runs a factory in nearby Macungie, but these operations are quite modest compared to what existed in the 1970s. Allentown today doesn't have many tourist attractions, but ironically, one of the biggest is the Mack Trucks Museum.

Everyone in the Tropiano family worked hard. At one point in the late 1950's Sal, who was a foreman in a local textile factory, decided to strike out on his own; Victor was then five years old. Initially he rented space in the neighborhood to open a small grocery store, and every morning he would get up early to pick up fresh milk, baked goods, and produce. He ultimately bought the building where the store was located and over the years acquired several others, all within a stone's throw from his home. Emma and Sal never moved from their home on Ninth Street.

Tropiano's was a family business, and Emma worked side by side with Sal. Sister Edda worked there as well, and occasionally young Victor helped out when he became old enough. Other family members pitched in too. Sal also hired a few neighbors with developmental disabilities, treated them well, and paid them fairly. These were people that might not have found gainful employment were it not for Sal's generosity and kind heart.

Stores like Tropiano's were neighborhood fixtures in the '50s and '60s, and most people who lived nearby would stop in regularly to pick up produce and household goods and then walk home with a brown paper bag in their arms. Unlike today, where suburbanites routinely drive to shop in huge, impersonal supermarkets (nearly fifty thousand square feet, on average), Tropiano's offered a feeling of intimacy.

I met with Victor Tropiano in Sarasota, Florida, in 2014. He is in his early sixties now, and while he left Pennsylvania years ago, he retains vivid memories of his childhood. His father Sal, who he described as both smart and stoic, left school after the sixth grade and worked like a bear his entire life. When he took a (rare) vacation, he was miserable. Tropiano's was open seven days a week, sixteen hours a day. Emma often worked the register, chatting up customers as they checked out. She had a type A personality and was always quick with a quip.

The Tropiano home was neat as a pin. Victor reluctantly complied with his mother's orders to straighten up his room and make his bed every morning. The living room was simply off limits to all family members. At the time, this was not considered all that unusual—Victor referred to an old joke among Italians about roping off the living room in case the Pope came to visit. Sal and Emma had a tremendous amount of pride in their home and in their business. In their minds, they were living the American dream.

Throughout the 1960s and most of the 1970s, Sal and Emma lived quietly, working devotedly in their family business. Emma had never demonstrated an interest in politics or a desire to run for public office. Victor himself observed, "My mother was not a politician." Fate, however, was to intervene and draw her into politics in a most unusual way.

As the '70s progressed, Allentown began to experience many conditions common to other American cities. To be charitable, downtown Allentown was not aging gracefully, and a weakening economy along with the first wave of job losses in the area no doubt accelerated this process. One of the most obvious results of urban decay was suburban flight, which first appeared in the years immediately following World War II and picked up momentum as time went on.

Oddly enough, while this exodus was occurring, a small, generally younger and highly educated group of individuals were being drawn to the concept of urban living, and Allentown was no exception. They were typically homeowners, not renters, and they were deeply committed to enhancing the quality of life in their neighborhoods. In later years they were to become known as yuppies. These new homeowners were interested in making home improvements that would boost property values. While many more residents were moving out of cities than were moving in, these professional newcomers attracted a lot of attention: they were smart, they were vocal, and because they represented what city government deemed to be a "positive influence," they almost always had the support of the political establishment.

The Old Allentown Preservation Association was founded in 1976, and its mission was centered on the preservation and revitalization of historically significant buildings located in downtown Allentown. Its founder, Benjamin Walbert III, was a young architect who had just purchased a new home on North Eighth Street, and he was attracted to the idea of creating a zone within the city that would promote the rehabilitation of historically significant buildings, consistent, of course, with the architecture of earlier times. Walbert began speaking with a few neighbors who shared similar goals, and within a matter of months, OAPA was born. OAPA lobbied tirelessly for its cause, and ultimately it was successful in persuading city council to establish the so-called "Historic Ordinance," which gave the newly created Historic Architectural Review Board (HARB) the power to approve or deny all exterior improvements made to buildings located within the Historic District itself.

The Historic Ordinance was born of idealism and hope. For many of Allentown's old-timers, however, it represented nothing more than an unnecessary and unneeded intrusion by government in their private lives. These people were more concerned with jobs, public safety, and basic municipal services than the fine points of architecture, ornate woodwork, or stained glass.

Incredibly, Emma Tropiano's entrance into municipal politics was the result of a dispute over a neighbor's casement window. In 1981, Franklin A. Koch, who lived one block away from Emma, replaced an original double-hung window with a triple casement window without receiving prior approval from the review board. HARB pursued the matter in court, and a magistrate ordered Koch to reinstall the original window and pay a fifty-dollar fine. For a number of downtown residents, this was the last straw. For several years, they had grumbled about HARB and its intrusions and regulations, and they were outraged over what had happened to Koch.

Angry neighbors soon coalesced to form CAHO, the Citizens Against Historic Ordinances. CAHO's goal was simple: repeal of the Historic Ordinance and the dissolution of HARB. In what was to become an alphabet war, CAHO lined up against OAPA and HARB, and these organizations fought each other head on for a number of years. Whenever a homeowner received HARB approval for work, OAPA provided him with a colorful banner he would be able to display at his front door. CAHO, not to be outdone, suggested that its adherents exhibit their own banners—in solid black.

Koch himself filed a counter lawsuit, which was supported and partially financed by CAHO. Even though Koch subsequently sold his home and moved to nearby Carbon County in 1984, appeals went on for another four years. Finally, in 1988, Judge David Mellenberg dismissed the suit. While he had lived in his Allentown home, Koch remained defiant and never took out the casement window. Before Koch left town, the city had no power to enforce its decision because the matter was under appeal. Interestingly, HARB also had no ability to compel the new owner to remove the casement window either. It was already there when he bought the home and, as such, was grandfathered. Seven years after the ruckus had started, nothing had changed.

In any event, Tropiano became very active in CAHO, which quickly became a powerful and organized special interest group within municipal politics. Apart from their common opposition to the Historic Ordinance and HARB, CAHO members shared other opinions on society, the economy, and government. CAHO adherents were almost entirely white, blue-collar, patriotic people who felt disenfranchised, neglected, and in some ways, betrayed by a society that seemed to have developed an entirely different agenda, whether it was about architectural restoration or affirmative action. Government seemed to act in a way that was hostile to their own perceived interests.

These folks—once called the silent majority by Richard Nixon—became angrier, more resentful, and less silent as the economy worsened in the 1970s. In Allentown, as in other industrial cities in the Northeast, there was no real recovery in the 1980s. As time moved along, more factories closed, job losses deepened, and frustration had reached a boiling point.

With CAHO's full support, Tropiano successfully ran for a seat on Allentown's City Council in 1983. At the time she was pretty much a one-trick pony, and she would be the first to admit that her antagonism toward Historic Ordinances was the dominant issue of her campaign. In time, her interests broadened. She later said, "I originally ran for the city council in 1983 in part as a result for my support for the Citizens Against Historic Ordinances, but since then my efforts have grown to embrace (other) issues affecting all of Allentown and its people."

The same could be said for CAHO. In 1984, CAHO contributed thousands of dollars to police officer Dennis Troccola's defense fund. Troccola had been accused of falsifying court appearance records, and immediately after the charges were brought, he was dismissed from the police force without pay. Apparently, the evidence against him was not airtight. Ultimately, after many weeks of hearings, the case was settled, but since Troccola was reinstated and received back pay, it was widely interpreted as a win for him.

It is hard to imagine how CAHO—an organization that came into existence to fight historical preservationists—could become deeply involved in the legal affairs of a suspended cop. CAHO President Francis Hartman said, "We felt he was being treated unfairly by the city...It's just a case where we felt a person's rights were being violated just like the Historic Ordinance violates rights."

Tropiano was at heart a populist, and she had a very strong, emotional connection with her many supporters. It really didn't matter whether the issue was a casement window, a suspended police officer, or a pothole. She stood up against government waste and inefficiency, and in the fifteen years that she was politically active, she became the most recognizable figure in local political affairs.

Her career ended as strangely as it started. In 1997 Tropiano was a candidate for mayor, and she was involved in a close, vigorous primary campaign against fellow councilman and Democrat Martin Velasquez III. On the day of the election, Victor Tropiano, standing outside one of the polling stations, was approached by a family friend who came by to offer his best. The man told Victor how much he thought of his mother and asked him to send along his best wishes. Victor thanked him for his support. The well-wisher then awkwardly replied that he was voting for Velasquez, but only because he didn't think a woman should be mayor. Tropiano lost by one vote.

Emma stayed active on the council for a few more years and was then defeated in 1999 in her last run for reelection. In the end, she served a total of sixteen years on city council and made three unsuccessful runs for mayor; before Velasquez, she first ran in a Democratic primary and again as an Independent in a general election, losing both times to incumbent Joe Daddona.

As the years wore on, her influence began to wane; the world was changing, but Emma wasn't. The silent majority was on the way to becoming the silent minority, and in Allentown, this was happening much faster than in the rest of the nation. The Latino population in the Allentown metropolitan area grew 261 percent between 1980 and 2000, and within the city itself, the rate of increase was substantially larger than that. By 2000, much of Emma's core support had either passed on or moved away.

If Emma believed in a cause, she took it on with vigor, even if her passion was not widely shared. Often she would latch onto a relatively unimportant issue and run with it for all it was worth—and sometimes for more than it was worth. She spoke out against fluoridating the municipal water supply, believing that the government was not obligated to involve itself in the dental care of children. After all, she reasoned, it's easy enough to use toothpaste or mouthwash.

Her second run against Mayor Joe Daddona was more memorable for outrageous sound bites than anything else. Emma's quips and outspoken nature sometimes received national attention, and she always maintained an intensely loyal cadre of supporters. During her 1989 mayoral campaign against him, she once camped out in a tent on Kline's Island next to a sewage treatment plant. There were two reasons for the stunt: first, to draw attention to the odor that occasionally permeated from this facility, and second, to protest Lehigh County's decision to open up the plant to businesses located outside Allentown itself. She also wanted to draw attention to Dadonna's claim, made ten years earlier, that he would go to Kline's Island one night a week until the stench disappeared. Daddona said, "I did go over there in the evening. I didn't stay overnight. But you don't have to stay overnight to realize the problem." Tropiano posed for photographers with a gas mask hanging around her neck before she retired for the evening. Emma was well aware that federal funds were being used to cover and seal off all of the treatment tanks, and that this work would be completed within a few months. She also knew that the plant was run by the county, and that neither she nor any other official in the city of Allentown had the authority to determine who would be able to use its services. None of it mattered to her. She saw Kline's Island as a mismanaged, inefficient example of government bureaucracy run amok—yet another instance of government failing to serve its constituents. When she saw an opportunity to get some free publicity and perhaps a few votes as well, she went all in.

She held herself out to be a "people's candidate." Her campaigns were always grassroots in nature. She spent no time on fund-raising because she didn't believe in it, putting her faith in God instead. Dozens of supporters volunteered their time and worked tirelessly on her behalf. In one campaign, the largest donation she accepted was ten dollars. She was proud beyond words. When she lost to Daddona in 1989, she received 8,974 votes, or only 41 percent of the total ballots cast. The results were not surprising. She ran with minimal financial support and was up against a popular incumbent who had the support of the Democratic Party.

On election night, she never called Daddona to congratulate him. Depending upon whose account you believe, she either gave no concession speech or a halfhearted one. Daddona, hardly the gracious winner, said "Mickey Mouse could have gotten 7,000 votes," implying that Emma's 8,974 total, all things considered, was quite pitiful. The two continued to lob Mickey Mouse grenades at each other, and then Daddona backed off. He said, "It's very nice to be important, but it's more important to be nice."

In politics, the two were more often than not adversaries, but they always got along reasonably well. Emma's son Victor described their relationship in very unusual terms. When asked if they were enemies, he said, "No. They just watched each other." Daddona represented the establishment, Tropiano the outsider. Apparently, there was a good deal of fondness and respect that existed between the two outside the political arena. They grew up in the same neighborhood and knew each other from childhood. Joe Daddona, in fact, delivered her eulogy. He said, "There will never, ever again be an Emma Tropiano. She was one of a kind."

Tropiano's supporters reveled in her populist appeal; her detractors labeled her a racist. For all of the sometimes humorous history connected with casement windows, Mickey Mouse, and camping out next to a sewage plant, this is where the conversation gets deadly serious. The issue of race has plagued the United States for many years. In Allentown it never really existed as a talking point until the 1980s, but after that, race-related issues assumed a front-and-center position almost overnight. In 1960, Allentown's population was over 99 percent white, with a very high proportion of those represented by German and Dutch residents who had lived in the area for a number of generations. Demographics began to change ever so slowly after that, accelerating in the 1980s, when the minority population began to swell.

Allentown's total population remained stagnant between 1960 and 2000. Connecting the demographic dots is very easy. For every white person who moved out of Allentown during this time, a nonwhite or Hispanic replaced him. Most of the newcomers were Puerto Rican, coming from either New York or New Jersey. They were attracted by cheap rents and a much lower cost of living in general. By 2000, the white population had declined to 72 percent; today, whites represent a minority (only 43 percent of the total), approximately the same share as Latinos. The balance is made up of blacks and Asians. Within the space of approximately thirty years, the face of the city was radically transformed.

Allentown's economy began to spiral downhill long before the Latino influx became noticeable, and a measurable increase in crime, poverty, and drug and alcohol abuse became apparent early on. In 1980 Allentown was still overwhelmingly white, but crime had exploded since the '50s and '60s. By then, the city had already become a fairly dangerous place, with 321 violent crimes (murder, rape, robbery, and aggravated assault) reported. Another 5,602 nonviolent property crimes occurred as well. The national recessions that began to appear in the '70s never really disappeared in Allentown; as we have seen, most manufacturing jobs that were lost never came back when the national economy recovered. Within a few years, Allentown was on its way to becoming one of the poorest and most violent cities in Pennsylvania.

The 1960s and 1970s represented a transitional time in American race relations. Far-reaching legislation had been passed concerning civil rights and voting rights, enfranchising vast numbers of Americans who had been pushed aside and discriminated against for decades. The ideals and goals that America's founding fathers had envisioned would now be extended to all citizens, who would henceforth be able to enjoy the full protection of the law. Yet for many people like the Tropianos—blue-collar, semi-skilled, self-reliant, patriotic—the attention (not to mention the money) that the government heaped upon minorities (and indigent whites as well) was thought to be undeserved if not shameful. The Tropianos and millions of others felt betrayed.

During the 1970s, *All in the Family* was an immensely popular television show that touched on many of the sensitive issues of the times. The central character, Archie Bunker, was a bigot and a racist, but because his character was occasionally humanized—buried under his prejudice, there really was a measure of decency and kindness—viewers could see racism in a different light. For many, they could actually see it in themselves. Gloria, Archie's daughter, and Mike, her husband, were young, extremely liberal and progressive—the perfect counterpoint to Archie's bigotry. Edith, his wife, was forever the peacemaker, a good woman who was instinctively honest. It's hard to imagine this airing on network television today:

> ARCHIE: Now wait a minute, Meathead. I never said your black beauties was lazy. You don't believe me...look it up.
> GLORIA: He's prejudiced, there's no hope for him at all.
> ARCHIE: I ain't prejudiced, any man deserves my respect and he's gonna get it regardless of his color.
> MIKE: Then why are you calling them black beauties?
> ARCHIE: Now that's where I got you, wise guy. There's a black guy who works down at the building with me. He's got a bumper sticker on his car that says "Black is Beautiful." So what's the matter with black beauties?
> EDITH: It's nicer than when he called them coons.

This scene, of course, was played for laughs, but it is hard not to cringe when reading it some forty years later. There aren't too many Archie Bunkers left in this world. Tolerance and cultural pluralism are now embraced everywhere in society—in government, religion, education, and business—but the transition that took place did not come easily.

During the years Emma served on city council, from the early '80s through the late '90s, the economy worsened, job losses deepened, unemployment rose, and crime increased. Emma's primary concerns were government waste and bureaucracy, the degradation of the city infrastructure, absentee slumlords, and crime. She was also angered by graffiti and poorly maintained homes. Invariably, the issue of race was brought into the conversation about the changes that had taken place in Allentown and the challenges that the city faced in the future. Emma herself was hardly the reluctant warrior; she was characteristically outspoken and short on diplomacy. Many of her remarks about Latinos were poorly chosen, and some, by her own admission, should have been left unsaid altogether.

In 1983, when Emma made her first run for city council, Latinos had already begun to move to the area, but they represented a very small slice of the demographic pie (only 5.1 percent according to the 1980 US census). As we know, it was Franklin Koch's casement window and CAHO that spurred her to run in the first place, and it was the central focus of her campaign.

As the years passed by, two things happened simultaneously: the Latino population began to swell, slowly at first, then almost exponentially, and the economy continued to sputter and stall. As the economy struggled, poverty and crime increased with numbing regularity. The startling increase in Latino influence as well as the economic difficulties during this time became the two most critical and talked-about issues of the era. For some whites, the two occurrences were joined at the hip and had a cause-and-effect relationship. Applying this false syllogism, one could conclude that 1) poor Latinos moved into the city, 2) the incidence of crime, drug use, and poverty increased dramatically, so *therefore* one must assume that the city went down the drain because Latinos from

New York and New Jersey moved there. There is no way of sugarcoating it. Among some whites, this sentiment did exist, and to a smaller extent today, it still does.

In 2000, the Lehigh County Historical Society published *Hidden from History: The Latino Community of Allentown, Pennsylvania.* This seminal work was written by Anna Adams, a professor of history and Spanish at Muhlenberg College. In the early '90s, she had discovered that Latinos were absent from Allentown's history books—literally hidden from history. She also noted, however, that significant evidence about the Latino community and its influence in local affairs was clearly present in many historical documents. Adams soon became fully engaged in research. *Hidden from History* touches on politics, culture, religion, the economy, and racism. Interestingly, an entire chapter is devoted to Emma Tropiano.

Adams writes, "There is ample evidence to support the beliefs of many people that Tropiano's outspokenness contributed to politicizing an otherwise fairly passive community and to uniting the Black and Latino communities for the first time." One would be hard pressed to disagree with this assessment after a quick review of the facts. Emma was beyond outspoken. She had a very loose tongue. Many of her statements, even when she was attempting to be conciliatory, inflamed her opponents, especially Latinos. Once, when defending herself, she claimed "I am not a racist." She should have stopped there, but she continued, "I don't have a problem with them." When used in this fashion, the word "them" is no mere object pronoun.

She saw the world in simple terms, with no shades of gray. She viewed herself as a populist in the mold of Harry Truman, "give 'em hell" Harry, who, like herself, never graduated from college. She idolized Truman for his truthfulness and shoot-from-the-hip style. Her decision to enter politics was made almost viscerally. She wanted to save "her" city and restore it to its former status. She felt she was doing God's work. Her son Victor remembers her sitting in the kitchen, reading the newspaper, and crying. She would often rhetorically ask, "What have they done to my city?" She took it all personally, but she never considered changing her residence.

She once introduced a proposal that required that police officers live in the city proper because they would "care more" if they did.

Victor Tropiano was quick to defend his mother against charges of racism. From the moment I first spoke to him, he said he would be happy to meet with me. He clearly felt his mother had been misunderstood, and he wanted to be able to set the record straight. In his mind, she was totally race agnostic. Others who knew her well also agreed with his assessment. Carol Cleveland wrote in the *Morning Call* that "one of Tropiano's friends, liberal Democrat Ted Fine...is convinced she is not a racist; instead, he says, she has strong convictions about what a citizen should be, namely law-abiding and eager to join the American mainstream." Cleveland also reported, "When a Hispanic told (Emma) his friends often felt blamed by whites for the crimes of a few, Tropiano said, 'You're good. Do your act. Don't worry about what bad Hispanics do, or bad Germans, or bad Italians.'" By all accounts she had a generous heart, and on a number of occasions, she gave away food from her store to impoverished Latino neighbors.

Yet she had an unfortunate habit of putting her foot in her mouth. In 1988 she claimed that 99 percent of the increase in local crime was attributable to Latinos. The truth turned out to be 34 percent. Frankly, it wouldn't have mattered a great deal if these numbers were reversed. Just by introducing the subject of race in this context, she was essentially guaranteeing that the entire conversation would have an unsuccessful and polarizing outcome. In any event, rather than apologize, Tropiano explained that she was fed inaccurate information by the police department, and to make matters worse, she rationalized her position by pointing out that many crimes go unreported in the first place. I suppose even if she had apologized, it may have made no difference; she would always be remembered for the accusation, not the apology. She knew it herself, admitting she would carry these words to her grave.

Allentown created its own Human Rights Commission in the 1960s following the passage of an antidiscrimination ordinance. The commission was empowered to enforce this ordinance to ensure that all citizens were given equal opportunity in housing, employment, and the use of public facilities. Emma derided the commission from day 1, saying that it was a waste of money, that it simply duplicated the work of a similar state commission, and that it only represented minorities instead of all the people. She fought against the commission for years unsuccessfully, hoping to cut its funding or abolish it entirely. In 1991 she attacked the HRC's practice of sending speakers on its payroll to outlying districts without receiving any compensation in return. "Let them (the other districts) pay for it," she said.

Her first run-in with the HRC was in the 1970s before she was active in politics. She had turned down an application by a single (minority) male who wanted to rent an apartment from her. She explained to him that she only rented to married couples, and that in her experience they were more reliable as tenants. A few weeks later, after the applicant had filed a complaint, she received a notice to attend an HRC hearing. She refused to show up and in fact talked to an attorney about fighting the matter in court. She was adamant in the belief that she had the right to pick and choose among prospective tenants, just like her mother had before her. Her husband Sal quietly paid the seventy-five-dollar fine that had been assessed when Emma failed to show up for the hearing.

By the early '90s, the HRC's role had expanded to include minority recruiting for city jobs. In this regard, Allentown maintained dual hiring lists for the police and fire departments, one for whites and another for minorities. This incensed Emma. "I'm for the good of everybody," she claimed. "Human Relations—they represent the Blacks, the Hispanics, the minority—that's all." Like many, she was angered by affirmative action, feeling that it victimized whites by denying *them* equal opportunity. This was a recurring theme with Tropiano, and she held on to these feelings for the rest of her life.

In 1987, this issue became front page news. The *Morning Call* broke a story revealing that James Ocasio, a Puerto Rican police officer who had been on the force for two years, was having difficulty writing police reports in English, and he was being tutored by another member of city council, Barbara Irvine. Tropiano remarked in her inimitable way, "Someone who is being tutored after he has been given a gun and a police uniform has me worried." All hell broke loose. Community activists Maria Melendez and Evelyn Bayo Antonsen both called for Tropiano's resignation.

Council President Watson Skinner did not join in this chorus but noted, "Sometimes I wish she (Tropiano) wouldn't say things in her unique way." He tried to be diplomatic and maintain neutrality. "I understand the concern of the Puerto Rican community," Skinner said. "But the method of reacting to it is perhaps overkill...It shouldn't be this big a deal." Mayor Joe Daddona was equally equivocal, saying, "No elected official should be rated just on one statement or perception." In time, the firestorm faded from public consciousness, but for many the bitterness and resentment lingered.

Tropiano was sometimes vocal about seemingly trivial matters. She chided some "newcomers" (code for Puerto Ricans) for moving indoor furniture, like upholstered sofas, out on their front porches. She spoke out against those who repaired cars while they were parked on city streets. She expressed outrage that garbage was put out before trash collection day, not fully sensitive to the fact that many Latinos lived in extremely overcrowded conditions, and the only alternative some of them had was to accumulate their trash indoors. Emma was exasperated with graffiti, crime, littering, drugs, and a government that coddled and favored specific minority groups. Of course, the minority groups and their more liberal and moderate supporters were equally exasperated with Emma. This hostility resulted in increased frustration, anger, hurt feelings, and resentment.

Nowhere was this seen more clearly than in the confrontation over making English the official language of city government. This was something that Tropiano strongly supported; it tied in very neatly with her core views regarding the value of hard work, playing by the rules, self-reliance, and American opportunity. She felt that the English language was as fundamental a part of America as was the Declaration of Independence, GI Joe, or baseball. Her parents, like many others, came to America from Italy and eagerly learned the language. In her mind, it was not only a waste of money to print documents in Spanish and otherwise introduce the Spanish language into daily government affairs, it was un-American. It was yet another example of the established order caving in to bestow special favors on a few rather than treat all people equally.

In September 1994, city council passed an ordinance by a 6-1 vote, which proclaimed that English was the city's official language, encouraging the use of English in all city business except when it would run afoul of state or federal law. This was a concept that Tropiano had supported for some time, always unsuccessfully. This particular ordinance was able to pass because it had no teeth and no mandates; essentially, it just expressed an opinion, similar to a governor's proclamation on physical fitness or the benefits of higher education.

The fallout was predictable. The ordinance received widespread media coverage. Hundreds of angry Latinos demonstrated outside city hall. Tropiano was, as usual, far from shy about expressing her opinions and was denounced by her opponents. Most of the established politicians tap-danced, even those that supported the measure. Councilman Ernest Toth supported the proposal because he felt it somehow was able to simultaneously preserve both "unity and diversity"—a rather extraordinary claim. Toth was quick to point out that the ordinance did not "in any way discriminate against or restrict the rights of any individual in the city of Allentown." Mayor William L. Heydt remained silent throughout the discussion that occurred prior to the council's vote. Perhaps this was the best strategy. Martin Velasquez, the only Latino councilman, was the lone dissenter. His opposition was not surprising, but the rationale behind it was. Robert Moran in the *Philadelphia Inquirer* reported that Velasquez had said, "There would be no need for the ordinance because it was already understood in the Latino community that to be successful, learning English is important."

A similar ordinance that required, rather than urged, the city to print all documents (not related to health or safety) was put up for vote two years later, but the idea was tabled, and a vote was never subsequently taken. Allentown's English-only ordinance, weak and powerless from its inception, did nothing except to increase the divide between Latinos and whites. This is particularly distressing considering that both Tropiano and many Latinos like Velasquez largely agreed on the major goal of the ordinance. Nevertheless, self-righteousness and resentment became firmly rooted on both sides, and this sabotaged any hope of compromise and cooperation.

Race-related issues remained on the front burner after Tropiano left politics. The Puerto Rican Day Parade held on June 25, 2000, was envisioned as both a celebration and demonstration of pride by its supporters, but it turned out to be a public relations disaster. Ron Devlin reported in the *Morning Call* that "rowdiness, vandalism, and threats in center city neighborhoods kept police busy for hours afterward...Allentown police worked 52 hours of overtime handling complaints of tires squealing, car stereos booming, and other incidents including threats to a city worker.... There were reports of fights and children hurling rocks and bottles." When a meeting of city council's Public Safety Committee was called to discuss the incident, Juan Orta, parade committee spokesman, responded defensively and implied that the committee's concern was racially inspired. He claimed that "the authorities do not respond with the same intensity to incidents after the St Patrick's Day and (other) parades." This debate continued in a twisted fashion. Council President Toth said matter-of-factly, "Nothing happens after the Irish parade and the Veteran's Day parades." US Congressman Pat Toomey's office produced a proclamation in support of the event. Shortly afterward, Orta made a surprising statement. He said, "The sun comes up for everyone. We live here, and we need to work together." He couldn't have been more correct, but unfortunately, years of distrust and bad karma had made this simple goal nearly unachievable.

In the end, Emma was unsuccessful in turning back the clock. She dreamed of seeing "her city" restored to its former glory. The dream turned out to be just that, a fantasy. Allentown experienced an economic tsunami during the '80s and '90s, suffering near permanent damage. High crime rates, drug abuse, difficult race relations, unemployment, and deteriorating conditions in the city's schools changed the fabric of life in the city. In retrospect, its fate was not all that surprising.

Her legacy is not so much related to what she did, but rather to what she represented. Proud, loyal, principled, and, yes, often insensitive and abrasive, Emma Tropiano did what many of us did not. She stood up for what she believed to be just causes, even when they sometimes became lost causes. She spoke her mind, often without a filter. She led her constituents tirelessly and created a loyal and passionate following—and agitated countless others. She was a living dichotomy, part patriot and part provocateur. You were either her friend, or you were not. No one was ever "undecided" about Emma.

10

JOE

JOE DADDONA WAS first elected mayor of Allentown in November 1973. Several months before the election, the Chamber of Commerce submitted an application for the National Municipal Council's "All-American City Award" for 1974–75. Subsequently Allentown became one of only ten cities in the country that achieved this honor when the list of winners was announced. It was a very proud moment for the new mayor, who had been in office for about a year.

A little over fifteen years later, in 1990, *Money* magazine ranked three hundred American cities in terms of the "best places to live," and Allentown came in dead last. While it is true that this survey, like many of its kind, is based almost entirely on a random mixture of facts, opinions, and intuition, no one could argue that the city was in a worse place in 1990 than it was in 1974. Last is last.

My mother grew up in New York City during the 1930s. The mayor of New York at that time was Fiorello LaGuardia. He was a lifelong public servant. As mayor he served three consecutive terms from 1934 to 1945, a period of extraordinarily difficult and trying times. The Great Depression and World War II represented the twentieth century's greatest economic and humanitarian disasters. This was a time of almost constant uncertainty and fear, yet LaGuardia stayed in office through it all, solid as a rock. He was consistently held in high esteem because of his integrity, optimism, and commitment to the people of New York. While he was occasionally domineering and outspoken, he had a natural ability to connect with the average citizen. He was sincere and effective in rooting out corruption within city government, and this enhanced his popularity.

He also had a good heart. Once, during a time when the city's newspaper deliverymen were on strike and many New Yorkers went without their papers, he read comic strips to children during his weekend radio show. He regularly showed up at fires to help the firemen on duty. He was a progressive Republican who enjoyed widespread support among Democrats. I am sure that today over 50 percent of New Yorkers have no idea how LaGuardia Airport got its name, but in his time, Fiorello LaGuardia was a New York icon.

LaGuardia graduated from law school in 1910. Five years later, he was deputy attorney general of New York, and in the following year, he was elected to Congress. Soon afterward, he resigned to volunteer for military service in World War I, where as Major LaGuardia he commanded a squadron of bombers in the US Army Air Service. After the war, he returned to politics. His entire life was devoted to public service.

Daddona's pathway was similar. He served in the US Navy during the Korean War and graduated from Lehigh University following his discharge from active duty. Within a few years, he too was in politics, and he served on Allentown's City Council (beginning in 1967) until he was elected to his first term as mayor in 1973. Joe Daddona remained in office for four terms, a lifetime in politics. Through all the trials and struggles of the '70s, '80s, and '90s, Daddona was a political miracle. After losing his first reelection bid in 1978 by a whisker, he returned to hold office for three more terms in succession from 1982 to 1994. He was Mr. Allentown.

Unlike the sometimes abrasive LaGuardia, Daddona was the perpetual optimist, cheerfully attending countless ribbon-cutting ceremonies and dedications as if they were the most important items on his daily agenda. Of course, he had political opponents, but he remained well liked and highly regarded by most. Everyone I spoke with who knew him said that he was a "good guy," and they also all observed that he *loved* being mayor.

When he announced his decision to retire at the end of 1992, longtime nemesis Emma Tropiano attended his press conference. Tropiano had run unsuccessfully against Daddona three years earlier and had been critical of his administration for years from her city council seat. Yet she openly praised Daddona when she said, "You've added a lot of credibility to the city," and then jokingly added, "I won't say this during the election." Daddona responded, "I know in your heart you think I've been a pretty good mayor." Tropiano got in the last one-liner, "Don't put words in my mouth." After twenty years of political combat, Daddona still retained his greatest adversary's genuine respect.

His only loss was understandable if not somewhat bizarre. Frank Fischl, a retired air force colonel, managed to edge him out in an extremely close contest in 1977. Two issues proved problematic for Daddona at the time. Allentown's manufacturing economy had already begun to weaken, and the reality of job layoffs and an aging city infrastructure obviously meant more to the electorate than the cachet of an All-American City award. Perhaps more damaging, though, was a scandal regarding campaign financing irregularities that surfaced shortly before the election. This sad story involved Dominic Falcone, a local contractor, who accused Daddona of soliciting illegal campaign contributions from him back in 1969 by linking the contribution to bogus "storage services" that were never performed. There is no doubt that a contribution was made, but a subsequent investigation by the county's attorney general found no link between Daddona himself and the sham arrangement. Daddona was cleared after the election, but the damage was done.

Interestingly, Falcone had been arrested just a few months beforehand for solicitation of a prostitute, and it was Daddona's belief that Falcone brought his charges to the public because he refused to "fix" the case and keep it quiet. The two men had been close for years; incredibly, Falcone was godfather to one of Daddona's children.

In any event, here Joe was, now forty-four years old and unemployed. This was the second time in which Daddona had been defeated as a mayoral candidate, the first coming years before in 1969. Many people in his position might have started to look at different career choices, but Daddona had no plan B. His heart was in public service and politics, and he steadily built up enough support to stage a successful run for reelection in 1981. There are nineteen wards in Allentown, and he was the top vote-getter in all of them. It was no contest. In the midst of a nasty recession, his victory was overwhelming.

Daddona's level of optimism remained unreasonably high, even when his health began to fail when he was in his sixties. In 1998 he was diagnosed with cancer; the disease dogged him for the remainder of his life. In that year, surgeons removed his left kidney, and when he fell ill again in 2002, his prostate and bladder were taken. Only a year later, physicians discovered yet another cancerous growth, this time near his remaining kidney. The tumor was inoperable, but when Daddona was told that the growth was treatable, he consented to endure both radiation and chemotherapy treatments. Notably, he did so with characteristically good humor. He said, "The docs say I may still be able to buy green bananas." Later, at a public ceremony where he was honored, he did a takeoff on David Letterman's "Top Ten" list by offering his own "Top 5 signs you are a candidate for hospice." Joe Daddona was able to see the bright side of everything, in spite of the fact that the city of Allentown was on the ropes throughout most of his reign as mayor.

I can find only one instance in his political career in which he was clearly put on the defensive and felt disheartened and dispirited. In 1986, a federal court awarded $400,000 in damages to two police officers who Daddona had demoted several years earlier. The men had claimed that their demotions were evidence of retaliation by Daddona for their having supported one of his Republican political opponents during a previous election campaign. Daddona testified that he demoted them because the two had been part of a clique that had threatened, intimidated, and (on one occasion) assaulted other officers. As in many civil suits, it is not so easy to definitively establish where the truth lies; often it rests neither with plaintiff nor defendant, but rather in a hazy area somewhere in between. In any event, Daddona was devastated by the court's decision. He said, "My faith in the justice system in this country has been shattered." This was an exceptionally rare sentiment for Daddona to express. As a rule, Joe's innate faith in America and its bountiful future was the touchstone of his very being.

This faith was challenged on multiple occasions during his time in office. Of these, the most difficult issue of all encompassed race relations. As we know, starting in the 1980s, Allentown experienced a huge influx of Latinos, and this radically changed the demographic profile of the city. Not surprisingly, life remained hard for the optimistic newcomers. Jobs, particularly factory jobs for semiskilled workers, were disappearing as fast as people moved in. Much of the rezoned housing stock in center city fell into the hands of slumlords. The weak economy also affected municipal government services—funding was cut for schools, police, fire, and public works. The streets of Allentown were not paved with gold after all.

It is difficult if not impossible for white Americans to think of life's challenges primarily in terms of race or ethnicity. Minority groups that have experienced discrimination understandably look at life through an entirely different lens. It is true that the economy was weak for everyone, that slums were slums no matter who paid the rent, and that city funding was cut across the board. Yet it is also inarguable that Puerto Rican residents of Allentown were not well represented in government and experienced a feeling of powerlessness as a result. Poor, powerless minority groups are generally not very content with their condition. They often have a heightened sensitivity to their minority status and tend to hold on to resentments related to it. Sometimes, when it is least expected or even unjustified, the race card gets played.

In November 1987, Raul Feliciano, a retired judge, asked Mayor Daddona for permission to fly the Puerto Rican flag from city hall as part of a celebration commemorating Columbus's discovery of Puerto Rico. Daddona, who had recently consented to a similar request during

Hispanic Awareness Month, respectfully declined. This set off a firestorm of accusations and hurt feelings. The *Morning Call* reported that Feliciano claimed, "The denial of the request was an offense against him and other Puerto Ricans." He said, "Puerto Rico is a nation; it's not a bunch of people." Actually, it's neither, but whatever the case, it appeared that the level of outrage was entirely disproportionate to the alleged slight.

Daddona was an establishment politician, but he was also a liberal Democrat. He was clearly caught off guard by charges of bias. At first, he said he didn't want two flag-raising ceremonies in one year. Then, he explained that even though he had not approved a flag raising several months beforehand, perhaps he would have done so a second time if he had been given enough time. Later, one of Daddona's assistants said the mayor would have granted permission for sure if the request had been made sooner, even though he simultaneously suggested it was a poor idea because it would be "impossible to raise every state flag and every territorial flag." Coming after the fact, this explanation seemed somewhat lame and satisfied no one. When a subsequent complaint was made to the Human Rights Commission, then Chairman Glenn Clark said that he (Clark) "had no prior knowledge" of any details. Newspaper headlines blared "Mayor Accused of Bias." This was but one of many seemingly innocuous events that diverted the attention of citizens and government from their core concerns: jobs, public safety, education, and city services.

Race relations remained a prickly subject throughout Daddona's administrations. In 1989, Fire Chief David Novosat suggested at a city council meeting that the department put a doorbell outside its six fire stations (instead of a telephone) "because some Hispanic will be running down the street with it." As soon as the words came out of his mouth, he tried to backtrack. "Don't put that down," he told reporter Tim Reeves. Reeves ignored the request. The quote appeared in the *Morning Call* on the following morning. Novosat went on to say that he was joking, that he was color-blind, and that the fire department had "no minorities... we only have firefighters." He made it sound as if the Allentown fire department was affiliated with Jesse Jackson's Rainbow Coalition. The fact was that there were four blacks and zero Latinos among Allentown's 142 firefighters.

Of course the matter didn't go away quietly. Some community activists called for Novosat's head. Novosat expressed his remorse publicly and said that he planned on writing a formal letter of apology to the city's Latino organizations. He also repeated his defense that his remarks were meant as a joke, he was not a bigot, and if (if?) anyone were offended by what he said, he was deeply sorry. Daddona immediately found himself in the middle of a three-ring circus, trying to pacify offended Puerto Ricans and give some measure of compassionate support and understanding to his loose-tongued fire chief, who did achieve a number of positive results during his many years on the job in spite of this awful gaffe.

After several weeks of mea culpas, Novosat's apology was ultimately accepted by Luis Goyzueta, the Hispanic Political Caucus president. The two shook hands and embraced at a joint press conference. Novosat quickly announced that he would join a newly formed committee on racism. Then, in an odd spin, he hypothesized that his inflammatory comments may well have been extremely helpful in the long run by bringing Latinos closer to government officials. To make it clear that he was truly misunderstood, Novosat let it be known that his aunt married a Hispanic man. Perhaps in his mind, having this family connection would convince his detractors as well as the entire Latino community that he was not the ogre some portrayed him to be. Clearly, he was humbled by the affair and appeared to be genuinely remorseful, but by this time, the damage had been done. Whatever the case, Daddona did not show up at Novosat's press conference, sending Community Affairs Assistant Joseph Rosenfeld in his place. Who could blame him?

Ultimately, the uproar subsided. Novosat had, in fact, served with distinction since he was appointed chief while still in his late twenties, and those who knew him well believed him to be a sincere and good man at his core. L'affaire Novosat soon faded into history. It is worth noting, though, that an enormous amount of time was spent during Daddona's mayoral terms on matters just like this, where an inappropriate remark would set off a chain reaction of charges, countercharges, hurt feelings, and amends.

Racial tension and charges of bias and discrimination remained part of the landscape long after Daddona left office. The first Puerto Rican Day Parade took place on Daddona's watch in 1989, but within a few years, problems emerged. By 2000, post parade rowdiness, violence, and vandalism led to a confused discussion: partly about security and police overtime and partly about race and its role in public safety. Some questioned whether or not the city should sanction the parade at all, given the collateral damage. Parade supporters claimed they were being singled out because they were Latinos. When Ernie Toth, a member of city council, suggested shortening the parade route or banning cars (there had been incidents of parade celebrants spinning wheels and burning rubber), his proposal was viewed by many Latinos as being hostile to Puerto Ricans. Daddona had left office six years earlier in 1994, but incidents like this had occurred frequently throughout his administrations as well.

In a sense, damage control defined many aspects of Daddona's years in office. Illegal drug use and the inevitable increase in crime that accompanied it quickly became front page news. In this respect, Allentown was probably no different than any other American city, but there is no question that the weak economy and the growing incidence of poverty in Allentown itself allowed the city's drug problem to quickly overwhelm its police department, its courts, and its prisons. Like many mayors, Daddona was forced to play defense; he simply didn't have the financial resources to wage an effective battle in the "war against drugs."

Court records, which I came across at random, reveal one indisputable fact: drug trafficking was out of control in Lehigh County and nearby Northampton County. Area courts were each processing nearly ten felony cases per week that resulted in criminal convictions on various drug-related charges. In a surprisingly large proportion of these, the defendants had been taken into custody after attempting to sell heroin, cocaine, or both to an undercover police officer. Judges routinely handed out sentences of two to four years and almost always attached an order that restitution be made to the police department for the money used to acquire the drugs. Normally, this ranged between $150 and $300. It is hard to imagine someone risking a stretch in state prison for a few hundred dollars, but in Joe Daddona's Allentown, it happened constantly. These were desperate times.

The war on drugs was brought into the American consciousness by the Reagan administration, with First Lady Nancy Reagan's "Just say no" message of abstinence resonating with millions and being ridiculed by millions of others. Continued by President George H.W. Bush, the War on Drugs became a war of attrition, something that we never won but seemingly endured for eternity. Brave pronouncements from Washington and the DEA reminded me of "body count" press briefings during the Vietnam War. Allentown faced long odds in its war on drugs, especially considering that the federal government had enormous resources in technology, people, machinery, and money—everything that city of Allentown did not possess.

The drug problem became an epidemic near the end of Daddona's terms. In just two years between 1986 and 1988, arrests in Allentown for drug-related crimes more than doubled, and charges for drug-related offenses such as possession tripled. A dramatic increase in the amount of cocaine smuggled into the United States sent prices tumbling throughout the '80s, making it increasingly affordable. Robert Csandl, a local treatment center administrator, claimed that by the end of the decade a vial of crack could be had for as little as three dollars. Local law enforcement and the criminal justice system were overwhelmed. In late 1988, after what had been a difficult problem had grown into a full-blown crisis, Daddona could only suggest impaneling another citizen task force to study ways of combating the problem. He was out of bullets and ideas, and truthfully no one could blame him.

His 1988 reelection bid focused on personality and leadership qualities, as Daddona once more squared off against longtime rival Emma Tropiano in a lively and entertaining campaign. He was one of many mayors who believed the war on drugs would become a lost cause unless

Washington was able to dramatically increase funding. As we know, the war on drugs was not won in Allentown or any town. It would not be fair to place any specific blame on Daddona's shoulders. Allentown's heroin and cocaine epidemic was symptomatic of a national crisis. It taxed the resources of law enforcement and health care, clogged the prison system, put city government on the defensive, and, of course, tragically claimed the lives of numerous victims of addiction.

An enormous amount of time and money was spent battling drug trafficking and drug-related crime. This seemingly endless struggle was similar to the effort to create racial tolerance and understanding between Puerto Ricans and working-class whites; both groups often harbored resentments against the other and frequently felt alienated from society as a whole. Daddona must have felt like a farmer trying to plant a crop while battling a swarm of locusts.

Daddona faced many significant challenges beyond drugs, crime, and racism. Allentown's deteriorating economy, infrastructure, and social fabric required immediate attention, and any solution required money. He appeared before Congress with a contingent of mayors from the National League of Cities, and in 1987, he testified at a House of Representatives banking and finance subcommittee. His words resonate today in describing the predicament that Allentown and other cities were facing at this time.

> "In the central part of our city, 61 percent of our residents are of lower income...This section of the city is the oldest, with the majority of the structures dating from the 1860s to the 1920s... Broad segments of our population must struggle with a severe housing problem...Since 1980 (federal) housing assistance has fallen from $30 billion to less than $10 billion and construction of new assisted housing units has come to a virtual halt."

Daddona then explained that the waiting list for subsidized housing units stood at an all-time high (at eighteen hundred) and predicted that reduced government funding would create a "time bomb" effect in the future. He envisioned a housing shortage made worse by the shrinking supply of existing subsidized units—as government subsidies aged out and/or mortgages were prepaid.

The shortage of affordable housing made Daddona's job more difficult and created a secondary problem of homelessness. Additionally, Daddona blamed reduced federal funding for the release of eleven hundred mental hospital patients in one year alone. I had heard anecdotal evidence from a few of my former classmates that one of the reasons suburban shoppers became uncomfortable going downtown was that many homeless and mentally ill people congregated there. It appears there was at least some truth in that assessment.

Money was a constant issue. Throughout the 1980s, the city's tax base was shrinking while the demand for city services was growing. Daddona had a hard time getting city council to go along with his $50 million 1991 budget, but ultimately he prevailed after a number of protracted hearings. The plain fact was that the city didn't have $50 million to spend, and it needed more than $50 million to dig itself out of the hole it was in. Just before approving the budget, council adopted a measure designed to reduce Allentown's operating deficit by $2 million. The action, not surprisingly, was nonbinding.

Council President Watson Skinner threw his support behind the budget. The *Morning Call* reported that he believed "that the lack of response from city residents was a signal to accept Daddona's proposal." Possibly, he was correct, but I am certain that public apathy and cynicism had by this time reached a tipping point.

The debate over funding for the police department was especially contentious. Daddona wanted authorization to add twelve new police positions. Three council members—Tropiano, Benjamin Howells, and Frank Palencar—opposed this on fiscal grounds. Howells claimed somewhat dramatically in early hearings, "I see us on a crash course to economic oblivion." There was further discussion over more details—how many officers should be allocated to community policing, to the vice squad, to administrative support, and so on. Ultimately, the budget passed 4–3, and afterward, Frank Palencar intoned, "Why did we waste all this time? We should have passed the budget the day he (Daddona) presented it. We would have saved electricity."

Just a few months earlier, Daddona had been reelected to his fourth mayoral term. When he and all of the city council members were sworn in, the atmosphere was quite festive. Daddona proclaimed, "The city is on the verge of exploding into the twenty-first century, with the potential of being not just a good city, but a great one." He then introduced a new slogan: "Allentown Together—Still Better than Ever." While ever the optimist, Daddona knew very well what he would be up against given the city's dwindling financial resources. Council President Skinner put it succinctly by saying, "Allentown is a city under stress."

Three years later Daddona had announced he would not run for reelection. By that time, with the local economy limping along if not atrophying, Daddona was forced to face reality. After city council refused to go along with his proposal for a property tax increase, Daddona admitted defeat and said he would be forced to lay off as many as eighty municipal workers to balance the budget. It was the first time in his four terms as mayor that he furloughed a city worker. He said, "I've never been in the position of being a lame duck before. I'm realistic and practical enough to know that the situation has changed dramatically."

In 1991, city officials introduced a comprehensive redevelopment plan for the deteriorating downtown area. The ambitious proposal, called the "Vision Plan," was developed by an independent consultant who confidently called it "a game plan for the rest of this century." The plan called for the construction of a large office building and the creation of a mini retail mall connected to Hess's. Additionally, various zones would be earmarked for residential, cultural, governmental, and commercial development. Existing real estate would be upgraded and/or modified to conform to the plan's goals.

Given the financial realities of the 1990s, I am not sure that Allentown's Vision Plan would have ever gotten off the ground, but its potential implementation was made next to impossible after Mark Mendelson bought the Americus Hotel. He had grand plans for its restoration, pledging to invest millions in improvements. Daddona could hardly restrain himself, calling it "the most exciting thing in this part of town in many years."

Daddona couldn't have been more accurate in this assessment, but not in the way he imagined. The Americus and Mendelson himself soon became long-term, oversized problems that would interfere with and ultimately thwart any serious proposal concerning urban redevelopment in the downtown area. The Americus was the largest hotel in the city and as prominent and well known a structure as Hess's and the PPL Tower. It had just been named to the National Register of Historic Places. A dilapidated Americus Hotel simply could not coexist with a downtown renaissance.

We've seen that Mendelson never put millions, as promised, into the hotel. He was habitually negligent in paying taxes, constantly involved in lawsuits over unpaid bills, and always played the part of the victim. He suggested he was the target of criticism because he was Jewish. He typically bought run-down properties and let them run down further, but meanwhile he often used them for collateral to pyramid his real estate footprint.

Early on, he was able to align the Americus with Radisson, but in 1994 this affiliation was terminated due to late payments and bad checks. The same thing happened with Clarion four years later. Mendelson had also acquired additional properties in the city with similar results. Among his other holdings was the Colonial Theater, a lovely venue where I used to take in first-run movies on Saturday afternoons. He let it go to seed.

City inspectors ultimately found the Americus in violation of numerous health and building codes. While the building's condition was deteriorating, Mendelson had accumulated $5 million in liens against the Americus. Soon afterward the hotel was put up for auction, but Mendelson managed to keep possession of the Americus because no one was willing to bid on it. The occupancy permit was pulled in 2002. The Americus collected dust for several more years.

Mendelson himself, who purportedly owned seventy cars in the mid-1980s, filed for bankruptcy in 2009, after which the city of Allentown took possession of the Americus. Nearly twenty-five years had passed since Joe Daddona had first lauded Mendelson as the savior of downtown.

A number of Daddona's major accomplishments were noted in his obituary. To be perfectly honest, they don't jump out at you. The introduction of 911 emergency dialing, the initiation of a waste recycling program, and the installation of sodium vapor street lights are not attention grabbers. The same could be said for the elimination of toxic fumes from a wastewater treatment plant or the repair of various aging roadways. Still, one must be fair when grading Joe Daddona's performance as mayor. During his time in office, Allentown suffered from increased crime, drug trafficking, and unemployment. It also experienced suburban flight, difficult race relations, and severe job losses. Affordable housing was in short supply, as was money in general, since the city's tax base was shrinking along with the economy. The deck was stacked against him. There was not much he could have done differently.

This much we know: Joe Daddona was a devoted public servant. He loved his job, and he gave it everything he had. He also loved the city of Allentown, and everyone knew it. His enthusiasm, if not entirely contagious, was certainly apparent. His sincerity was as well. Without his energy and what I call "unreasonable optimism," it is entirely possible that Allentown could have gone completely off the rails during these difficult years. Often he may have been pushing on a string, but he never stopped trying.

11

ESTAMOS AQUI

IT WAS NOT until the 1980s and 1990s that the influx of Hispanics picked up full steam. As we have seen, these newcomers to Allentown were largely transplanted Puerto Ricans residing in New York and New Jersey, who were attracted by Allentown's relatively low cost of living and less expensive housing. Over time, this migration gathered momentum and became the defining demographic event in the city's recent history. Within the space of thirty years, the Hispanic population in Allentown increased exponentially. Currently, nearly 50 percent of Allentown's population is Hispanic.

This spurt was sudden, improbable, and unpredictable. Had it not been for the collapse in manufacturing employment, especially in the steel and textile industries, the white suburban exodus from downtown Allentown would still have taken place, but at a much slower pace. The city would never have experienced the housing vacuum that it did, real estate values wouldn't have collapsed in a historic fashion, nor would rents have tumbled so quickly. These factors coalesced simultaneously as the local economy continued to struggle year after year. Every measure of economic activity declined. Sadly, the Latinos who came to Allentown had no more luck in finding good jobs than the resident whites they began to replace.

The first meaningful numbers of Latinos showed up in Allentown after World War II. Most were from Puerto Rico itself, not New York or New Jersey, and came to the Lehigh Valley as migrant agricultural workers. Many traveled back home after harvest and worked only seasonally. But as time went on, a fair number did settle in permanently, and a viable Puerto Rican community began to take shape.

John "Jack" McHugh was the principal of the Horne School in 1962 when a number of Puerto Rican students unexpectedly enrolled on opening day. Anna Adams revealed in *Hidden from History* that McHugh was both startled and unprepared. He said, "We weren't ready. We didn't understand the culture and couldn't speak the language." He was able to recruit a native Puerto Rican teacher, Ramonita Sanabria, to fill a badly needed void. McHugh later would say, "Allentown refused to prepare itself for a changing population in schools or in city government. There was no attempt to hire minority personnel."

A word about Jack McHugh is in order. It turns out he was my fifth-grade teacher at Muhlenberg School, and I never expected to come across his name in my research about the Latino influence upon life in Allentown. He was a good man, a skilled educator, and in my mind, the best teacher I ever had. He involved his students in a number of creative projects. One was "Brotherhood Week," where each student picked two nationally known figures, typically one from the entertainment industry and one from politics, and wrote a letter asking them to be "brotherhood buddies." (How ironic that within a few years his idealism and sensitivity would manifest itself in such an unexpected way.) I remember my new pen pals were Red Blake, the legendary coach of the football team at West Point, and the governor of New Jersey, Robert Meyner. I was thrilled and held on to the letters I received back from them for many years.

McHugh, a Korean War veteran, returned to Allentown as a young man and began teaching in the Allentown School District. He was filled with ambition and energy. He earned a PhD from Lehigh University in the late '60s and became principal of William Allen High School in 1971. After retiring from the school district in 1982, he ran successfully for

Lehigh County commissioner and held that post for nineteen years. His obituary, which was published in the *Morning Call*, reveals a remarkable man, one with an unusual appreciation of history and a thirst for travel. The *Morning Call* reported that "Jack wrote extensive daily diaries, travel logs...and, during his waning months, an essay on his personal spiritual sojourn...He thoroughly enjoyed his years in public education and for the remainder of his life he loved meeting his former students and faculty."

McHugh died in September 2010, just a short time before I became involved in the research for this book. I still have the autobiography I wrote for him as part of a classroom project, which took all of us the better part of that year to complete. On the front page, he wrote, "I enjoyed having you in class and I am positive your life will continue to be a success because you have many fine abilities....If ever you need a friend, come around." This was written in 1958. I never did take him up on his offer, and I was deeply disappointed not to have reconnected with him before he passed.

McHugh was obviously sensitive to the needs of new students from Puerto Rico in 1962, but he could never have foreseen that the Hispanic population would grow to become—within his own lifetime—the largest ethnic group in the city. The Allentown Puerto Rican community in the 1960s was extremely small, an insignificant speck in statistical terms. At first, this community grew slowly. The first Spanish mass was said in 1965; two years later, Iglesia Betania, a Latino Pentecostal Church, opened its doors. Worship began in the home of the founders, Francisco and Miriam Vega; initially there were only seven members. The Puerto Rican population was augmented by small numbers of other Latinos from Central and South America; by 1960, their total number was perhaps a little more than one thousand.

Hispanics were initially attracted to Allentown for a variety of reasons: a reasonable cost of living, open space, low crime, ample housing, and most important, jobs. In the '60s, the economy was strong, and the city's manufacturing industries were humming; by the late 1970s, there were approximately ten thousand Latinos in residence. At this time, most of them had moved from elsewhere within the United States, spoke English, and had become acclimated to life in America. Anna Adams wrote that "the Allentown of the 1970s was beginning to operate as a suburb for already urbanized Latinos seeking work and peace." In time, though, these feelings of contentment and optimism began to disappear as economic circumstances were altered.

Within a generation, a sea change would occur. Today a travel guide about Allentown ominously warns visitors in very explicit terms, "Much of the crime is gang related, so it is advisable to avoid poor neighborhoods and housing projects...Active gangs in the city include Eighteenth Street, Black Dragons, Bloods, Crips, Latin Kings, Los Solidos, Mexican Mafia, GGU and MS-13....Theft is an issue, so be sure to lock cars and stay out of poorer areas at night. Prostitution and street racing are also issues in Allentown. Don't walk alone late at night or on dimly lit streets."

Of course, gang violence and criminal activity are not exclusive to the Latino community. Yet it is clear that as the Latino population swelled and the economy worsened, there was a palpable increase in tension among longtime white residents, who saw their own neighborhoods slowly change and erode before their own eyes. No doubt the waves of layoffs and factory closings heightened these feelings of insecurity and anxiety. More than a few blamed Latinos for the process of decay that was visible to all.

Many of the newer arrivals from New York and Northern New Jersey had escaped from exceptionally poor and high-crime areas, hoping to find a better way of life. They didn't. There were no jobs for whites, and there were no jobs for Latinos either. Joblessness, at least in this time and place, did not discriminate. It affected everyone. Each group, however, saw things in a much different light. Latinos sometimes viewed themselves as an oppressed minority, the object of discrimination by an entrenched white establishment. Many whites, especially those hit hardest by factory job layoffs, blamed Latinos for crime, drug use, and deteriorating living conditions in general. Each group made the other a scapegoat. I am certain the atmosphere would have been much different if jobs (and hope) were more plentiful.

Outspoken city council member Emma Tropiano incensed the Latino community virtually every time she spoke. Emma believed in the melting pot concept, the vision of America that drew her parents to the United States from Italy in the early 1900s. Her unique idea of pluralism was that in this nation, all Old World identities would melt away and disappear and be replaced by a distinctive, self-reliant, English-speaking "American" persona. People would work their way up the ladder, without government help, just like her parents (and she and her husband) did.

The way in which she expressed herself, as we have seen, was quite inflammatory. "The Puerto Ricans that came here 25 years ago, they're established, they did melt, you don't realize they are here. It's just this new breed coming from New York and New Jersey...They're brazen, and they think they can take over this town...Nobody wants to live here anymore. People who can afford it are selling their homes and running to the suburbs."

Tropiano's repeated, ill-chosen remarks unified the Latino community, and no doubt fueled the fires of anger and resentment, but incredibly, they did not serve as a catalyst for substantive political action. In fact, it was apathy that ruled. By the early 1990s, the Latino community was well established and had significant numbers. It could have represented a reasonably powerful voting bloc. Yet only one in five *registered* Latino voters bothered to vote in the 1993 municipal election, a participation rate 60 percent lower than the rest of the electorate. This followed a well-established pattern that had begun years earlier. Even in the presidential elections of 1988, only half of the city's registered Latino voters cast a ballot versus nearly 85 percent of those who lived in the largely white West End.

Tropiano fought tirelessly to promote the use of English as the official language of Allentown. She opposed bilingual forms in city hall and bilingual education in the Allentown School District. As we have seen, when council ultimately passed a resolution sanctifying the use of English in city documents, it issued a toothless decree because the ordinance did not mandate any specific action or compliance. All it did was offend nearly all Spanish-speaking people, who (it must be pointed out again) were mostly American citizens with American passports. One can imagine many of them asking themselves, "What kind of America is this?"

William Heydt, who was mayor at the time, refused to veto the ordinance, saying, "It didn't mean anything, so why should I veto it? I didn't approve it, either." Heydt was a straight shooter. Whether he was being cavalier or just unusually honest is open to debate, but his comments may have served to deepen the wedge that had developed between city officials and the Latino community. Heydt's statement was made a few weeks before the Allentown Latino Council was scheduled to meet and celebrate its first anniversary. That meeting never took place; it was postponed while the council huddled to discuss its own future. Teresa Willis wrote in the *Morning Call*, "The Council has been plagued by political naiveté, weakened spirits, and a continuing conflict with Mayor William Heydt over its mission. Those who helped create the advisory council remembered talk of building bridges. Instead, chasms have emerged between the Latino community and sometimes hostile city officials." It was never clear to me that Heydt or anyone in his administration was "hostile" as Willis described, but during these years, race was frequently injected into conversations where it never really belonged.

The Latino Advisory Council had been created during Joe Daddona's last mayoral term, but it never had specific marching orders. What Daddona, Heydt, and the council members themselves were able to define as "advisory" was open to differing interpretation. Clearly, the council envisioned itself having some real power and influence. When confronted with the reality that it did not, it quietly disbanded.

Relations worsened when yet another advisory council called the Governor's Advisory Commission on Latino Affairs released a report in 1993. This report itself was fairly pedestrian. It contained a number of findings and recommendations related to the living conditions and needs of Latinos in Pennsylvania. Created in 1989, the commission had been established by Gov. Robert Casey to "counteract discriminatory practices and institutional barriers" faced by Latinos in Pennsylvania, and to act as a sounding board for ideas to enhance the quality of their lives. Tropiano denounced the findings as a "crybaby report" and was especially incensed over the Spanish-English issue, which was forever paramount in her mind. She said, "The report's tone is paternalistic, patronizing, and condescending in general, but particularly to Latinos. It seems to assume that Latinos aren't capable of change." She went so far as to say the commission implied that "key elements of American society must learn Spanish as a second language and adopt Latino culture instead."

This report and, of course, Tropiano's response created quite a stir, somewhat surprising when one considers what little influence the commission had. It had no prescribed powers. Its annual budget was slightly over $200,000. The governor was out of town on the day the report was issued, and his press secretary, John Taylor, said at the time he could not make a comment about it; in fact, he wasn't even sure if Gov. Casey had read the report before it was released. Chuck Ayers reported in the *Morning Call* that Taylor told him "*generally* someone on the Governor's staff reads such reports before they are issued."

If someone on staff had not read the report before its issuance, I am certain they did afterward. Whatever the case, it is amazing to consider how a benign report issued by a toothless advisory council could generate such outrage. Yet this pattern of behavior became all too commonplace; one side provoking the other, and each accusation followed by a counter-accusation. Like most family disagreements, political debates often end up with exhausted participants and no consensus.

Racism and bigotry have existed throughout recorded history. The concepts of ethnicity and race have subtle but important differences. Ethnic groups typically share a common culture. Americans may be black, white, or Asian, but they are all still considered "Americans." Many Americans are naturalized citizens who have adopted our culture, language, and customs.

Race refers to shared physical and genetic characteristics that people are born with. These characteristics are not chosen and can never be changed. All Americans are guaranteed equal protection under law, but they have often been unable to obtain this protection due to racial discrimination.

The Puerto Rican experience is in some respects unusual if not unique. Puerto Ricans are American citizens with a nebulous status. I call them quasi-American. Residents carry an American passport but cannot vote for president. They have no representation in Congress. The official language of Puerto Rico is Spanish, but English is also spoken virtually everywhere on the island. In 2012, voters approved a local referendum for statehood, but there has been very little actual movement from Washington to make Puerto Rico our fifty-first state. To confuse matters further, there is no Puerto Rican race, any more than there is a racial identity for Texans or Floridians. Native Puerto Ricans do not share a common skin color or facial features. Puerto Rico, in fact, is very likely more racially diverse than any state within the United States.

There are, however, unique cultural elements that extend far beyond a common Spanish language. They exist in matters as diverse as cuisine, music, or religion, where Catholics and to a lesser degree Pentecostals, dominate. Nationalistic pride abounds, even though Puerto Rico has been controlled for the past five hundred years by foreign powers, first Spain and then the United States.

Family life is central to this culture as well. To many Puerto Ricans, family has a special meaning, extending well beyond the nuclear family, across generations, to many cousins, second cousins, nieces, and nephews. They often live in close proximity to one another and are deeply involved in each other's lives.

One thing is undeniable: Puerto Ricans who flocked to Allentown to live in the 1980s and 1990s were not welcomed with open arms and were often subjected to discrimination. Discrimination can sometimes be overt, but today in America, more often than not, it tends to be a bit more subtle, like a bank quietly redlining a poor neighborhood by refusing to open a branch office within its boundaries or make loans within those boundaries. Whatever form it takes, discrimination stings, and often the hurt and resentment it fosters can fester endlessly.

Margarita Ortiz first came to Allentown in the 1950s and settled there permanently. For a number of years, she worked long hours at factory jobs at Queen City Poultry, Western Electric, and GE. As part of the Puerto Rican Day Parade celebration in 1996, she was named Mother of the Year. When she reminisced with *Morning Call* reporter Yvette Cabrera about her first days on the mainland, she recalled being harassed every day by a group of fellow workers. "They screamed 'spic' at us," she said. This was long before hate crimes were recognized as such, and she recalled that this type of behavior was allowed to continue without interference or punishment.

Ortiz had kind words for her former employers but added that others "wouldn't flat out say no to Latinos, but some employers would give any excuse—they'd say, 'Oh, we already found a person for the job.'" While Margarita Ortiz and other early residents endured insults and intolerance, I was attending grade school in Allentown's West End, totally oblivious to everything going on around me. I think the same could be said for my parents. We truly lived in a different world.

The assimilation of Allentown's Latinos has been exceedingly slow, as Anna Adams points out in *Hidden from History.* She categorizes this traditional German-Dutch influenced society as being particularly closed and unwelcoming, and she wrote that the "majority of the people interviewed for (her) book claim to have felt some sort of subtle or blatant discrimination...Many believe that the problem has grown worse in recent years."

Adams also points out that racial stereotyping sometimes manifests itself in strange and perverse ways. Some whites have assigned geographic labels, judging Puerto Ricans from Puerto Rico as being "good" and those from New York and New Jersey as "bad." Adams also found instances of an odd sort of reverse discrimination, revealing that some Latinos shunned treatment from Latino physicians, assuming they would receive better treatment from Anglos. She also cited a study (unnamed) that suggested that Puerto Ricans in Allentown live in one of the most segregated societies in the nation. Even today, thirty years after Puerto Ricans began to come to Allentown in significant numbers, the vast majority of them live in the same two wards they first settled.

Jennifer Lin of the *Philadelphia Inquirer* attended a public hearing on Latino affairs in 1992 and picked up on a sense of alienation that seemed pervasive. Allentown Latinos spoke of government agencies that had no bilingual employees, hospitals without interpreters, police brutality, cuts in public education, and an escalating drop-out rate because "*students felt disconnected from school* (my italics)." I have no evidence that would indicate whether any of these conditions were commonplace, rare, or somewhere in the middle. In a sense, it doesn't really matter because our feelings represent an authentic truth of their own, even if they are based on simplistic or partially correct assumptions.

To me, it seems hard to accept that someone could justify dropping out of school due to a "disconnected feeling." Of course, white, middle-class Americans like me don't ordinarily feel disconnected, and they aren't. Many Anglos in Allentown no doubt could identify (at least silently) with Emma Tropiano when she talked about "crybabies." This can be a very touchy subject, a lightning rod, really, for conflict and misunderstanding. It is an extremely awkward matter for whites to discuss openly, and they rarely if ever do so in the presence of minorities.

This could be seen very clearly when a community group (Puerto Ricans/Latinos United) circulated a petition in 1991 calling for the resignation of two school board members, Thomas Ruhe and Willard Clewell. Ruhe and Clewell were both Republicans; Clewell was the former head of the science department at Allen High School, and Ruhe was a production supervisor at Western Electric. They spoke openly about violence in the schools and the inability of school administrators to deal with it. Much of this violence was racially inspired and pitted Latino against Anglo. It was undeniable that the cultural and racial divisions that plagued the city of

Allentown extended into the city's schools. It was not racist per se to recognize that reality and speak out against it. The problem was that Latinos felt that Ruhe and Clewell were pointing the finger at *them*. Ruhe and Clewell felt they were just being truthful.

The Ruhe-Clewell petition was symptomatic of the challenges of that era. The petition expressed outrage over various statements from "racists Thom Ruhe and Willard Clewell" and called for their resignations. Both of them either denied making the statements altogether, or in certain cases when they did, they said that their comments were taken entirely out of context and had been misunderstood. The *Morning Call* ran a nine-hundred-word article about the incident. In the end, nearly three weeks after the board meeting in question, Puerto Ricans/Latinos United had gathered a total of only twenty-four signatures on its petition. Once again, apathy prevailed, and both Ruhe and Clewell continued to serve out their terms.

Statistics suggest that the quality of life for many Latinos in Allentown has not improved materially over time. When the credit crisis first hit in 2008, approximately 28 percent of the Latinos living in the Lehigh Valley were living in poverty. When the Lehigh Valley Research Consortium (LVRC) issued a report in 2012, several years into the nation's economic recovery, the poverty percentage had actually *risen* to 35 percent. In both cases, their poverty level was much higher than in the nation at large. Truthfully, it is hard to imagine how there can ever be a meaningful improvement in racial harmony and understanding unless Allentown's Latinos are able to break out of the cycle of poverty that has shadowed them for so long. In some ways, powerlessness and poverty have been self-perpetuating, so the reality of "two worlds" endures.

It is axiomatic that individuals need educational training and job skills to find good jobs. The Allentown School District has struggled to meet statewide educational standards for many years, and the performance gap that exists for Latino students has not improved with time. Another report issued by the LVRC in 2009 focused entirely on education, and the statistics were equally disturbing. Graduation rates and SAT scores for

Latinos lagged behind those of white, non-Hispanic, Asian, and black students. The Pennsylvania System of Student Achievement (PSSA) scores for all students in Allentown were discouraging enough, but for Latinos they were materially worse; in the period 2006–07, less than half of the Latino students in Allentown achieved proficiency in math, and only 39 percent did so in reading. Some improvement was made in subsequent years, but in relative terms, there was no significant progress for Latinos as a group. After the state raised its proficiency standards, the number of school districts in Allentown that underperformed remained constant. PSSA tests were not administered after 2012, but the tests that replaced them produced equally grim results.

The drop-out rate speaks for itself. Allentown's graduation rate has remained at or near the bottom when compared to all of the other school districts in the Valley. Enrollment in Allen High School, the city's largest high school and the third largest in the entire state, is highest for ninth-grade students, with dramatic losses starting as early as tenth grade. In the end, nearly 40 percent of all students who enrolled in Allen High School failed to graduate. Only 20 percent of all students who did graduate took SATs or planned to attend four-year colleges, and the number of Latinos who did so was—not surprisingly—the smallest among all ethnic groups. It was equally predictable that the drop-out rate for Latino students was higher than for any other group.

The Allentown School District is beset by many problems, and chief among them is a lack of financial resources. Interestingly, it ranks near the top of all districts in the state when one considers how much of its annual budget goes directly into classroom instruction. At the same time, it is near the bottom when measuring how much revenue is actually spent per student. This is hardly a surprise given the economic changes that have taken place over the years and how poor in reality the city has become. The city is poor because its residents are poor. Eighty percent of all students at William Allen High qualify for subsidized or free lunches.

Ron Skinner, a former fourth-grade classmate of mine, served on the school board between 1971 and 1991. He provided me with some very interesting information. During the 1970s, while the economy was weak and the suburban exodus first began (but before Latinos began to arrive in large numbers), the number of children in Allentown schools declined from nineteen thousand to thirteen thousand. The school district prepared to shrink itself, closing schools and losing teachers and other employees through attrition. The tables turned in the 1980s, and the student population suddenly climbed back from thirteen thousand to nineteen thousand. During this upsurge, the total assessed tax base throughout the city remained flat, due to underutilized if not abandoned factories whose fair market value had plunged dramatically when economic conditions worsened. Property taxes on these buildings declined in lockstep with their shrinking valuations.

The Allentown School District was suddenly short on facilities, resources, money, and Latino teachers—just as thousands of new Latino students were enrolling. These challenging circumstances were further complicated by the fact that during this time, the teachers were represented by two rival unions: the Allentown Education Association and an insurgent Allentown Federation of Teachers that was affiliated with the AFL-CIO. If this situation appeared to have been a bit chaotic, there is one reason: it was.

The inability of the Latino community to fully assimilate, whether due to a feeling of strong cultural identity, recurrent discrimination, or both, has been a constant feature of life in Allentown for the past twenty years. Lawsuits alleging discrimination against Latinos have been filed with mind-numbing frequency. In one instance, Ernesto Galarza, falsely suspected of being an illegal immigrant in 2012, was jailed for three days before being released. Initially he had been taken into custody when detectives suspected him of being part of a drug deal, which occurred at a construction site where he was working. At the time, he happened to be in the immediate vicinity of three Latino coworkers who were apprehended in the act. Clearly, Galarza was in the wrong place at the wrong time.

Detectives became suspicious when they ID'd the other three and had reason to believe they were in the country illegally. Like the others, Galarza had initially been booked on charges of distributing a controlled substance, but they were dropped almost immediately when he was able to establish his innocence. He was nevertheless detained over the weekend until Mark Szalczyk, an Immigration and Customs Enforcement (ICE) agent, was able to confirm his identity and authorize his release.

He filed two separate lawsuits, one against the city of Allentown and the other against ICE; each of them was settled for $25,000. In addition, a third lawsuit was filed against the detective who made the arrest, Christie Correa, as well as ICE agent Szalczyk. That suit was still active and pending appeal several years later. A fourth complaint against Lehigh County itself was subsequently dismissed by a federal court. There is no doubt whatsoever that Galarza was wronged, a totally innocent victim of circumstances and quite possibly of racial stereotyping as well. One can fully understand his need for payback. The fact that he filed four different lawsuits is testament to the emotional pain he experienced. He will never forget those three days.

Evelyn Antonsen was a Latino educator who became embroiled in several discrimination lawsuits against the Allentown School District. In the 1990s, she applied for seven different principal or assistant principal positions, and after failing to land one of them, sued the school district alleging racial bias. The suit was ultimately settled for $60,000, but with an unusual twist—Antonsen admitted she had no clear proof of discrimination. She was later hired as a principal in the Harrisburg school system. Surprisingly she attempted to return to Allentown, applying once more for three open principal positions. At the time, she said of her past struggle with the school district: "It has been behind me. We move on in life." Unfortunately, it turned out not much had changed. Again, she was passed over, and again, she sued the Allentown School District. The second case was also settled, this time for an undisclosed amount.

At first glance, one might dismiss Antonsen's behavior as being an odd mix of opportunism and sour grapes. While there may not have been hard evidence of outright bias in the hiring practices of the Allentown School District, events have demonstrated that such problems existed. Many Latino administrators were unhappy with the direction of the school department, often becoming vocal critics, or in some case, ex-employees.

Sometimes a lawsuit would appear that seemed worthy of inclusion in *Ripley's Believe It or Not!* In 2012 Leif Henry, a veteran (Hispanic) Allentown police officer, filed an unusual suit against the city alleging discrimination. However, connecting the dots in this particular case presented a bit of a challenge. Henry worked in the K-9 unit; his dog, Valka, sadly died of liver cancer in 2010. He was subsequently reassigned out of the unit, according to the Allentown Police Department, after mishandling Valka's replacement. Henry claimed this was a demotion, not a transfer. The department disagreed, saying that Henry was never suspended and continued to earn his normal salary. Henry made his situation more difficult by claiming migraine headaches prevented him from working nights. It may be entirely true that his headaches worsened in the evening, but this peculiar medical condition hardly served to endear him to his superiors. In any event, the court system found it difficult to correlate Henry's Hispanic heritage with any of his legal claims. Henry's lawsuit was first filed in 2012, subsequently amended three times, and finally dismissed in 2014 after a federal judge failed to find even "minimal proof" of discrimination based upon race.

Allegations of racial discrimination even cropped up against the Allentown School District. In 2013, the US Department of Education's Office of Civil Rights (OCR) surprisingly launched a widespread investigation of local practices regarding hiring of minority teachers and administrators. Previously, several community groups had expressed concern that only 5 percent of Allentown's teachers and administrators were represented by minorities. The school district claimed—with justification—that the pool of state-certified Latino applicants for positions in

Allentown's schools was relatively small, and it could only hire qualified candidates. Yet hard feelings persisted.

Additionally, as Colin McEvoy reported in the *Express Times*, an additional compliance review was undertaken "to determine whether the district (had) included policies, procedures, or practices that excluded Hispanic or English Language Learner students from high level courses offered by the district." School District Superintendent Russell Mayo appeared blindsided. He said, "I don't consider it an investigation in the sense that we are doing something wrong. It's more of a review, or an audit." He expressed ignorance of any issue or incident that prompted the investigation and appeared baffled by the suggestion that minority students were channeled away from honors programs. "On the contrary," he said, "we actually attempt to push those kids and challenge them into AP and dual-enrollment courses, particularly at the high school level."

Mayo pledged to be totally cooperative and open to the OCR's recommendations for improvement. He did not hide behind the fact that there were two thousand students within his district for whom English was a second language. He clearly could have. A lack of proficiency in English certainly cannot make it easier for minority students to achieve at a high level, nor could the limited and dwindling financial resources that the ASD had at its disposal—funds that could have been used to augment its ESL programs. In fact, two days after the story of the OCR audit was released to the public, the Allentown School District announced a new budget, which saw 151 jobs eliminated, including 127 teacher positions. This budget, of course, was not racially inspired, but simply a sad commentary on the financial realities that plagued the city at this time.

There are numerous factors responsible for differing levels of student achievement—whether in Allentown or anywhere else—and an analysis of those factors requires both broad vision and careful scrutiny. Racial discrimination can certainly be part of the mix, especially when economic opportunity is denied to the parents of the schoolchildren in question. Poverty can affect someone's self-esteem as well as his wallet, and despair and cynicism can trickle down through multiple generations. This can be a team sport, where everybody in the family gets to play. Still, we need to remember when the issue of race is introduced, the conversation often stops and confrontation begins.

In Allentown, like many other cities in America, poverty has been joined by crime and drug trafficking, creating a trifecta of hopelessness and misery. The Latino community in Allentown and in neighboring towns has been plagued by this. Some of the cases are especially horrifying. In 2010, the US Department of Justice issued an indictment naming dozens of Lehigh Valley Latin King members; the charges included numerous firearms offenses, drug trafficking, assault, kidnapping, and conspiracy to murder.

A 2014 drug sweep in center city Allentown netted fourteen arrests in one day. Most of those who were apprehended were Latino, and all were in their twenties and thirties, with the exception of Ernesto Gonzalez, a fifty-nine-year-old Allentown resident. Police saw Gonzalez selling drugs from his car at 9th and Linden Street, just a few blocks from the new hockey arena and much of the city's massive redevelopment project. In the chase that ensued, Gonzalez threw bags of cocaine and heroin from his car window. Both the drugs and Gonzalez were quickly recovered. Gonzalez was booked on multiple charges and held on $150,000 bail. He told police he sold drugs because he needed the money. After this, he was going to need more.

Latinos, of course, hold no monopoly on crime or drug trafficking, whether in Allentown or anywhere else. The explosion in drug-related crime nationally has been testament to the failure of our "War on Drugs." Currently, the United States holds 5 percent of the world's population and houses 24 percent of its prisoners, but our diligent prosecution of drug trafficking has had minimal effect upon the spread of drug use throughout society. The Latino community in Allentown has experienced more than its fair share of crime, and no doubt its chronic level of poverty and widespread alienation contribute to this condition. It is a severe handicap.

Many Latinos realize that they cannot rely entirely on the largesse of government to produce positive change. Founded in 2003, the Hispanic Chamber of Commerce of the Lehigh Valley has gotten off to a booming start. It now boasts three hundred members who collectively employ over ten thousand people. Apart from the usual events, promotions, and networking opportunities common to most Chambers of Commerce, it offers a special program for Hispanic youth, called the Fé (faith) program. FE is also the acronym for Futuros Empresarios, or Future Entrepreneurs. It is a summer work study program initially launched with the support of Aetna Insurance and has since been embraced by several dozen of the area's largest employers. Over thirty high school students cycle through each summer, learning work skills and gaining job experience through internships.

The Hispanic Center Lehigh Valley, first founded in 1968, has grown steadily in size and influence. It oversees a variety of community-based programs, including an active senior center, pro bono legal advice, and broad-based assistance in employment searching. Revealingly, one of the organization's areas of focus is a "Fatherhood Initiative," whose mission is to address what the center refers to as "the epidemic of father absenteeism." Another active organization includes the Latino Leadership Alliance of the Lehigh Valley, whose principal goal is to engage young future Latino leaders through education, training, and mentoring. This group recently awarded nearly fifty partial scholarships to promising students.

The Hispanic American Organization (HAO) provides a wide variety of community supports: affordable housing referrals, counseling, GED preparation, ESL instruction, and nutritional guidance. The HAO was founded in 1976 by Lupe Pearce and operated initially with one volunteer. Today, it is a beehive of activity, with sixty staff members. Pearce and the HAO were behind the establishment of the Roberto Clement Charter School, which has been an unqualified success. Student proficiency there has increased steadily for a number of years, and most recently, the school has been able to claim a 100 percent rate of graduation.

Latinos have also been able to make significant inroads in politics. Martin Velasquez, who edged out Emma Tropiano in a mayoral primary, served a number of terms on city council. Currently, the council features two Latino members, Cynthia Mota and Julio Guridy, the latter who serves as its president, and two Latinos also serve on Allentown School District's Board of Directors. It is clear, though, that the level of political representation is disproportionately small relative to the size of the Latino population.

Allentown's population stabilized around one hundred thousand after World War II and remained near that level for decades. Recently, however, its population has begun to increase significantly, and virtually all of this growth can be attributed to the influx of Latinos. This demographic change, which first gained traction in the 1980s and accelerated as time went on, has created a much more diverse, multicultural society. What happened was entirely unplanned and unexpected, and this made many older white residents uncomfortable and insecure. The steady loss of manufacturing jobs contributed to this feeling of anxiousness for Latinos as well as Anglos.

Both sides have experienced growing pains, and this will likely continue for some time. As we have seen, assimilation has progressed slowly. Perhaps it should not be all that shocking. New York City became a true melting pot in the late 1800s, when waves of European immigrants came to the United States. Jews, Greeks, Italians, Poles, and many other nationalities settled there. There existed a wide variety of different ethnic groups, all longing to belong and to become "American." Nevertheless, it often took two or three generations for the pot to melt.

Also, it is useful to remember that a strong sense of Latino identity continued to exist in New York and New Jersey, years after Puerto Ricans settled there. It should not be surprising that it has also remained strong in Pennsylvania. In this respect, what we call "assimilation" today may have a different meaning than it did over one hundred years ago. That is not necessarily a tragedy. There is nothing praiseworthy about seeing a language, a culture, or an ethnic identity vaporized.

Sometimes quickly, more often slowly, progress is being made. One can see it in the establishment of Latino businesses and in organizations that support them. It is evident in politics, education, and any number of entities that serve the local Hispanic community. Most importantly, it is visible in the unmistakable pride that resonates so clearly in schools, in church, and in places of work.

Allentown's economic struggles brought great hardship to many, but the toll this took on area Latinos was especially acute since they were most vulnerable to begin with. Crime, drug use, and a high drop-out rate among Latino high school students were the obvious symptoms of alienation and estrangement. Racial tension and instances of bias added fuel to the fire of resentment. In the final analysis, though, it was Allentown's thirty-year recession, the lack of jobs, and the inability to create new work opportunities that retarded the economic well-being of many Hispanic residents. Evidence exists, however, that conditions have recently begun to improve as both government and private industry have committed significant resources to the city. Perhaps this will prove to be the beginning of a meaningful recovery, but in the end it will take higher levels of educational achievement, strong family and community support, and above all, decent job prospects for this turnaround to get real traction.

12

Reinvention Part 1

By the end of the 1960s, the suburbanization of American cities had been progressing for nearly twenty-five years, and Allentown was no exception. As a very young child, this evolution was barely perceptible; in those days, I recall there being clear boundaries between the downtown business district, a mature residential area in the city's West End, and farmland. Yet it was clear that change was afoot. In 1955 my father, who was a builder, put in a small, fourteen-unit subdivision of inexpensive split-level homes near the northern perimeter of the city in an area that can best be described as suburban. All of the homes were sold in two weeks.

As time progressed, the movement of people from city to newly created suburbs gained momentum. Lower Macungie Township, which lies a few miles west of Allentown proper, saw its population more than double between 1960 and 1970 (from thirty-eight hundred to eighty-eight hundred), and it continued to increase steadily for the remainder of the century. By 2000 the number of residents had risen to nearly twenty thousand, and by 2010 approximately thirty thousand. Macungie is now a prototypical suburb, with lovely, meticulously maintained homes, excellent schools, and ample recreational resources for both children and adults.

To the north, both North and South Whitehall Townships experienced similar growth and an identical bulge in population. Today nearly forty thousand people live in Whitehall—when I was a child it was largely rural. Yet while both Macungie and Whitehall boomed, the city of Allentown stagnated. Its population remained level for fifty years, and as the suburbs prospered, the city suffered.

What happened here was commonplace in America and really should come as no surprise. Suburbanization gained momentum because land was cheap and plentiful, the country was in the midst of a postwar economic boom, and more and more families were able to afford two cars, making long-distance commuting a mainstream activity. Traditional downtown urban centers began to struggle on many levels, and the movement of people from city to suburb made their predicament more difficult with every passing day. Phrases like "urban blight" and "urban decay" became part of our everyday vocabulary.

After the Lehigh Valley Thruway (US Route 22) was completed in 1954, a number of retailers opened stores on adjacent land that heretofore had been vacant. Shoppers were attracted by the ease of access and ample free parking. Allentown got its first mall in 1966, when the Whitehall Mall opened on MacArthur Road north of Route 22. Soon afterward, plans were hatched to develop a large, enclosed shopping mall nearby, one that promised to be the largest in the state of Pennsylvania, at least at that time. Although the Lehigh Valley Mall did not open for business until 1976, it had already become obvious that urban exodus and suburban development were going to impact Allentown's downtown business district in a profound way. As early as the 1960s, city officials were becoming increasingly aware that downtown Allentown, like downtowns everywhere, faced an uncertain future, and they began to take a serious look at ways in which the city could adapt to the changes that were taking place.

The first step the city took with an eye toward reinventing itself was the Hamilton Mall. Today we think of shopping malls as either strip malls or large, enclosed structures housing dozens of individual businesses. The Hamilton Mall was neither. Simply put, four blocks of Hamilton Street in the heart of Allentown's shopping district were turned into a "semimall." The Hamilton Mall was really not much more than Hamilton Street with a facelift. Sidewalks were expanded from twelve to twenty-nine feet, and designers reduced the roadway from five lanes to two. Some areas of the sidewalk were bricked, plantings were added, and an attractive system of overhead canopies was constructed along the length of the mall to protect pedestrians from the elements.

There was confusion and debate concerning roadway access. The mall was initially visualized as an auto-free zone, with free shuttle buses available for shoppers. However, when merchants squawked about the difficulties small trucks and vans faced when making deliveries, limited auto traffic was ultimately permitted. Conventional traffic, though, still needed to be diverted, and this created numerous bottlenecks. Construction of the mall took nearly two years, and rubble often piled up on the storefront sidewalks. The Hamilton Mall was a well-intentioned attempt to revitalize the city's downtown business district, but it was apparent early on that it wasn't going to succeed—in spite of the city's claim to the contrary made in its 1974 application for "All-American City" status. After the mall opened, there was a small bump in retail activity, but it did not prove to be enduring.

After the Lehigh Valley Mall opened in 1976, business in the downtown area began to dry up. The trend of suburbanization had become irreversible. In subsequent years, officials experimented with the Hamilton Mall's appearance, but these changes were only cosmetic and had no discernible impact upon the ongoing decline in retail sales. Today, few if any vestiges of the Hamilton Mall remain. Businesses that used to use "Hamilton Mall" as a street address have reverted to Hamilton Street. It's as if the mall has been erased from history.

Zollinger's Department Store closed in 1977. The Rialto Theater, a lovely venue that accommodated nearly nineteen hundred people, closed a year later. A few blocks east, the Colonial Theater, an equally impressive Beaux Arts-styled structure, struggled on for several years until it was sold to the notorious Mark Mendelson in the late 1980s. Mendelson, true to form, made no improvements to the Colonial. This did not dissuade him, however, from using it as collateral to further pyramid his real estate holdings, all of which ultimately went up in a cloud of smoke years later. This pattern of behavior was standard operating procedure for Mendelson, whose history of deceit was, if nothing else, consistent—unpaid bills and taxes, broken promises, and neglected, run-down properties. The theater continued to deteriorate badly, and all the while, the city of Allentown fought with Mendelson in a white-collar death match. Ultimately, the city "won" and gained control of the Colonial as a result of a court order in 2003; two years later it demolished the building and covered the now-vacant lot with crushed stone. The Colonial had achieved dubious notoriety in 1990 when Allentown came in dead last in *Money* magazine's list of three hundred places to live in America; *Money* included a photo of the once-grand Colonial, along with the caption "Vacant movie theater in Allentown."

Then, in the mid-1990s, Leh's Department Store and the legendary Hess's both closed. If there had been any doubt about this story having a happy ending, and I doubt that there ever was, the closure of Leh's and Hess's erased it. From this point on, downtown Allentown became terribly quiet. Sadly, it had lost its mojo long before. Apart from municipal and county offices and business as usual at PPL headquarters, there wasn't much else happening. Many storefronts were vacant, and most of those that were not featured services that most Chambers of Commerce would scarcely brag about, like check cashing, pawn shops, bail bonds, and adult entertainment. Some had one word signs like "Eat" or "Nails." Others just read "Closed."

For a long time in the 1980s, the watchword was survival, and there was not much conversation about urban renewal, especially projects that required large capital outlays. First of all, the national economy didn't begin to improve until the latter part of Ronald Reagan's initial term in office, and it was understandable for locals to think that Allentown would snap back when the rest of the country did. It never happened. As time passed and it became obvious that such prosperity was passing the region by, watchful waiting was replaced by denial and then despair. President Reagan was both principled and sincere in his support of a free market economy, but the plain fact is that Allentown was a casualty of competition and change, not a beneficiary. There wasn't much that "trickled down" here.

The Allentown Economic Development Corporation was founded in 1979. AEDC is a nonprofit entity that was created by several dozen area corporations (dubbed Cornerstone Members), each of which put in some seed money, as did the city itself. The AEDC's mission was to attract business investment. That noble goal was more easily said than done. The AEDC started slowly and made its first splash in the mid-1980s, purchasing two large Mack Truck assembly plants, which that company had shut down a few years beforehand. It took four years to redevelop the site, but ultimately a refurbished Bridgeworks Enterprise Center, an incubator for small business startups, opened in 1989. Since then, the AEDC has enlarged the scope of its project, and next to the Enterprise Center now sits the Bridgeworks Industrial Center, home to several more established businesses.

The AEDC's early activities were reasonably successful, and that success was tangible, but if truth be told, somewhat limited. The city of Allentown was losing businesses far faster than it was attracting them. Today there are still many vacant factories, a number of which sit on brownfield sites. I asked Kurt Zwikl, AEDC's executive director from 1996–2004, "Can all of the old, empty factory buildings be saved? Can they be gutted and redeveloped as lofts, light industrial space, or commercial offices?" He replied, "Sure. All you need is a tenant."

The AEDC was at its core involved with real estate redevelopment. Given its somewhat limited financial resources, to its credit the AEDC accomplished quite a bit. At the time that Kurt Zwikl got involved, there was a noticeable pickup in activity. Zwikl focused his attention on real estate development in several core areas: commercial and government offices, as well as facilities serving education and the arts.

The Lehigh Portland Cement Building between 7th and 8th on Hamilton was a total gut job and became a new home to the Lehigh Carbon Community College's Allentown satellite, which until then had been housed somewhere inside a courthouse building nearby. At Lehigh Landing in East Allentown, there now sits the America on Wheels Museum—the building is situated on land formerly occupied by a meat-packing plant. The Arts Walk, one of Zwikl's ideas, was designed to create a campus-like setting that integrated a number of different elements, such as the Allentown Arts Museum, Symphony Hall, and the Baum Art School. The Arts Walk incorporated a design that included pedestrian walkways, performance areas, and dedicated parking. Additionally, after a number of false starts and disappointments, a new "green" office building for PPL was finally constructed on land that once had been occupied by Hess's.

While these more modest achievements took place, Zwikl and other public officials had struggled seemingly without end to put together a large redevelopment project, one that could be truly transformative. For years after Hess's closed, the building had remained vacant, a sad, ghostly reminder of what it was and tangible evidence of what it became. During these years, city officials, as we have seen, considered various proposals for the Hess property, none of which panned out.

By far the most ambitious of these was the original Arena Project, the brainchild of sports agent Terry Bender and accountant David Stortz, who formed a partnership called B&S Real Estate. The two had been in negotiations for some time with William Heydt, a two-term mayor who had succeeded Joe Daddona in 1994. Heydt was no stranger to the risks of real estate. Only two months into his first term, the city's newest office building, a seven-story structure called Corporate Plaza, literally collapsed into a giant sinkhole. Experts concluded the building's sudden failure was brought on by unusually porous soil, which had been made even more unstable by a heavy concentration of limestone. The demise of Corporate Plaza gave Allentown a celebrity it neither desired nor needed. The disaster proved to be a huge distraction and served as a caution sign for other downtown redevelopment projects like a large arena.

Corporate Plaza's design incorporated support columns placed on top of spread footings, which were intended to distribute the weight over a large area. The overall scheme, given the composition of the soil below, was fatally flawed, and Frank Moyer, the engineer who made the recommendations, bravely admitted his error. A few hours before the collapse, workers at a municipal water plant were astonished by a sudden two-foot drop in nearby reservoirs. Heydt was quickly awakened in the middle of the night, and he drove downtown to meet up with officials from the fire and water departments. At 4:00 a.m. he saw the building shake and several windows pop loose. Within a few hours, Corporate Plaza suddenly crumpled, appearing as if it had been cleaved in two pieces. Several months later, it was imploded before three thousand onlookers, each of whom had paid the city three dollars to watch the spectacle. The rubble was ultimately cleared away to make way for an open-air parking lot, operated by none other than Mark Mendelson.

With the memory of the Corporate Plaza disaster fading as years passed, Mayor Heydt began to look aggressively at a variety of new redevelopment proposals. When Hess's closed and the city took title to the building site, Heydt saw an opportunity that could both transform downtown and at the same time create a personal legacy. His initial response to Bender and Stortz's project was clearly positive. His support was reinforced after B&S said the venture would not require any public funds. However, as the two of them were to learn, securing investment capital proved to be an ongoing challenge.

The arena certainly would have benefited from government backing of some sort. Construction estimates increased regularly, and Bender and Stortz found it increasingly difficult to move forward. Some potential investors may have been scared off because the arena's primary tenant was to have been a hockey team owned by Bender himself—and the team had never played a game. There were no committed secondary tenants—only prospects.

The original plans they presented to Heydt included a seven-thousand seat arena, which would serve as the home rink for Bender's Lehigh Valley Xtreme. The fledgling team was envisioned to be part of a low-level professional hockey league, the United Hockey League, which began life in 1991 as the Colonial Hockey League and ended as the International Hockey League—before folding its tent in 2010. It operated in such places as Binghamton, New York, St. Thomas, Ontario, and Muskegon, Michigan. Bender and Stortz signed former NHL defenseman Dave "The Hammer" Schultz to serve as the team's coach and general manager. Schultz, who played for the Philadelphia Flyers in the 1970s, still holds the NHL record for penalty minutes in a single season. He was regarded as a hero in Philadelphia and a goon everywhere else. His fights with Boston's Terry O'Reilly were legendary. I have no idea whether Schultz would have succeeded as either a coach or an executive, but he certainly would have provided great theater.

He never coached a game, nor did the Xtreme play one, for a very simple reason: the arena was never built. At the beginning, though, there was a tremendous amount of optimism about its prospects. Many possibilities were talked about—an arena football team, USBL (professional) and college basketball, concerts, and professional wrestling—all of which could comfortably coexist with the arena's anchor tenant, the Xtreme. It was also thought the project would include a conference center and space for retailers. When Heydt officially announced the city's approval on January 20, 2000, Bender called it "a dream come true."

Five months later came a reality check. A *Morning Call* headline said it all: "Allentown Arena's Timetable in Doubt as Risk of Sinkholes Forces New Test." I can't imagine how this came as a surprise to anyone given that the proposed arena was only a short walk away from the site of the now-infamous Corporate Plaza. In any event, the city revealed that dozens of additional test drillings would have to be made and an unknown number of extra steel support beams would need to be utilized during the arena's construction; the drilling tests, the modified design, and the use of the extra steel beams were expected to add as much as $2 million to the project's planned expense. Bender was understandably distressed and found himself somewhere between disbelief and denial. He said, "I thought maybe the rock (bedrock) was closer to the surface…The Hess's building was there for how long and nothing ever happened. Now we have to deal with it."

During the next several months, the estimated project cost continued to increase, from $12 million to nearly $17 million. In August Heydt simply said that design changes and modifications of the arena's "basic systems" were responsible for the additional overrun. He bravely claimed he was "confident" that the project would go forward but admitted he was looking at other alternatives. At the same time, Bender and Stortz were considering a plan B that would take the project elsewhere in the Lehigh Valley. Neither attended Heydt's press conference that summer, when the mayor delivered the grim news about the project's unexpected detour. Bender's only comment was, "I think the mayor did well today. He said what he had to say."

By December, B&S announced that they were experiencing some difficulty in getting all of the financing they needed to proceed with construction. Without investors, lenders were unwilling to lend; without lenders, investors were unwilling to invest. Officials put on a brave face, denying that the project was dead. The usually loquacious Bender was silent. It seemed clear to others that the game was over. Revealingly, the city immediately made plans to reinstall decorative lampposts in front of the construction site on Hamilton Street.

Days passed, then weeks, and finally months. While the arena project struggled, paralysis seemed to grip municipal government. Kurt Zwikl had thought the run-down buildings and storefronts on the south side of Hamilton (directly opposite the arena) would be prime parcels for future restaurants, shops, and bars. When the arena ran into trouble, Zwikl wanted to solicit formal bids for alternative redevelopment. Heydt, an arena booster, resisted, and the area became increasingly grimy and dilapidated with every passing month. In truth, Zwikl shouldn't have been surprised. Several months earlier, Heydt had told Michael Rosenfeld, the head of the Allentown Redevelopment Authority, not to solicit alternative proposals for the Hess's site, hoping to give Bender and Stortz time to cobble together a viable deal.

Late in 2000, Stortz had brought in local businessman Jeff Trainer for a fresh perspective and a dose of new energy. When B&S's original deal fell apart, Trainer immediately went to work to come up with an alternative. Trainer was successful in attracting several new investors, a feat that in retrospect seems particularly noteworthy in light of the many difficulties the project had faced in the past. Trainer in fact told his investors to be prepared to lose money initially and to brace themselves for the prospect of owning an arena that would remain idle over 50 percent of the time.

In March 2001, it looked as if Trainer had caught lightning in a bottle. The Allentown Commercial and Industrial Development Authority announced that it had reached an agreement in principle with his new, reformulated investor group and had granted them a lease option to develop the downtown arena. ACIDA, a sister organization to the AEDC, is an entity that describes itself as a "conduit" financing organization—it doesn't borrow money directly, but rather provides a vehicle for many public or quasi-public projects to do so. Often hospitals, schools, airports, parking lots, and yes, arenas, are financed in this manner.

In spite of the obstacles he faced, Trainer remained committed, perhaps unreasonably so. He told *Morning Call* reporter Daryl Nerl, "If the deal was that good and that easy, believe me, it would have been done immediately. We need to be prepared to lose money. You've got to have guys who believe in the area."

Trainer undoubtedly had some believers, but they did not serve on the AEDC. Just two months after the arena project was brought back from the dead, it collapsed. On May 1, the AEDC executive committee voted to deny the lease option that had previously been granted. Two days later, the Lehigh Valley Xtreme let go its entire staff, including Dave "The Hammer" Schultz. Terry Bender, who owned the Xtreme, didn't even appear at the press conference.

Trainer bravely announced that his investor group would be looking at alternative development sites elsewhere in the Lehigh Valley. It is hard to imagine, given the project's history and bad karma, if he ever would have been successful, but after the terrorist attacks of September 11, 2001, it became a moot point. The US economy sank immediately into recession, one that was to hit the travel and leisure industries particularly hard. A year later, in the fall of 2002, Trainer's group was in negotiation to build a recreational skating complex on former Bethlehem Steel property. Ultimately PPL purchased the former Hess's site from the city and put an additional office building on the property.

The Xtreme had become "xtinct"—almost. Bender was interviewed a few years later and seemed to have gained some degree of acceptance regarding the Xtreme's fate. When asked what happened to his team, he replied, "They're in a filing cabinet in a drawer in my office." Apparently cured of the desire to develop an arena, Bender still believed his team could get an opportunity to play hockey—someday, somewhere. After all, he still owned the team, such as it was. In fact he recently had been approached by a potential buyer from New York, and he and his partners declined to sell. Some dreams die hard.

Meanwhile during December 2001, just three months after the terrorist attacks on the World Trade Center and the Pentagon, plans were unveiled to redevelop the former Harold's furniture store site on Hamilton Street as a data center, or a "telecommunications hotel" as it was described at the time. The man behind this was Richard Welkowitz, CEO of Blackford Development, who was also closely connected with Jeff Trainer. Blackford, in fact, was to be one of the equity investors in the failed arena project. It is amazing to think that what was once prime (and pricey) retail space was being considered as a home for computer servers.

Within two months, that project was dead as well. Originally, Franklin Gillespie Jr. and Anthony Boyle had been given the exclusive right to redevelop Harold's, but they had trouble getting lease commitments. They then attempted to transfer their option to Welkowitz, and in this regard, they were supported by Mayor Heydt. In the end, the city's Redevelopment Authority denied the transfer. Gillespie and Boyle were through; they let their option expire on January 8. It was another five years before the old Harold's site came to life as the new home of Allentown Brew Works.

Progress was even slower at Schoen's Furniture, yet another defunct business in center city. In early 2001, Heydt had the city purchase the building, which had been vacant since 1990, with the hope of turning it into an arts incubator. As he was preparing to leave office late in 2002, the *Morning Call* ran this headline: "Financing for Allentown Arts Incubator in Old Furniture Store Is Still in Limbo." Ten years later, in 2012, Schoen's was still vacant, and its future uncertain. The dream of an "arts incubator" had died long ago. Finally, in 2013, more than twenty years after Schoen's closed, construction finally began on redeveloping the site as a mixed use retail/office facility, and it is worth noting that a significant amount of public money had to be made available before construction could proceed.

Then there was the Americus Hotel. As we know Mark Mendelson bought the once-grand hotel in 1985 for short money and promised to restore it to its former grandeur. He never made good on his promise. Today, thirty years after Mendelson purchased the Americus, the building remains a vacant eyesore.

Allentown had made a number of attempts, small and large, to reinvent itself. The successes, and there were a number of them, were quite modest when compared to obstacles that the city faced. There were missteps, missed opportunities, and sometimes a few outright blunders. Lack of cohesion and coordination between the mayor's office, city council, and various county agencies contributed to political gridlock and periodic turf battles.

The Hamilton Mall, the collapse of Corporate Plaza, the arena project and the Lehigh Valley Xtreme, Schoen's, Harold's, Leh's, Hess's, Zollinger's and the Americus—it seemed as if life in Allentown was similar to a Shakespearean tragedy, with a seemingly endless stream of disappointments, suffering, embarrassment, and failure. What is there left to say when a respected national magazine ranks three hundred US cities in order of their attractiveness and your hometown comes in last? Every passing year seemed to present new challenges that no one could have realistically expected or planned for in advance. Many well-intentioned civic leaders tried mightily to turn the ship around. Nothing seemed to work. It was as if the Corporate Plaza disaster cast a spell of misfortune over the city that no amount of effort could overcome. Sadly, when it seemed the situation could not possibly have gotten worse, it did.

Another year, another mayor, and once more, Allentown soon found itself in the breakdown lane with an empty gas tank. For many years, the city's economic difficulties could usually be debated or even explained away. Millions of manufacturing jobs were lost in the United States, not just Allentown; similarly, almost all cities in the Northeast and Midwest were experiencing aging infrastructures, rising crime, changing demographics, and a shrinking tax base. Allentown's struggles were sometimes made worse by occasional errors of omission and because different government agencies or their officials failed to collaborate effectively. In addition, it must be said, the city seemed to experience more than its fair share of bad luck, or it may have turned a blind eye to reality—but never before had it shot itself in the foot as it did in 2004 when it was obligated to pay pension benefits that it could not afford.

Democrat Roy Afflerbach won the election as Allentown's fortieth mayor in 2002. His administration is best remembered for a near-death financial experience of its own making. Afflerbach privately agreed to changes in vesting formulas and other provisions for the police and fire department pension plans, changes that were so extreme that even before his first and only term came to an end, Allentown was struggling for its financial life. Almost immediately, city council found itself in a perpetual state of war with the mayor. A few weeks after Afflerbach left office, the now-desperate city of Allentown actually went to court in an attempt to have its *own* pension plan and related liabilities invalidated.

Afflerbach had agreed to a change applicable to the police department's pension crediting formula, which pegged future benefits to the highest thirty *days* of compensation earned by each participant. This change encouraged policemen who would have been eligible for early retirement to game the system, and a number of them did just that by packing as many overtime hours as possible into a thirty-day period. As a result, a large number of individuals were able to create lifetime pensions for themselves, which actually *exceeded* their previous annual pay. One policeman who left the force earning \$60,000 became eligible for a pension of \$91,000. Another police officer, who had somehow managed to accumulate eighty-four hours of overtime in one week, retired at age forty-two with a pension in excess of \$60,000; his base pay had been \$48,000 just before he left. Over eighty policemen retired in 2005, leaving the department with a gaping manpower void and the city with a financial migraine.

The fire department's pension plan was not quite as generous, but it was sweet enough to encourage approximately one-third of all active firefighters to elect early retirement in 2011, the first year a more liberal benefit formula kicked in. Between the police and fire departments, Allentown suddenly found itself with an unfunded pension liability of \$150 million. When incoming Mayor Ed Pawlowski took office in 2006, the situation appeared hopeless. Allentown was nearly broke. Soon afterward, the credit crisis of 2008 and the Great Recession that it spawned promised even more dire consequences. For approximately thirty years, Allentown had been on a slippery slope downward, and now it appeared that the end was near, this time largely from self-inflicted wounds.

13

Reinvention Part II

In September 2008, the developing credit crisis quickly took on the characteristics of a full-blown financial panic. Within a matter of weeks, the US government bailed out Fannie Mae, Freddie Mac, and AIG. Lehman Brothers went bankrupt, and Merrill Lynch, fearful that it would meet the same fate, hurriedly agreed to be acquired by Bank of America. Later in the month, federal regulators seized the giant thrift Washington Mutual and facilitated its acquisition by JPMorgan Chase. Chase thus obtained control of a bank that ostensibly had $300 billion in assets for less than $2 billion; it turned out that WaMu was a paper tiger, overwhelmed by an inventory of delinquent mortgages, underwater collateral, and bad business practices.

The stock market, which had already suffered significant losses in the previous twelve months, experienced a violent plunge. It was not to hit bottom for six more months, after it had lost an *additional* 30 percent of its value. Credit dried up in a heartbeat. Perfectly solid citizens found themselves unable to borrow money because fearful financial institutions were unwilling to lend it. The national economy had in a sense locked up and was in a state of paralysis.

It was in this environment that Allentown's Patrick Browne, state senator from Lehigh County, was busy hatching a scheme that he believed would in time transform the city he represented. Detractors or cynics would dismiss Browne's ideas as being both misguided and naïve. After all, they would argue, the city of Allentown had spent the last thirty years trying to create a new future for itself, and in spite of the best of intentions, its effort was largely futile.

Pat Browne was born and raised in Allentown, and he lives there today. After attending college at Notre Dame and then law school at Temple University, Browne worked for the next nine years in accounting, finishing up as a tax manager at Price Waterhouse Coopers. In the mid-1990s, he successfully entered politics, when he was elected to the Pennsylvania House of Representatives in the 131st district. He served there until 2005, when he was elected to the state senate. He has had a long and distinguished career in public service, drafting and sponsoring a number of key laws. His signature achievement in the eyes of many was the Neighborhood Improvement Zone program (NIZ), something first established by the Pennsylvania legislature in 2009 under Act 50.

Act 50 is complicated, but one thing was clear: it represented a huge investment by the taxpayers of Pennsylvania to revitalize the city of Allentown. When Browne first introduced the legislation, it was labeled by some as social engineering of the worst sort: corporate welfare. Many others were simply hesitant or uncertain. Even good ideas can get lost in a sea of distrust. Remember, this was 2009, as America was suffering through the credit crisis and the Great Recession. Feelings of alienation and suspicion were commonplace, especially toward government.

The NIZ encompasses 128 acres in Allentown's central business district and along the Lehigh River. Act 50 had big goals from the very start: attract capital, spur massive redevelopment, stimulate economic growth, and transform the city. Even in the beginning, the conversation about the project's size *started* at several hundred million dollars.

Debt financing for the real estate development would be made available through bonds issued by ANIZDA (the Allentown Neighborhood Improvement Zone Development Authority), but in this scheme, the authority was not much more than a financing conduit. ANIZDA itself guaranteed nothing. Browne's legislation allowed for the state to recycle tax dollars it collected within the NIZ sector directly back to ANIZDA; the authority in turn would apply these funds against the developers' debt service. Simply said, the Commonwealth of Pennsylvania would be subsidizing mortgage payments with tax dollars. With this assistance, the thinking was that these developers would be able to offer bargain below-market rents to prospective tenants. Browne's vision was that first-class space and low rents would prove to be a highly irresistible combination.

The plan was groundbreaking and extremely generous. Pennsylvania was going to kick back a tremendous amount of revenue to ANIZDA—including all corporate income taxes, business privilege taxes and fees, and licensing fees related to the operation of any business within the NIZ. Personal income taxes would be applicable as well and would include state income taxes withheld from an employee's paycheck. Liquor licenses, sales and use taxes, and amusement taxes were also included. In fact, the language of Act 50 was crystal clear, plainly stating that *any* state or local taxes other than real estate taxes would be fair game.

A few years after Act 50 passed, the Pennsylvania legislature created the City Revitalization and Improvement Zone program (CRIZ). Based on the Allentown NIZ, it was designed to help other cities in need. Compared with the open checkbook of the NIZ program, it is much more limited both in scope and largesse. For example, Lancaster's CRIZ earmarked only seven state taxes for a redevelopment subsidy, not twenty that are eligible in NIZ; it mandated that relocating business must come from outside Pennsylvania, a requirement that never applied to Allentown; and it limited state subsidies to the future *increase* in state taxes and fees, not the entire amount collected. Compared to NIZ, CRIZ was downright stingy. Allentown got a very good deal indeed. By early 2013, the value of proposed development was approaching $800 million. Mayor Ed Pawlowski, a Democrat, praised the Republican Browne as "one of the greatest legislators this state has."

Browne himself was always low-key and matter-of-fact about defending his creation. Recognizing that there was a meaningful amount of opposition to NIZ on principle, Browne essentially just shrugged his shoulders. In his mind, tax revenue generated within the NIZ was found money. Without NIZ, there would be no redevelopment, and without redevelopment, no chance for recovery and future growth.

It was as if the city of Allentown had hit the lottery. Browne was convinced NIZ legislation would produce not just a short-term building boom but also help to create permanent jobs and long-term economic activity, which of course would create a surge in tax revenues. Absent NIZ legislation, he felt there would be no chance of revitalization, and that the tax base in downtown Allentown would continue to erode as it had for the last several decades. To him, the "debate" about NIZ was really a nonstarter because continued government inaction would do nothing except insure ongoing failure and urban decay.

The centerpiece of the proposed project was a multipurpose sports and entertainment arena anchored by a minor-league hockey team. It had been only a half dozen years since Bender, Stortz, and Trainer had seen their own proposed arena project fail ignominiously, and in 2009, both the national economy and Allentown's financial health were more precarious than ever. Many residents greeted the announcement of another arena proposal with skepticism if not outright disbelief. Much had changed, however, since Bender and his associates tried vainly to find financial backing and political support for their arena project some years earlier.

One difference was obvious: the hockey team was real. Even better, it was looking for a home. The Philadelphia Flyers' top minor-league affiliate, the Philadelphia Phantoms, had played hockey in Philly's Spectrum until it was torn down in 2009. The team then made a move to Glens Falls, New York, and operated there for several years as the Adirondack Phantoms.

Team owners Jim and Rob Brooks actually considered shutting the team down ("going dark" in their words) because they wanted to bring the team to Allentown and were willing to wait for the arena to be built. The city of Glens Falls was both understanding and accommodating, welcoming the Phantoms as a temporary guest and letting the team renew short-term leases. It was always expected that the Phantoms would soon be moving on. Glens Falls only wanted to prove to the NHL that their city could support another minor-league franchise at some point in the future.

NIZ was a game changer. The Adirondack Phantoms ultimately became the Lehigh Valley Phantoms, and the team began play in its new home in October 2014. Moving the team to Allentown made a great deal of strategic sense. Allentown is only fifty miles from Philadelphia, and all of Philadelphia's major-league sports teams enjoy a strong following in the Lehigh Valley. It would be a mistake to underestimate the value of that connection. Allentown's proximity to Philadelphia gives the team a unique advantage: the Phantoms would be able to count on a loyal and large fan base before they even played their first game. Additionally, being only an hour's drive from the parent Flyers would serve to facilitate player movement, as well as communication between the teams.

The arena project was the centerpiece of Allentown's revitalization plan, but not the only piece. NIZ spawned massive redevelopment, projected to exceed $1 billion by the end of 2015, and it gave Allentown its first positive national attention in generations. Arguably the key figure for the entire project was homegrown real estate developer J. B. Reilly. Unlike Terry Bender, who was a (sports) marketing entrepreneur, and Dave Stortz, a CPA, Reilly had spent his life in real estate.

Reilly was experienced and had a stellar track record. Beginning with modest projects when he was just in his twenties, Reilly became one of the most successful and best-known developers in the state. He started small and proceeded cautiously. Over time, he moved from single-family homes to apartment buildings, fifty-five plus retirement communities, and office buildings. He understood the difference between risk and recklessness and steadily built his fortune—one brick at a time. When the NIZ program became law, Reilly made a decision to become an active participant in Allentown's revitalization. It would prove to be the defining moment in his business career. Apart from his pedigree, and his deep pockets, he had an intuitive understanding of what was ailing Allentown and what could be done to engineer a turnaround.

His partner in the venture was Joseph Topper, CEO of Allentown-based (and NYSE-listed) Lehigh Gas Partners, a regional distributor of motor fuels. Topper brought with him a wealth of business experience and, if truth be told, some personal wealth besides. Together Topper and Reilly formed City Center Lehigh Valley, which soon became synonymous with NIZ redevelopment. Reilly, however, was generally regarded as the face of City Center.

His plan was far reaching. Reilly made that clear from the outset when he said, “It’s not that we don’t have great companies here and great job opportunities, it’s that we don’t have the urban environment the young people want…We’re looking at a live, work, play 24/7 environment anchored around a world class hockey arena…This project improves the standard of living for all, makes business more competitive and makes the community more attractive.” His initial ten-year plan announced in 2012 included the arena, along with a Marriott Renaissance hotel and an office complex linked to it, as well as several other substantial office buildings nearby. Two City Center, the eleven-story building next to the arena, opened in 2014 and was fully leased before it opened its doors. As time went on and Reilly was able to obtain new lease commitments, he began to acquire additional property within the NIZ. More shovels were put in the ground, and downtown Allentown soon became a huge construction zone. Apart from additional office buildings, new activity included luxury as well as market-rate apartments, restaurants, retail, and additional parking.

A number of cities have been involved in urban renewal projects in the recent past, and not all of them have been successful. One of the biggest disappointments occurred in Boston’s working-class West End in the 1950s. Sadly, what transpired there resembled a scorched-earth policy more closely than urban renewal. In short, the entire neighborhood was leveled, and twenty-seven hundred families were displaced, all in the name of progress. Developers then built five huge high-rise apartment buildings, which together contained less than five hundred units, and to make matters worse, the monthly rents were so high that few if any of the former residents could afford to live in them. City officials had felt they could increase tax revenue by replacing older and/or substandard housing with modern apartment buildings. They regarded the West End as an eyesore, a slum, or worse. The displaced residents were made to feel powerless. In truth, they were.

The human price for the West End's "renewal," however, was immense. At the end of the day, all that was left were memories. Almost fifty acres of residential housing were vaporized. After this "renewal," not much remained in the West End except for the Massachusetts General Hospital and the Charles Street Jail. A few years ago, after the city of Boston closed the jail, MGH bought it and turned it into a luxury hotel. Equally ironic, the West End Museum opened in 1992, nearly forty years after the old neighborhood was razed. The museum honors what city government destroyed.

Eager to avoid this type of experience, city officials in Allentown were committed early on to make sure the NIZ program would bring enduring value to the city and its residents. The challenge was obvious: to make sure that future redevelopment was not just a big construction project, but rather something that was truly transformative and that could help to create viable long-term job growth among local residents, especially those that lived in or near the NIZ itself. It would be almost tragic if the revitalization failed to touch those people who were most vulnerable and heavily in need.

In April 2014, the city completed and published its "Reindustrialization Strategy." It was clear that many of the same people behind the NIZ program were behind this white paper and supported its fundamental conclusion that NIZ without jobs would lead to a fiasco, a billion-dollar boondoggle of inspiring architecture and not much else. The Reindustrialization Strategy was an important follow-up to the city's long-term strategic plan "Allentown 2020," which had been issued late in 2008, just as the NIZ was about to get life. Both documents pay attention to critically important issues like brownfield remediation and workforce education, both essential components of new business creation.

The NIZ program has gotten off to a very impressive start. Its $1 billion price tag is a staggering sum considering the population of Allentown. It is entirely possible that a true urban renaissance is at hand, one which could serve as a blueprint for other American cities. Nevertheless, there still are many detractors and nonbelievers; some are cynical, strident, and self-righteous. The most vocal of them are bloggers Bernie O'Hare and Mike Molovinsky. To call either outspoken would be an understatement. Always judgmental, sometimes outrageous, *Molovinsky on Allentown* and O'Hare's *Lehigh Valley Ramblings* are, if nothing else, clear evidence that our Constitution has a First Amendment. O'Hare has claimed, among other things, that J. B. Reilly was "luring" business into Allentown's NIZ with rent subsidies that should have been spent on Allentown's failing schools. (I must point out that without NIZ redevelopment, there would be no new money created to provide subsidies of any sort.) He also charged that J. B. Reilly "bought" the Northampton County executive seat; his proof was that Reilly had made a $25,000 campaign contribution to the Pennsylvania State Republican Committee!

Molovinsky takes O'Hare's bitterness and distrust to even higher levels. He lauds the merchants of Hamilton Street for "a lifetime of work, loyalty, and investment" and claims that their reward from city government has been only "deceit and threats." He calls the NIZ program and the arena project a white elephant and predicts it will take the city thirty years to recover from certain disaster. He is critical of every individual associated with the NIZ program and every project within it. He ran for mayor in 2005 and got 4 percent of the vote.

Even though the opposition that comes from people like O'Hare and Molovinsky has as much nuisance value as substance, the NIZ program has in fact faced a variety of serious challenges and obstacles in the past. In the spring of 2012, a bevy of lawsuits were filed that threatened to derail redevelopment within the NIZ. As usual, the dispute was over money. Tax subsidies allowed Reilly's City Center Investment Corporation to offer subsidized rents at eight to twelve dollars per square foot—about half the going rate for prime space elsewhere in the Lehigh Valley. A number of neighboring townships cried foul, concerned that state earned income taxes from their own communities, i.e. taxes paid by commuters, would be funneled directly into the NIZ. Ultimately both sides were able to reach a satisfactory settlement.

Some local real estate developers were displeased as well, fearful that the tax incentives that made the NIZ possible would harm them financially. Suburban buildings they already owned and operated could face a future loss of tenants; besides that, bargain leases in Allentown could in time force them to lower their own rents as well. Also worrisome were their prospects for future construction—how would they be able to compete on a playing field that was not level?

Several dozen developers met privately during the spring of 2012 to discuss their grievances, and for a time, they considered joining the townships in a lawsuit lawsuit. At one such meeting, Sara Hailstone, community and economic development director, came to represent the city. She had never been invited to the meeting and was asked to leave the room as soon as she arrived. She did so, remaining in the hallway just outside the meeting room. At that point, she was again asked to leave the building. She innocently told Matt Assad of the *Morning Call*, "I was there to help and answer any questions they might have. I don't know why they were all worked up." Ultimately the developers' opposition went nowhere, as they had no legal basis or popular support to obstruct NIZ construction.

In any event, a few days after Hailstone was shown the door, she found herself at another meeting, this time with a group of Hamilton Street merchants. It must be said that these merchants have had an uneasy, insecure feeling about NIZ redevelopment from the beginning, feeling small, unimportant, and relatively powerless. One really couldn't blame them. For decades they were regarded as part of the problem, not the solution. Their meeting with Hailstone was testy, but reasonably productive. Hailstone, who chaired the meeting, began by asking Matt Assad why he was present. He told her he had been asked by the merchants and was allowed to stay. Once discussions began, many of the business owners complained that they had been pressured to sell their property by an unknown entity or face seizure by eminent domain. Hailstone admitted that the city was the straw buyer and promised better communication in the future. "We do value small business and we want you to stay in Allentown," Hailstone said. Then she added, "We can't make any guarantees, but I promise you my staff can help you with relocation, maybe even in the same neighborhood." Change is rarely easy.

Another thorny issue was the Americus Hotel, which had become city property after Mark Mendelson went bankrupt in 2009. Mendelson's bankruptcy did have one silver lining. It made possible a court-approved sale of the building to the city of Allentown, which quickly auctioned it off. Local businessman Albert Abdouche ended up taking title to the Americus for $676,000, not much more than its original owners paid for the lot alone one hundred years earlier. The auction, to be kind, did not attract a tremendous amount of interest. One out-of-town investment group had to remain on the sidelines because it couldn't produce a certified check representing a 10 percent down payment. That left Abdouche and another investor, Joe Clark, as the only bidders. Abdouche won, although there have probably been a number of occasions in the past several years when he wished he had lost.

Abdouche, who had a history of purchasing distressed properties, rehabilitating them, and turning them around, was a credible investor. He had purchased a recreational skating arena in East Allentown and turned it into a highly successful banquet and conference center. However, in this venture, the stars did not align perfectly for him, and his experience with the Americus was difficult from the start. By the time he purchased the Americus in 2009, it was more than an eyesore—it was a danger and a public health hazard. Abdouche understood the severity of the situation. He also put on a brave face, saying that the building basically had good bones; the rooms just needed to be cleaned, painted, and recarpeted. Mayor Ed Pawlowski was a bit more direct. He said, "I don't think the roof will last the winter."

Shortly after the purchase, Abdouche and his partner John Haik decided to give the *Morning Call*'s Jarrett Renshaw a tour of the Americus. Renshaw was not impressed. He wrote there were only "glimpses of the hotel's past glory. The ornate lobby is covered in dust and dirt. Portions of the ceiling are missing. Pipes and electrical wiring are exposed. The rooms on the upper floors show signs of neglect."

The Americus was not originally part of the 128-acre NIZ, and for this reason, as well as a weak economy and a tight credit market, Abdouche was in no rush to push ahead with redevelopment. It may well have been suicidal if he had. For a number of years, he had struggled with the thought that it would take many millions to restore the Americus, and without the benefit of NIZ subsidies, he would be placed at a severe long-term competitive disadvantage. Surprisingly, he revealed this uncertainty within days of purchasing the Americus, saying "We're taking our time looking at the property, seeing what needs to be done, how much it will cost...But if the right price came along, we'll consider selling it as well."

It turns out that Abdouche actually had a brief opportunity to apply for NIZ funding but turned away from it in 2010, opting instead to continue to be included in the Keystone Opportunity Zone. This program, administered by the state, is very similar in concept to the NIZ but offered less generous and far-reaching subsidies. Abdouche complained that neither Mayor Ed Pawlowski nor anyone else in his administration could explain how NIZ would work. Abdouche said, "I took the tax incentives I understood, rather than the ones I didn't. Had I known what the NIZ could do, I'd have chosen NIZ." Pawlowski subsequently told me Abdouche was sitting "right here in my office" when he explained the nuances of each program and gave Abdouche the ability to choose between them.

Sour grapes or not, Abdouche was stuck, unable to get serious financing commitments and equally unable to attract a buyer (on terms acceptable to him), so in 2010, he slowly began to put his own money to work. His expectations were initially quite limited—to make the Americus safe enough that the city of Allentown would no longer consider it to be "blighted." Unless he was able to have this dubious distinction removed, Abdouche would find it impossible to secure any financing or grant money.

In 2010, hundreds of windows were replaced, the facade repaired, and electrical and plumbing systems were brought up to code. Abdouche spoke of much more ambitious future plans to renovate the ground floor retail shops and then, over time, the lobby, banquet and dining areas, and all of the hotel rooms. He felt he could complete the job for $10 million. The city believed the final cost would be more than double that. Perhaps Abdouche may have harbored some doubts himself because he made no secret of the fact that the Americus was still for sale. Potential buyers, however, remained on strike, discouraged by Abdouche's estimate of its value and the realization that without NIZ money, they would face the same roadblock as he had.

In the spring of 2011, the scaffolding, which had been up for several years, was finally removed after exterior repairs were completed. By 2012 Abdouche had made over $2 million in additional improvements, but the project continued to proceed in slow motion. Abdouche optimistically spoke about renovating the first floor for retail tenants—targeting availability within twelve months. He maintained his long-term goal of operating the Americus as a first-class hotel and revealed he had been in negotiations with both Marriott and Wyndham. Nearly three years after he had purchased the Americus, the building still needed a gut job to become commercially viable, let alone have its former grandeur restored. Simply getting off the "blighted" list wasn't good enough.

The Americus as well as a number of other buildings lay just outside the zone that had been originally approved for NIZ funding. This frustrated Abdouche immensely, especially having witnessed the financial incentives that were made available for a succession of J. B. Reilly's projects. Abdouche had taken his case to the city and ANIZDA several times before without luck. He had publicly appeared before ANIZDA and said, "How can I be in the NIZ? Who should I talk to? Nobody can give me an answer."

In 2012, it appeared that Abdouche finally caught a break and received some unexpected good news. By this time, Allentown's downtown redevelopment had begun to gather a good deal of momentum, and many early doubts about the viability of NIZ had begun to disappear. When the Pennsylvania Department of Revenue gave its blessing to a small modification of the original NIZ boundaries, one which included the Americus, it looked like Abdouche's pleadings for reconsideration had been serendipitously answered and that the long-dormant construction project had received a jump start.

It didn't. The key sticking point was money. ANIZDA felt that Abdouche's $10 million estimate for a total renovation was far too low, and it was unwilling to sign off on a project that it felt was doomed to fail. As time passed, of course, even Abdouche's original estimate was bumped up periodically—from $13 million, to $16 million, then $17 million "tops"—but the gap between Abdouche and ANIZDA remained insurmountable. Time and inflation increased ANIZDA's numbers as well. In addition, Abdouche didn't evoke the same sort of confidence as did J. B. Reilly, whose projects seemed to fly through the approval process with ease. Abdouche's pockets weren't nearly as deep, and while he had created a successful record as a real estate developer, his experience in large commercial projects was limited. He had never been involved with a hotel. He was working with an out-of-town construction firm and an out-of-state bank—neither of which were well known in the area.

ANIZDA repeatedly denied Abdouche's requests for NIZ funding. ANIZDA member Alan Jennings summed it up, "He's never done a project this large, has no experience in hotels, and wants to do the project with an amount of money no one thinks is enough....It's not just another building project. It deserves every bit of scrutiny we're giving it." Pat Browne concurred by saying, "They (ANIZDA) absolutely have the authority to deny a project they believe will fail."

In the summer of 2014, Abdouche lost his financing commitment and abandoned his hope of renovating the Americus with NIZ funding.

Frustrated and deeply disappointed, he said he would nevertheless proceed with the project using his own money—starting with the ground floor. His hope was that he would be able to lease this space up to retail tenants and then go back to ANIZDA once again for approval. If not, he was prepared to take on the renovation himself, one floor at a time. Abdouche realized that this could add years onto his timeline. He defiantly said, "I'll prove them all wrong...This is my building and I'm here to stay." By this time, he was in too deep to walk away. Currently the Americus remains an empty shell, and it has been one ever since the city of Allentown pulled its occupancy permit in 2002.

Virtually all of the people or organizations who have expressed dissatisfaction with the NIZ program share one thought in common: they are resentful that they never got the keys to the candy store. Whether it was a group of suburban developers, outlying townships, Hamilton Street merchants, or Albert Abdouche himself, the refrain was the same—"What about me?"

Nowhere was this feeling of alienation and anxiety felt more acutely than among the poorest of the poor. The residential districts in the city's downtown, which had the highest unemployment, crime, poverty, and school drop-out rates, are literally in the shadow of the hockey arena and all of the surrounding construction. How would the quality of life in these neighborhoods change, if at all? Without good jobs, safe streets, and successful schools, how could one seriously talk about "revitalization"? Of course it was beyond the intended scope of Pat Browne's NIZ program to provide job training and eradicate poverty in Allentown's urban core, but at the same time, it is perfectly understandable why local residents would feel resentful and betrayed if their lot remained unaffected by all of the activity (and wealth) created by the NIZ.

The challenges are real. Good jobs are not given away; they are offered to applicants who can demonstrate they possess the education and training that are required of them. Allentown currently ranks 485th out of 498 school districts in Pennsylvania. Only two of its twenty-two schools achieved what Pennsylvania considers to be "adequate yearly progress."

Approximately 40 percent of high school students drop out before graduation. Funding for local schools is scarce; the 2014 school budget included the elimination of ninety-eight jobs, most of them in teaching. Without a dramatic turnaround in educational achievement, it is hard to imagine a future much different or more promising than the past.

The issue of hiring local residents for NIZ jobs didn't begin to get much traction until 2013. Almost immediately, it provoked dissension, even within ANIZDA itself. ANIZDA Chairman Sy Traub believed that the NIZ program's mission was to attract businesses to Allentown's core, not to direct or get involved in their hiring practices; long-time ANIZDA board member Alan Jennings, however, felt that the authority was entirely justified in taking a more activist role in promoting local hiring and employment practices. Jennings, in fact, suggested that a wage floor of twelve dollars per hour be set for city residents working in the NIZ.

It's important to keep in mind that many of the "new" jobs (as opposed to those that simply moved from the suburbs to downtown) would normally pay only minimum wage or perhaps a bit more. The arena and the surrounding commercial buildings would need janitors, security guards, and food servers; the same could be said for the new hotels. Traub immediately jumped on Jennings's suggestion as being counterproductive and more likely to scare business away than attract it. "We have no business manipulating the free market the way he wants," Traub said.

Traub's view certainly represents a consensus for business, but it was by no means widely shared by all constituents. Community activist and school board member Ce Gerlach speaks eloquently on the subject: "We must ensure that in the effort to improve the quality of life downtown that we focus on the current residents of Allentown and not just the new buildings...The best way to ensure real benefits from development is to have tangible, measurable goals stipulated in a *Community Benefits Agreement.*" Among them, she proposed hiring goals, along with job training, for women, minorities, and local residents.

Her point is well taken to be sure, but there is also an underlying tone in this conversation (in fact, it is almost impossible to escape) that somehow the NIZ program was designed to reward real estate developers and corporations at the expense of the urban poor. It seems a bit of a stretch to assume that NIZ supporters are engaged in some sort of conspiratorial behavior. NIZ's core mission, after all, was limited from the outset—to revitalize the city by attracting new business downtown. It was widely expected that people, rich and poor alike, would be the beneficiaries of this surge in economic activity, but the creators of NIZ never intended to mandate social change. They just wanted to help it along.

Trying to align and then meet all of the needs of different interest groups will be an ongoing challenge. It will involve compromise and change, and neither ever comes easily. One thing is certain: a quick solution is not at hand. Faced with the difficulty of persuading business and community interests to find common ground, ANIZDA came up with a timeworn "solution." It appointed a committee to study what it should do.

Some of the changes that have taken place have already created discomfort. Residents were upset when two popular stores (Family Dollar and Rite Aid) were demolished; for years they had offered a convenient place to go for clothing, food, and prescription drugs. A genuine void was created after Rite Aid closed, leaving the nearest pharmacy nearly a mile away. A similar loss was felt when Family Dollar closed. Currently, groceries can be procured only at small convenience stores.

Fear of gentrification sent shudders through the neighborhood; locals were worried that rising real estate values and new construction would push rents sky high, forcing many to leave their homes. In late 2013, J. B. Reilly began discussions with Starbucks about signing a lease at his eleven-story office building, Two City Center. He joked, "We couldn't get Dunkin' Donuts, but we're working on a Starbucks." Not everyone laughed.

There have been many instances where government has taken an activist role in economic affairs. Even the best-known and most successful such initiatives, like the Marshall Plan or the New Deal's WPA, had their detractors, and sometimes their most ardent supporters would admit to occasional flaws, omissions, and incidents of waste. When the final record is written, it will probably be no different with Allentown's grand experiment. The NIZ program by itself will not erase crime and poverty, eliminate unemployment, or create top-notch schools. It cannot perform miracles, yet it has already made a difference and a big one.

Just a short time ago, Allentown was a city with a grim past and a dreary future. Now a sense of genuine optimism resonates in many quarters. If the city is in fact successful in reinventing itself, it will owe itself a huge pat on the back. Allentown suffered, struggled, and stumbled for forty years, and then at a most unlikely time, it experienced an unexpected reversal of fortune. Some might debate forever when and why conditions finally stabilized and how the pieces of recovery actually were put in place. I am fortunate to know the answer. It is something my mother told me in 1956, when I was nine years old: "God helps those who help themselves."

14

CROSSROADS

AMERICAN AUTHOR BILL Bryson—a baby boomer like me—recently penned a memoir of his youth in Des Moines, Iowa. *The Life and Times of the Thunderbolt Kid,* like many of his works, was written mostly to amuse and entertain, but Bryson can also be reflective and insightful. I could easily identify with his sentiments when he reminisced about Winfield, Iowa, where his grandparents lived:

> Winfield is barely alive. All the businesses on Main Street—the dime store, the pool hall, the newspaper office, the banks, the grocery stores—long ago disappeared. There is nowhere to buy Nehi pop. You can't purchase a single item of food within the town limits. My grandparents' house is still there—at least it was the last time I passed—but the barn is gone as is its porch swing and the shade tree out back and the orchard and everything else that made it what it was. The best I can say is that I saw the last of something really special. It's something I seem to say a lot these days.

What is nostalgia if not a sentimental yearning for an idealized vision of the past? Iowa today has fewer farms and fewer farmers than it did fifty years ago, but the farms are larger and far more productive. The state now produces more food for Iowans and the rest of us to eat. In Iowa, like Pennsylvania, and virtually anywhere else on the planet, change can often have two sides, positive and negative. Change is frequently subtle and complex. Bryson knows that economic growth and technological innovation have had, on balance, a positive influence on the lives of Iowans and many other Americans, yet the loss of a way of life as he remembers it has left a huge hole in his soul.

Many of us are guilty of this sort of selective memory. I know I am. For some reason, The World War II era holds a special fascination for me, even though I was born two years after the war ended. There were larger-than-life figures like FDR and Churchill and heroes like Eddie Rickenbacker, Audie Murphy, and Jimmy Doolittle. After the Philippines fell to Japan, Douglas MacArthur prophetically exclaimed, "I shall return." His words echo to this day. Dwight Eisenhower, on the eve of the Normandy invasion, told his troops: "We are about to embark upon the Great Crusade...Let us beseech the blessing of Almighty God upon this great and noble undertaking." Then our nation was united in purpose and spirit as never before. Sacrifices were made on the battlefield and at home. Tom Brokaw refers to the men and women of this era as "the greatest generation." Who would argue with him?

Of course there is another side to this story. Many traumatized soldiers who returned home after the war didn't speak about their experiences—ever. World War II was an unprecedented human catastrophe, with over forty million civilian and military casualties. The Holocaust speaks for itself. So do Hiroshima and Nagasaki. When I ponder the amount of suffering the planet endured, I can acknowledge my misplaced romanticism and misreading of history. I suppose that's what nostalgia brings about—a filtered look at the past—even when bad things did happen.

Bad things also happened in Allentown, even during its glory days. Hardship and struggle are simply part of life. I am no doubt guilty of looking back at my own youth through rose-colored glasses, if only because my memories are that of a nine-year-old child. Perhaps that is why I, like

Bryson did in Winfield, felt so indescribably moved when I first came back to Allentown after a thirty-plus-year absence, expecting to find something that no longer existed and becoming deflated when I didn't.

Elizabeth Kübler-Ross's *On Death and Dying* identified five stages of grief many people experience as they mourn the passing of a loved one. In order, they are denial, anger, bargaining, depression, and acceptance. This algorithm can be applied broadly in life, not just with respect to mourning. I actually experienced all of these emotions to some degree when I recently stood alone behind my boyhood home on Ott Street, gazing at a parking lot that had replaced what had once been picturesque, rolling hills.

I have had a chance to visit the city on a number of occasions during the past few years, and on each successive trip, I have been witness to dramatic change. Downtown Allentown looked like a ghost town in 2010, a construction zone in 2012, and most recently, in 2015, a city about to be transformed. Apart from the obvious physical changes within the NIZ, there has been a sea change in the attitudes and expectations of local residents. Most are now hopeful and believe that their city's future is indeed brighter than its recent past. Even ten or fifteen years ago, apathy and defeatism abounded. Americans elsewhere were convinced that places like Allentown were not much more than zombie cities, without a sense of possibility or hopefulness.

On a recent trip, I had the chance to speak with a number of individuals who played an active part in many of the changes that took place in the city during the recent past. First up was Bill Heydt, former two-term mayor who served between 1995 and 2003. Still reasonably active in his insurance business at seventy-six, he exudes the self-confident, no-nonsense aura of an individual who tells it like it is without loudly advertising the fact that he really does tell it like it is. He was never a career politician. He made it very clear that he sought political office because he saw there was work to be done and things that needed to be fixed.

He is proud of his record. Allentown's finances were in very rough shape when Heydt took office. In a matter of weeks, he was forced to lay off fifty-two city workers as a result of a reduced budget that was handed to him by city council, one which mandated a 5 percent across-the-board cut in payroll. Since Heydt couldn't lay off 5 percent of a person, these layoffs were his only option.

Heydt was ultimately able to bring all of those workers back by finding waste and inefficiencies in existing practices and processes. He oversaw a turnaround in the city's ambulance service and was actually able to expand several other departments including the police force. Heydt also successfully privatized city-owned parking facilities. At the end of his time in office, the city of Allentown had an $8 million surplus and a pension plan that was overfunded by $34 million. He often butted heads with city council, a largely Democratic body, but he felt he had a decent working relationship with its members. He seemed genuinely sincere when he said he did not place a great deal of importance on political party affiliation. In fact, Heydt once served on Democrat Joe Daddona's Finance Committee the first time Daddona ran for mayor and, like most people, remembers him with fondness.

He was not shy in talking about his struggles with PPL, the electric utility that maintains its corporate headquarters in downtown Allentown and employs approximately two thousand people in the city. It seemed almost amusing to me that Heydt, a Republican, would find himself in conflict with a large public utility, but their differences had very little to do with political philosophy. At the root of the hostility was a turf battle over the redevelopment of the Hess's site.

Under Heydt, Allentown acquired Hess's for approximately $2 million and then sold the parking deck for roughly the same amount, leaving the city in debt-free possession of the store (really, at this point a future building site) itself. With respect to redevelopment, Heydt supported the first arena project (Trainor, Stortz, et al.), feeling that it had the potential to jump-start the transformation of Allentown's urban core. PPL coveted the land, which was directly across the street from its headquarters, for its own future expansion needs. With the support of the AEDC and city council, PPL won the day and ultimately built a low-rise office building where Hess's once stood.

There clearly was some bad blood between Heydt and PPL. Heydt felt that the company paid nowhere near its fair share of property taxes. He claimed too that PPL was extremely tightfisted in supporting community projects and events. He mentioned that during the Hess negotiations, PPL threatened to leave Allentown altogether if it didn't get its way. Heydt told PPL's CEO William Hecht, "Go ahead." Diplomacy was not Bill Heydt's strong suit.

Heydt surprised me when he said that Trainor and Stortz had financing for their project secured. My own research had suggested that they did not, but it also suggested that the AEDC and council members were always far more comfortable with PPL's financial strength along with the security it offered. Most likely as long as PPL made a concerted effort to obtain this parcel, no one else—let alone a high-risk startup—was going to get it. The demolition of Hess's and the discussion regarding its redevelopment consumed thousands of man-hours. Private investors and government officials spent years in intense negotiations, encountering numerous impasses and dead ends. That's the way government works—slowly, sometimes maddeningly so—but in the end, it does work. PPL got its building, and although it took ten more years, Allentown finally got its arena.

Heydt retired in 2003 after completing his second term. He looks back at the time he spent in office with fondness. He admitted, "I like being the boss." There's probably not a mayor in America who would disagree. He feels he did his part. He inherited a fiscal mess and restored financial order and soundness.

He was brought back into the political fray four years later after Roy Afflerbach's disastrous single term as mayor, again hoping to play the role of the "fixer." This time it didn't work out for him as he had hoped. He was defeated rather decisively by Democrat Ed Pawlowski, Afflerbach's former community and economic development director.

Pawlowski in fact had resigned one year earlier, in 2004, over a dispute with Afflerbach regarding budget cuts. (It seems that Afflerbach had few defenders, Republican or Democrat.) Pawlowski, a Polish Catholic from Chicago, was an outsider in more ways than one. In fact, he had never held elected public office. This no doubt worked to his advantage with an electorate that was infuriated by the financial horrors that emerged during Afflerbach's term. Pawlowski also benefited from the continuing influx of Latinos, who traditionally supported Democratic candidates.

Whatever the case, Heydt was more than gracious in recalling his only political defeat, casting only a few rather mild verbal barbs in Pawlowski's direction; after all, they once had a powerfully adversarial relationship. In the end, though, Heydt seemed completely content with his career in politics and with his life afterward. He spoke positively about all of the NIZ-related redevelopment activity that has occurred since he left office and believes the city has a bright future. In his heart he may have always felt that way, even in the darkest days of the 1980s and 1990s. When I asked him if he had ever considered just picking up and leaving the area, it took him about one second to answer, "No."

I met with Ed Pawlowski later that afternoon. He is clearly on a roll. Now in the middle of his third term as mayor, he enjoys broad support—so broad, in fact, that he ran unopposed in his 2012 reelection bid. He seems very much at home in the world of politics, even though there was very little early evidence that his life was going to take him in that direction. In fact, Pawlowski attended the Moody Bible Institute in Chicago, where he prepared to enter a career in ministry; even though he did not, it was clear his early idealism was to play a central role in his life. He first worked as a community organizer in Chicago, assisting residents in obtaining housing, and then he earned a master's degree in urban planning at the University of Illinois. He subsequently continued his career at the Chicago Housing Authority.

Pawlowski came to Allentown in his early thirties as executive director of the Lehigh Housing Development Corporation before being named community and economic development director. The dust up with Afflerbach occurred shortly thereafter. At that point, gainfully unemployed, while weighing another job offer in the housing field, local Democratic Party leaders suggested that he make a run for mayor. He decided to throw his hat in the ring, and his political career was born.

The most visible object in his office is a huge map of the NIZ construction zone and of the various projects within it. Pawlowski spends a great deal of his time on NIZ-related issues and points to its achievements with great pride. Some of his detractors have minimized his connection with NIZ's success, awarding most of the kudos to Pat Browne and J. B. Reilly—and with good reason. Nevertheless, Pawlowski deserves some credit as well. He was quick to point out that the city did indeed play a critical role in the NIZ project, especially in its early years, when it floated a large bond issue to acquire property for future redevelopment. At that time there was no assurance that such development would take place on time, if at all. NIZ was a highly experimental piece of legislation, and if it didn't work, his own political career would have been in jeopardy.

Some community activists have expressed concern that the real beneficiaries of NIZ are real estate developers and their corporate tenants who get to pay below-market rents, and that the lives of Allentown's poor who reside just outside the NIZ boundaries will remain unaffected by all the current activity. I attempted to introduce the subject in our conversation, but Pawlowski didn't buy into it. He said that 80 percent of all new NIZ jobs were held by residents of Allentown, and while he admitted that many of them were low paying, they were nevertheless real jobs that could give true opportunity to the chronically unemployed. He then pulled out his iPad and played a video of a TV reporter interviewing a local woman who had been unemployed for several years; she had just been hired by a NIZ employer, as had three of her children, and was moved to tears with gratitude over her family's newfound good fortune. It was good theatre but also a very effective rebuttal.

The mayor is a steady, resolute pragmatist. Oddly enough, many of his personality characteristics mirror those of Bill Heydt. Both men had a history of placing results before ideology and, as a consequence, were consistently able to attract a large cross section of voters and special interests. In this regard, Pawlowski's appeal across party lines is almost without parallel. Certainly, he was in the right place at the right time and benefited from a rising tide of positive NIZ-related economic growth and PR. However, this fortuitous timing should not detract from his own success, nor should it minimize his accomplishments.

Pawlowski admitted that housing and education are still troubling issues and will require long-term workouts. Still, he has accomplished much during his terms in office and deserves high marks. By 2015, the unemployment rate in Allentown was one of the lowest in the state, and crime had dropped significantly—as much as 30 percent since 2005. Pawlowski recently engineered a sale/leaseback of the city's water and sewer systems with the Lehigh County Authority for more than $200 million. By doing so, a sufficient amount of cash was raised to plug the holes in the city's underfunded pension plan. In spite of widespread opposition, he got the deal done.

New businesses are flourishing in the city, from light industrial to technology and biotech. Allentown currently has an investment grade credit rating and is no longer considered a high-risk borrower by would-be lenders. Recently, Pawlowski has even talked about acquiring blighted properties and vacant lots to create small parks and organic farms for inner-city residents. It is an understatement to say he is enthusiastic about the future.

Ed Pawlowski didn't come across to me as someone who would like to be mayor for life. He made an unsuccessful run for governor of Pennsylvania in 2013 but was quickly forced to drop out because his campaign was unable to attract enough money to remain viable. He does not possess personal wealth and does not have an impressive rolodex of financial supporters. Apart from that, next to Philadelphia and Pittsburgh, the Lehigh Valley has always been somewhat marginalized in the world of Pennsylvania politics. I never asked him what his future plans are, and I am not sure at this point that even he knows the answer. Whatever the case, I am certain that one day he will look back at his time in office with fondness—his own good old days.

Frank Whelan is a local institution. A *Morning Call* feature writer for more than twenty years, Whelan has authored seven books about Allentown and its history. When he first came to the city in the early '80s, the worm had already begun to turn, but Allentown still had more in common with the place I remember as a child than what it was to become. Almost immediately, Whelan witnessed the start of an economic death spiral and the political backbiting it spawned.

Allentown had always had a small number of blacks, Whelan recalled, but until the 1970s, the city remained overwhelmingly white and English speaking, its population having largely Northern European roots. When Hispanics moved in, he noted that many old guard residents were unprepared for the change. Certainly that was the case in the Allentown School District, which did not have the resources to deal with thousands of Spanish-speaking students who suddenly appeared in class. Many older residents were absolutely bewildered by the changes that were taking place. Some probably still are.

As an ex-newspaper man, Whelan jokingly describes himself as a cynic. In truth, he is anything but, although as recently as two years ago, he expressed doubt that the NIZ would ever amount to much. NIZ, he said, was just a zone, not a neighborhood. As a long-term downtown resident, he cares deeply about the quality of life for the people who live there and was fearful that NIZ redevelopment would not influence them in any meaningful way.

I was surprised to hear that he is now a convert. There is now a viable restaurant business at night, he says, and people are out and about. Thousands swarmed into center city when the Eagles officially opened the PPL Center, and they stayed long after the concert was over. Don Shula's upscale Steakhouse created quite a buzz when it announced it was moving downtown from the Promenade Mall to the ground floor of Strata Flats, one of J. B. Reilly's new apartment buildings. The Lehigh Valley Phantoms have been successful in their inaugural hockey season, with frequent sell-outs. Truthfully, this is the first evidence we have had in fifty years or more that conditions in the heart of the city are actually improving.

None of this, of course, would have been possible without the NIZ legislation that was the brainchild of Senator Pat Browne. When I asked Browne if there was an "aha moment" or epiphany that gave him the inspiration to create NIZ, he answered no in a matter-of-fact manner. Browne is almost professorial in nature. He carefully explained that public-private partnerships are not new, and that he had an opportunity during his legislative career to become familiar with a number of them, some of which, of course, were more successful than others.

Most financings of this sort are project specific—for example, an airport, a football stadium, or a parking garage, but NIZ was much more far reaching. Browne told me, "Look at history. Cities cannot prosper without a vibrant urban core." He was looking to effect permanent and meaningful change and to do so on a broad scale. He initially encountered a reasonable amount of skepticism. When I asked him how much time he spent in conversation with fellow legislators and business interests prior to the creation of NIZ, he laughed. "For several years," he said, "it was a part-time job." Between him and his staff, perhaps several thousand man-hours were devoted to this legislation.

I brought up the point that others have made: NIZ will enrich real estate developers and have no positive impact on the lives of the city's urban poor. Browne was quick to point out that without a strengthening of the city's tax base, basic issues like sustainability and quality of life would become problematic. Education, police, fire protection, roadway maintenance, and other municipal services all cost money, and in Browne's mind, the alternative to NIZ or something like it would be continuing deterioration. His point is well taken. Two City Center, an eleven-story office building that is fully occupied, sits on land that was vacant for nearly twenty years.

During my research, I learned about some local manufacturing businesses that managed to hang on during the difficult years and wrote about several, like Aetna Felt, Anda Industries, and Schiff Silk and Ribbon. I have always been intrigued and inspired by the underdog who comes out on top. From a historical perspective, I felt it was important to show that even in dire circumstances, creativity and persistence can overcome what many assume to be insurmountable odds.

Over a year ago, I came across Monalisa Fashions, a small textile firm located in East Allentown. The company is a traditional CMT (cut, make, and trim) manufacturer, where seamstresses take finished fabric and piece it together to form a finished product like a shirt or a pair of pants. This is low-tech work that hasn't changed much over the years, and nearly all such labor has been moved overseas, especially to East Asia. The business was founded in 1984, a terrible time to enter the textile business in America. The fact that it survived for over thirty years was to my mind nothing short of a miracle.

I attempted to speak—without success—with Nagib and Mona Najm, the founders of Monalisa Fashions, and their daughter, Mereille, for the better part of a year. Always gracious, the family nevertheless appeared to be completely immersed in their business and couldn't find the time to talk. Ten minutes? Not now. Five minutes? Sorry. I felt like an obnoxious journalist chasing after an unwilling victim, shoving a microphone in the face of my prey.

On my way out of town, I nevertheless decided to stop by the factory, a small building of perhaps five thousand square feet. I had nothing to lose. I was standing outside the front door and about to enter when a woman who had just left her car approached me and said, "May I help you?" Of course, she was probably trying to figure out what I wanted to sell. For some reason, I simply blurted out, "Are you Mereille?" More than a little surprised at my psychic abilities, she said she was, and then we exchanged some small talk. Yes, she remembered our earlier conversations, and yes, she could give me five minutes. I probably shamed her into it. We went into a small office and began to talk. I told her I wanted to learn about the business and how it began. What obstacles did the company face? How did it manage to succeed in the face of intense foreign competition that practically wiped out the American textile industry? And, of course, since this was a family business, I told her I wanted to learn about her family. When she asked me if I wanted a cup of coffee, I was floored. We had apparently just come a long way from "not now" and "sorry." The story that Mereille told me was worth the wait.

The Najms are from Lebanon. Nagib and Mona came to the United States in the 1970s as a young couple, leaving the Lebanese Civil War behind. They had no money and could scarcely speak English. Both took menial jobs at Phoenix Clothes (an astonishing coincidence to me) and acquired basic skills in the needle trades. At the time, Phoenix was paying some workers by the piece, not by the hour, and Nagib, who was a quick learner and a quicker worker, was soon able to begin putting a little extra money aside. Meanwhile Mona bought a sewing machine, and she began to do some tailoring for friends and neighbors in her basement. Her reputation grew, and as her workload increased, she got another machine and hired a seamstress to assist her.

Soon enough, it became obvious that while Mona's cottage business was growing, the basement in her house was not. Around the same time, Phoenix reverted to straight hourly pay, so the Najms took the plunge and opened Monalisa Fashions in 1984. They are still heavily involved in the business on a daily basis, and they were both there on the day of my unannounced visit. In fact, when Mereille brought me over to meet her parents, Mona was sitting behind a sewing machine, working as she had for the past thirty plus years. The company has never had it easy. Apart from foreign competition, it is saddled with chronically high turnover among its own workers. Mereille is also fearful that a significant increase in the minimum wage here at home could virtually wipe out its razor-thin margin of profit.

Since joining her parents in business a few years ago, Mereille has used the Internet proactively to attract new customers and has diversified the company's product capabilities. These initiatives have certainly helped, as has the company's ongoing commitment to customer service. In one respect, having a Pennsylvania location isn't all bad, because you can ship a product to Chicago much more quickly from Allentown than you can from Kuala Lumpur. Monalisa Fashions has faced a world of challenges, but the family has always met them successfully. I have never seen a work ethic quite like theirs.

When I left the Najms, they were all beaming. Mona told me she loved history and wanted to read my book when it was out. And so she shall, and no doubt will be surprised to learn that she and her family will have star billing. The Najms have not had it easy over the years, but they have proven to be resilient, resourceful, and committed. They are proud of what they've accomplished and look forward to the future. The same could be said for the city where they live. Once regarded as a disaster zone, seemingly down for the count, Allentown now appears to be firmly in transition and on the road to recovery. Almost everywhere, there is a palpable sense of pride and optimism.

When I first went back home a few years ago, I felt like many of us do when we attend a high school reunion and reconnect with once-close friends for the first time in many years—curious, tentative, and a bit uncertain. Occasionally we can't even recognize faces of old classmates. Conversations can stall or become awkward. We all have a strong affinity with the past but a nebulous connection in the present. That's how I felt in 2010, driving through suburban developments that were once farms and looking at factory buildings that had been abandoned or storefronts that were boarded up. It was certainly not a pretty picture, but just within the past five years, I have seen the pendulum swing dramatically.

In any event I believe my days as a time traveler are now behind me. I am not nine years old anymore, and this is not 1956. Memoirists and historians may write about the past, but they don't live in it. None of us does. We all exist in the present—and so does Allentown, Pennsylvania, once the center of my universe, and now a treasured childhood memory I shall always hold close to my heart.

Made in the USA
Lexington, KY
10 August 2018